THE NEW KOREA

AN INSIDE LOOK AT SOUTH KOREA'S ECONOMIC RISE

Myung Oak Kim

Sam Jaffe

AMACOM

AMERICAN MANAGEMENT ASSOCIATION

New York • Atlanta • Brussels • Chicago • Mexico City • San Francisco
Shanghai • Tokyo • Toronto • Washington, D.C.

Bulk discounts available. For details visit:
www.amacombooks.org/go/specialsales
Or contact special sales:
Phone: 800-250-5308
E-mail: specialsls@amanet.org
View all the AMACOM titles at: www.amacombooks.org

This publication is designed to provide accurate and authoritative information in regard to the subject matter covered. It is sold with the understanding that the publisher is not engaged in rendering legal, accounting, or other professional service. If legal advice or other expert assistance is required, the services of a competent professional person should be sought.

Although this book does not always specifically identify trademarked names, AMACOM uses them for editorial purposes only, with no intention of trademark violation.

Library of Congress Cataloging-in-Publication Data

Kim, Myung Oak, 1971–
    The new Korea : an inside look at South Korea's economic rise / Myung Oak Kim, Sam Jaffe.
        p. cm.
    Includes index.
    ISBN-13: 978-0-8144-1489-7 (hbk.)
    ISBN-10: 0-8144-1489-3 (hbk.)
    1. Korea (South)—Economic conditions—1988– 2. Korea (South)—Economic policy—1988– 3. Korea (South)—Foreign economic relations. I. Jaffe, Sam. II. Title.
    HC467.96.K47 2010
    330.95195—dc22
                                                                                            2009037626

About AMA
American Management Association (www.amanet.org) is a world leader in talent development, advancing the skills of individuals to drive business success. Our mission is to support the goals of individuals and organizations through a complete range of products and services, including classroom and virtual seminars, webcasts, webinars, podcasts, conferences, corporate and government solutions, business books, and research. AMA's approach to improving performance combines experiential learning—learning through doing—with opportunities for ongoing professional growth at every step of one's career journey.

Printing number
10 9 8 7 6 5 4 3 2 1

CONTENTS

PART ONE

HISTORY

PART TWO

ECONOMICS AND TRADE

PART FIVE

THE FUTURE

This book is dedicated to our Abogee, Dr. Kim Chung-gil, who gave us the courage, insight, and motivation to tell the story of an amazing country and people.

ACKNOWLEDGMENTS

We would like to thank the following people in Korea, Europe, and the United States, all of whom helped us enormously:

Gary Heidt, our agent, filled our quiver with confidence and enthusiasm. The acquiring editor, Robert Shuman, helped us visualize the target. Robert Nirkind's content editing ensured that our aim was true. Karen Brogno and Erika Spelman and everyone else at Amacom improved our follow-through.

We are especially grateful to family and friends, including our mothers, Kim Soon-kyung and Amy Jaffe, for taking on our other duties while we worked on this book; our children, Anna Livia Jee Yun Jaffe, Naomi Soo Yun Jaffe, and Cai Yun Ho Jaffe, who patiently put up with a lack of attention from us on countless nights and weekends while we worked; Paul Sung Cha and Nina Young Hee Han, who listened to our stories and guided our work; and "Dew" Lee Sul who helped with interviews and research. Two organizations in Korea—the Academy of Korean Studies and the Presidential Council on Nation Branding—also provided crucial support with information and interviews.

Finally, we would especially like to thank our Abogee, Dr. Kim Chung-gil, who worked tirelessly on our behalf and instilled in us a deep love for Korea.

Introduction

ABOUT A MILE from Kyungbok Palace in northern Seoul, South Korea's frenetic capital, a narrow road winds up a hillside, past a small police station, a school, and a children's library. Near the top of the road, a parking lot leads to a steep set of stone steps. At the top of those steps you'll find an ornate pagoda that was originally built in 1898 on the orders of Emperor Gojong, who once ruled over the Korean peninsula. This place is called the Hwang Hak Jeong, which means Yellow Crane Pavilion. It is a traditional Korean archery range.

On a weekday afternoon in March 2009, Park Min-young, a law professor at Dongguk University, stood on a platform below the pavilion, gazing off toward a set of tall wooden targets 145 meters away. The platform also offers a clear view of the surrounding city landscape, including the central government complex, the U.S. Embassy, the Dong-a-Ilbo newspaper building, and the endless rows of high-rise apartment buildings that are home to Seoul's 10 million people. Standing alongside Park are a half dozen men and women, all holding laminate bows in their left hands. Around their waists, a bright-colored sash holds five arrows.

Park, who is in his early fifties, has been doing archery since he was about eight years old. His grandfathers did it. So did his father and uncles. So do his sons. Korean archery, called *kuk kung*, is different from other types of archery practiced around the world. It utilizes a short bow (traditionally made out of ox-horn) that bends significantly. The arrow (traditionally made out of bamboo) travels a considerable 145 meters (compared to 70 meters in Olympic archery) and forms a bell-curve-like trajectory (whereas most other archery styles create a straight linear trajectory). The key to kuk kung, because of its idiosyncrasies, is mental discipline. A kuk kung aficionado spends decades firing millions of arrows at the distant target before earning the title of master.

Park comes to the club about once every two weeks. When he does, he always practices on his traditional horn bow with bamboo arrows. Most of the others use newer laminate bows. He plays for exercise and to get away from the hectic lifestyle in Seoul. But most of all, he says, "We do this for our traditional Korean spirit."

Park's voice is filled with pride as he talks about the rich history of Korean archery. He knows that Koreans have excelled at archery since before Korea was its own country. He knows that the sport requires deep mental skill and a work ethic that Koreans have long ago mastered. And he also knows that the Korean spirit, exemplified in the success in both traditional and Olympic-style archery, is the key to the economic success his country has seen in its young existence.

Indeed, Korea's work ethic and collective spirit have been the backbone of the country's economic growth since the 1960s. Forty years of spectacular growth and transformation catapulted Korea to the status of an industrial powerhouse and the fifteenth largest economy in the world, according to 2008 World Bank data, despite its small landmass.

That growth came from centralized planning, an emphasis on exports, ambitious industrialization goals, and a dedicated, well-educated labor force. Let's call that initial growth trajectory Korea 1.0. It succeeded beyond the wildest dreams of President Park Chung-hee when he unleashed the economic juggernaut on the world in the early 1960s. Korea 1.0 specialized in building cars and ships—big brawny industries that took advantage of the country's disciplined work ethic and its low wages.

The work ethic is still there. But the low wages are gone. South Korea now has a per capita income that is greater than $20,000 per person. That puts it in the league of the European countries and within striking distance of Japan (where per capita income is $38,000) and even opens up the door to competing with the United States (where per capita income is $47,000).

The fundamental problem Korea faces today is how to continue to progress and elevate worker income from $20,000 to $40,000 while competing against low-wage countries like China and India. The rules of Korea 1.0 will no longer work for the next phase of the country's economic growth.

Despite the fact that most people still think of Korea 1.0 when they think of Korea at all, Korea 2.0 is already here. The economy is now dominated by new industries, such as entertainment, software, and telecommunications equipment manufacturing. Such businesses promise higher average wages, but they must be cultivated slowly and carefully—they can't be created from the edict of a president in the way that Korea 1.0 conjured up its steel and auto industries.

The culture and society of South Korea have also changed significantly in the last ten years. The ethnic homogeneity of the country has been replaced by a form of multiculturalism as more foreign laborers and more executives and their spouses have made Korea their home. In addition, women are moving into the workforce at a growing rate, leaving behind their roles as homemakers, so the traditional social structures are crumbling fast.

But Korea 2.0 is not entirely different from Korea 1.0 because the country continues to maintain ties with the past. In Korea, history is always a vital part of the present. That's why we start this book with an examination of how history has shaped, and continues to shape, the country. The division of the peninsula into two countries—one democratic and the other communist—has been one of the most important aspects of South Korea's past, and promises to be remain critical to the country's future.

Part two of the book deals with economics and trade. We delve into the economic catastrophe of 1997–98 and then explore South Korea's relationship with Japan, China, and the United States. Then, in part three, we also look at specific industries, such as the automobile sector, and individual companies, such as LG and Samsung. These chapters put the focus on a much smaller subject in order to learn the larger lessons they can impart for understanding Korea as a whole.

Part four of the book explores modern Korean society, including its obsession with golf, what it is like to work for a Korean firm, and how Confucianism dominates the cultural landscape of the country. Business moves at an incredible pace, but it requires a social finesse and patience in relationship building that Westerners may find confounding.

The book concludes with a look at the future. The first chapter in part five deals with the future of North Korea—an extremely important issue for the entire peninsula—and lays out four hypothetical courses for the communist country. The final chapter of the book explains what further leaps must be made to arrive at Korea 3.0, which we define as the complete development of the economy to the point where Koreans stand on an equal economic footing with the United States.

In *The New Korea*, we transliterated Korean words and place names according to the Revised Romanization method, which has quickly become the de facto standard for transliterating the Korean language into English. We took exception, however, in the transliteration of names, as many people choose to spell their names in English according to their own rules. Thus, when mentioning or quoting individuals in this book, we tried to respect their preferred spelling of their own names. One unifying factor in all the Korean names listed in this book is that we chose the "Korean" method of referring to names: The family name is listed first and the "first name" is capitalized and hyphenated (since most Korean "first names" comprise two names). The only exception to this naming rule is on the front cover, where one of the authors, Myung Oak Kim, chooses to use the "Americanized" order of her name.

We also use the terms *Korea, Republic of Korea,* and *South Korea* interchangeably. We have two chapters about North Korea, where we are careful to differentiate the two countries. Otherwise, you can assume that when we say Korea, we mean South Korea.

And now back to our archers. Kuk kung isn't the only style of archery popular in Korea. Korean men have dominated Olympic archery since 1988, but the Korean women have owned the sport. They won every gold medal—both in individual and team competition—since the Los Angeles games of 1984. The winning streak seemed unstoppable. Until the 2008 summer games in Beijing.

That summer, Chinese archer Zhang Juan Juan stood on the podium with the individual gold medal hanging from her neck. Koreans Park Sung-hyun and Yun Ok-hee stood glumly beside her, their silver and bronze medals dangling listlessly from their necks. This was a difficult blow to the Korean team and to the country.

The outcome of that contest is eerily similar to what Korea faces in its economic outlook. Koreans had dominated archery through hard work and mental toughness. But their formula for success couldn't last forever, and when their successful coaches began leaving to work for other teams, including China, the dynasty's days were numbered.

Korea is, and should be, concerned about competition from its much larger neighbor. China's economy is fast catching up to the Land of Morning Calm. And Korea will need to find a new model for success that goes beyond hard work and determination. The world is changing fast: China is rising, globalization has leveled the playing field, and Korea is playing with the big dogs now. Earning yesterday's awards may not necessarily be the goals Koreans should be shooting for in the future. In this new world, success will look a lot different.

PART ONE

HISTORY

CHAPTER 1

Still Living in the Past: Why History Matters

ASK KOREANS ABOUT their first taste of *doenjang* soup and their reply will probably be that they don't remember. There was no first taste: They have always been eating the soybean-based soup. But the first taste of doenjang can be a big surprise for a non-Korean. When the spoon first hits the mouth, the milky brown broth tastes like it looks: earth-like. Far from being subtle and cleansing, one's taste buds are instead flooded with a sensation of raw pungency. Unlike other Korean foods, which are prepared so that yin and yang are carefully balanced, doenjang is pure yang.

A taste for doenjang is what defines one's Korean-ness. North Korea's founder Kim Il-sung is rumored to have proclaimed, "You're not really Korean if you don't like doenjang." No matter how many foreigners claim to like *kimchi* (pickled cabbage) or *bulgogi* (barbecued ribs), very few will go as far as to claim that they "like" doenjang.

Koreans have been making doenjang for centuries. They store the brown soybean paste in dark clay vessels called *onggi*. The paste is used in soups and sauces. It also is considered to have healing properties. In recent years, scientists have confirmed that the process of making the bullion (which involves allowing soybean curd to ferment) probably encourages the same blue mold that produces penicillin.

Doenjang is so old that it is mentioned in one of the first written accounts of the Korean people. The *Samkuk Sagi* ("History of the Three Kingdoms"), written in the twelfth century, associated the Goguryeo people with the smell of doenjang (the Goguryeo Kingdom being one of the original Korean regions that included parts of Manchuria).

Simply put, Koreans eat their history. Their connection to foods like doenjang is one of many examples of why history is so important to the psyche of Korea. History is as much a part of the present as it was of the past. History, to a Korean, is not what happened. It is who you are, and what you do, and why you do it.

THE COLLECTIVE SPIRIT OF KOREA

On January 22, 2009, the head of the Federation of Korean Trade Unions, an organization that claims one million members, sat next to the leader of the Korea Employers Federation, which represents thousands of businesses, to publicly call for an emergency meeting among a variety of groups to find solutions to the global economic crisis.

"At this moment, when even more difficulties are expected than at the financial crisis of 1997, business turnaround and job security are all people's wishes," the groups said in a joint statement. "Job creation and a strong social safety net for the unemployed or the vulnerable can be achieved through cooperation by all social constituents."

A large-scale conference began the next week and the parties reached an agreement at the end of February. Nine leaders, most of them middle-aged men in dark suits, joined hands in a line during a press conference to announce the news. The deal essentially called for no layoffs in exchange for wage freezes, concessions, and job sharing by union workers. At the same time, the groups promised to find ways to improve profitability.

A month after the agreement was reached, a government survey of more than 6,000 companies found that almost one in four firms was using job sharing—the practice of avoiding layoffs by reducing work hours or, in some cases, having employees share jobs at reduced wages—as a way to reduce costs. The "pain sharing" pact represented drastic action taken to address serious economic troubles. The last time such an agreement was made was during the 1997 financial crisis.

The impact of this latest meeting and agreement remains to be seen. But the concept of "pain sharing" is a strong part of the mindset of Koreans, whose intense collective spirit and pride can be an enormous asset, especially in hard times. Like so much else in Korean culture, this mind-set goes back to Confucianism.

The philosophy is based on the importance of the well-being of the group and harmony among the members. Among the five relationships that form the foundation of Confucianism, one relates to the tie between the king and his subjects, who must show loyalty and trust.

But the collective spirit goes beyond the virtues of loyalty and harmony. It also incorporates a can-do attitude.

That attitude was key to a national campaign launched in the early 1970s by the Park Chung-hee administration. Park served as president of South Korea between 1963 and 1979 and led a huge push toward economic development. At this point in the country's young history, the Park administration faced criticism that it was focusing solely on the well-being and modernization of the cities, at the expense of rural villages and farmers.

The president's response to this criticism was an initiative called *Saemauel Undong*—also known as the New Community Movement. The campaign focused on modernizing and assisting rural areas. The government trained farmers on more advanced farming techniques, introducing a newer strain of rice and better equipment. The government also helped farmers replace thatch roofs with those made of cement and tile, and provided asphalt and cement to build roads.

The campaign garnered some criticism of its own in later years when it expanded to cities and factories and appeared to push for political support for the Park regime. Still, the New Community Movement was credited with creating an attitude shift and persuading people to believe that hard work and a positive outlook will lead to success for the entire community. Today, bright green flags with the campaign slogan and a yellow symbol of a plant still hang in a few areas of Seoul.

During the 1997 financial crisis, another campaign took place on a smaller scale. At that time, the country faced massive debt to foreign creditors. Among its responses, the central government put out a call to the public, asking people to contribute gold coins or jewelry. Thousands of people—many of them middle-aged housewives—showed up at collection stations across the country and handed over gold jewelry, including tiny rings given to babies when they turn one year old, to melt down into gold bars. In all, people gave 225 tons of gold, raising $1.8 billion, which was mostly used to pay off foreign debt.

The gold-gathering campaign did not make a significant dent in the economic crisis, but it showed how different segments of the population, including average citizens, were willing to step forward to sacrifice and help during a difficult time.

Koreans have also demonstrated a strong collective spirit in matters that are not clearly economic. On December 7, 2007, a barge owned by Samsung Heavy Industries struck a Chinese oil tanker during a storm at sea. The collision caused the vessel to spill more than 10,000 tons of crude oil into the Yellow Sea. Much of that oil washed onto a series of beaches in the area around Taean in South Chungcheong Province, a popular and scenic tourist area and stopover for migratory birds.

Gobs of thick, black, smelly oil coated the beaches and floated in the sea. Birds and other sea creatures were covered in oil, and many died. The slick affected at least 181 aquatic farms producing abalone, seaweed, littleneck clams, and sea cucumbers. The fishing and tourist industry that had flourished in that region suffered huge losses. It was the largest oil spill in the country's history.

More than 100 ships, including vessels from the U.S. Coast Guard, quickly arrived at the scene to assist with the cleanup. The government mobilized thousands of public workers. And within a day or two, thousands of volunteers arrived at the beach ready to help.

The volunteers included movie stars, students, and schoolteachers. Each day for weeks, roughly 6,000 to 7,000 volunteers donned suits, gloves, and rubber boots to help with the cleanup. They endured headaches, dizziness, and nausea from the stench of the oil. And while the numbers diminished after the first month, dozens of volunteers kept coming for months afterward. As one government official in the region put it, the public response to the disaster should have put Korea in the *Guinness Book of World Records* for most volunteers responding to an environmental disaster.

THE ENDURING IMPACT OF REGIONALISM

While Koreans show a fierce collective spirit, they also display strong differences based on a person's home region. There are many stereotypes about people based on where they come from. And people show strong loyalties to their own regions. Especially in presidential politics.

At first glance, military experience and a penchant to use authoritarian rule seemed to be the common link among the early presidents of South Korea. Park Chung-hee, Chun Doo-hwan, and Roh Tae-woo all had successful military careers, rising to the rank of army general, before they took the political helm of the country.

But Korea's top leaders had something else in common—their birthplace. Six of the eight presidents of the Republic of Korea came from North Gyeongsang Province in southeast Korea. Presidents Park Chung-hee and Chun Doo-hwan (1980–88) both came from the city of Daegu, and Roh Tae-woo (1988–93) was born in another part of North Gyeongsang Province. Kim Young-sam (1993–98) was born in South Gyeongsang Province.

The two most recent presidents, Roh Moo-hyun (2003–2008) and Lee Myung-bak, elected in 2008, came from South Gyeongsang Province, at the southeastern tip of the peninsula. Only two presidents bucked this trend. Rhee Syng-man, the first president, serving between 1948 and 1960, came from a province just north of the 38th parallel in what is now North Korea. And Kim Dae-jung (1998–2003) came from a small village in South Jeolla Province in the southwestern tip of the peninsula.

These geographical distinctions may seem minor, or even coincidental. They're not. In fact, geography plays a critical role in explaining modern politics. And it demonstrates why ancient Korean history is still important today. To understand the significance of these geographical issues, we need to look back more than 2,000 years—back to the time when the peninsula was divided into three kingdoms: Silla, Baekje, and Goguryeo. Although their boundaries shifted over the years, in general, Goguryeo occupied the northern part of the peninsula and parts of what is now China. Silla controlled the east and southeast swaths of the peninsula, and Baekje covered the smallest area in the southwestern tip of the country.

Goguryeo was generally the largest kingdom and had the most military power during that period, even overtaking large swaths of China at certain points. Baekje was the earliest kingdom to adopt Buddhism and made advancements in science, philosophy, and art. Silla developed last and also chose Buddhism as the predominant religion.

Because of the military power of Goguryeo, Silla formed an alliance with Baekje to protect against southward advancement by Goguryeo. The two kingdoms kept this alliance for many years, and then together overtook Goguryeo territory. But then Silla turned on Baekje and attacked the Baekje forces. Baekje, in response, partnered with what remained of the Goguryeo Kingdom to fight Silla. But Silla turned to the Chinese for help and ended up victorious.

In the end, Baekje ended up with the short end of the stick—dominated by Goguryeo and then by Silla in later years. According to some historical accounts, Goguryeo worked to pit Silla and Baekje against each other as a way to maintain power. Over the years, the people of Silla and Baekje maintained a strong distrust of each other. This enmity continued even when the names Silla and Baekje no longer were used.

Today, North Korea occupies the historical Goguryeo territory. A handful of provinces, mainly North and South Gyeongsang provinces, occupy what had been the Silla territory. And Chungcheong and North and South Jeolla provinces cover what had historically been Baekje.

Historically, the Baekje region was the center of rice farming. The people there also developed a reputation as being strong-willed, rebellious, and calculating. When King Taejo (formerly known as Wang Kon) established the Goryeo Dynasty in the late 900s, he remembered the troubles he had with Baekje people. He described the region as containing people who were treacherous and disharmonious. From then on, political leaders often excluded Baekje people from joining government.

During the Joseon Dynasty (1392–1910), in the mid-1400s, a geographical report on the country's eight regions described Jeolla people as "kindhearted and gentle, but also highly intelligent, manipulative, and calculating." They were ardent followers of shamanism, and not well educated. A local official in a report to the king in 1474 described the Jeolla people as thieves, murderers, and pirates.

The political marginalization worsened problems in the area. Baekje land was considered the rice bowl of the country—a farming area where a small number of government officials ruled over a large number of poorly educated farmers. The peasants suffered worse treatment, and more tax burdens, which spurred more resentment and call for rebellion.

So it was a vicious circle. Negative treatment by the government worsened the conditions in the area, leading to more disharmony and rebellion.

At the same time, the southwestern region had a thriving folk culture, including the *pansori* (narrative operatic performances). The Tonghak Movement—a nineteenth-century rebellion against the corrupt governors and a class struggle in favor of equality for the peasants—grew out of the folk culture tradition in this area. The struggles continued into the modern period, and even after the creation of the Republic of Korea in 1948.

Intent on solidifying his power as a military dictator, President Park Chung-hee took advantage of the stigma against Jeolla residents. He took power away from government officials who were not from his province. He forged strong relations with officials from his province. During Park's sixteen years as president, the people of Gyeongsang Province were more than two and a half times over-represented while Jeolla people were 0.7 times under-represented. Major government agencies, including the intelligence service, the Economic Planning Board, and the Ministry of Home Affairs, were run by people from Gyeongsang Province. Park was eventually as-sassinated by Kim Jae-gyu, the director of the Korean Central Intel-ligence Agency (also from Gyeongsang Province). But Park's legacy of putting people from Gyeongsang Province into positions of power continued with the presidents succeeding him.

The election of Kim Dae-jung in 1998—and the more liberal polit-ical policies of the even more recent presidents—reduced the stigma against Jeolla people. But social prejudice is still widespread. In tele-vision dramas set during the Joseon Dynasty, the farmers, thieves, murderers, and other low-class characters speak with a Jeolla ac-cent. Some people from Jeolla use a Seoul accent when they are looking for work. In Seoul, Jeolla people tend to be heavily concen-trated in the poorer suburbs. Some residents in apartment buildings try to stop Jeolla people from moving into their building because they fear a drop in property value.

WHY THE HERMIT ATTITUDE PERSISTS

Koreans can hold even stronger suspicion of foreigners, including Americans. Some Westerners are perplexed by anti-Americanism in Korea, which is frequently expressed in street protests. These demon-strations are often filled with young Koreans who did not experience the Korean War or the Japanese occupation. Many older Koreans who lived through those times lament that the younger generation does not understand the aid that the United States gave their country during the war and at other points. And these protests also are sometimes strongly tinged with political attitudes, such as opposition to restrictive policies under the George W. Bush administration, and are not connected with attitudes about the United States in general. That's why you will find Korean politicians speaking publicly against a Free Trade Agreement with the United States, but also sending their children to study at an American university.

The anti-Americanism expressed in demonstrations—like the ones that occurred in the spring and summer of 2008 against U.S. beef imports—reflects more than just the political attitude of the day. It shows that many Koreans still have the same basic attitude that their ancestors had centuries ago—a strong resistance to outsiders and foreign influence. With a fierce pride in their self-reliance and historical roots, Koreans have long held a strong suspicion of outside powers.

The Korean people can trace their ancestors back thousands of years before the birth of Jesus. They probably arrived on the peninsula after emigrating from the area now known as Mongolia, but the exact nature of the origin of the Korean people is marked by scientific controversy.

Many Koreans today trace their ancestors to a pristine lake high in the magnificent Baekdu Mountains on the Chinese border of North Korea. The lake is called Cheonji, or Heavenly Lake, and is part of a dormant volcano. It is in this area that the fabled Tangun Wangom was supposedly born. The first Korean, according to folk tales, Tangun was the son of a god (known as Hwanung) and a woman incarnated from a bear. According to legend, Tangun created the kingdom of Gojoseon in 2333 BC, during the Bronze Age. That kingdom was centered in the Liaoning area of Manchuria.

By the time of the birth of Jesus, the Korean peninsula was occupied by the three kingdoms—Goguryeo in the north, Silla in the

east and southeast, and Baekje in the southwest. For a time, another
kingdom known as Kaya existed, but it was engulfed by Baekje.

Over the years, the three kingdoms formed alliances among
each other and with leaders in China and Japan. They also defended
themselves against foreign invaders. But by AD 668, Silla emerged
victorious, overtaking the other two kingdoms, and the first unified dynasty began. To the north of Silla, the Parhae Dynasty ruled
the northern edge of the peninsula and northeastern China. During
the first century, Koreans built one of the world's first astronomical
observatories, which is still standing today. They also developed a
unique residential heating system known as *gudeul* or *ondol* (which
means "warm rock").

The long-lasting dynasties came later. The Goryeo Kingdom
(918–1392) was established by Wang Kon, later known as King Taejo.
He established his capital in Gaeseong (now in North Korea) and
ruled for almost thirty years.

By far the most enduring dynasty was the Joseon Kingdom
(1392–1910), established by General Yi Song-gye, with its capital in
Hanyang, which is present-day Seoul.

Over the centuries, Korea was greatly influenced by Japan and
China, and in turn Japan adopted aspects of Korean painting, sculp-
ture, and architecture. The Korean nation adopted Confucian systems regarding family and government relations. The sons of aristocrats studied Chinese classics. Some kings chose Buddhism as
the national religion. Society was based on farming, and strict class
divisions lasted for centuries. Slaves also were commonly used by
the ruling elite.

The country was repeatedly invaded by Chinese, Japanese, and
Mongol forces. In fact, Korea on several occasions could have become the territory of China or Japan—had it not been for the courage and ingenuity of two formidable military leaders: Ulchi Mundok
and Yi Sun-shin.

Ulchi Mundok lived so long ago that historians don't know when he was born or died. Born in a remote village in South Pyeongan Province, General Ulchi Mundok became a master scholar and soldier. General Ulchi was also a great writer. He became prime minister and commanding officer of Goguryeo, which had a standing army of about 50,000 men that would grow to more than 300,000 men in times of war. His forces were divided into specialties: archers, crossbow-men, spearmen, catapult operators, horsemen, and wall-climbers, among others.

In AD 612, an army of more than one million men from the Sui Dynasty in China invaded Goguryeo. Ulchi Mundok deployed his outnumbered men along the southern bank of the Yalu River. He "surrendered" to the enemy in order to spy on the enemy strength. After learning that the Sui soldiers were tired and demoralized, the general escaped across the Yalu.

He feigned numerous defeats to lure enemy soldiers toward Pyongyang, tiring them and stretching their supplies. Just north of Pyongyang, Ulchi Mundok sent a poem to the Chinese commander:

Your divine plans have plumbed the heavens;
Your subtle reckoning has spanned the earth.
You win every battle, your military merit is great.
Why then not be content and stop the war?

The poem worked. It lured the enemy commanders into thinking that the Koreans were on the verge of surrender. Instead, they ferociously attacked. The Goguryeo forces destroyed the Sui, with as few as several thousand soldiers surviving. That defeat was a factor in the fall of the Sui Dynasty. This defeat helped save Korea from long-term control by the Chinese.

Korea faced another formidable outside threat less than 1,000 years later. Warlord Toyotomi Hideyoshi of Japan invaded with plans to use the country as an entry point to invade China. Again, another ingenious military leader would help protect the country.

Admiral Yi Sun-shin (1545–98) was born to a poor *yangban* (aristocratic) family. As an adult, he worked hard to learn military arts and weaponry. At age twenty-eight, he took the military service exam, but failed after he fell off a horse during one test. He would have to wait four years before being permitted to take the test again. This time, he passed and was given a position in the navy.

Yi succeeded in the military and was promoted quickly. He became naval commander in Jeolla Province. That's where he designed the world's first ironclad ship. The ships were called Geobuk-seon, or turtle ships, because of their design. Some ships, spanning sixty-five feet long and fifteen feet wide, were covered with plated armor for protection. An imposing dragon head at the front covered guns that could shoot at enemies. The Koreans burned sulfur and saltpeter to create a cloud that came out of the dragon's mouth to provide a smoke screen during battle. And cannons were shot out of the front.

When the Japanese invaded in 1592, Admiral Yi deployed his new ships and easily destroyed the enemy fleet with the aid of Chinese allies. Five years later, Yi faced another invasion by the Japanese. This time, his ships also defeated the Japanese—leading to their withdrawal and an abandonment of expansion interests for about 300 years. During the battle, a stray bullet hit Yi and killed him.

In more modern times, Korean peasants staged their own campaign against the influence of other nations with song, leaflets, demonstrations, and even force. It began in the mid-1800s, when peasants were taxed to extremes to fund the aristocracy. The foundation of the economy was agriculture, so workers who tilled the fields faced the most economic hardships. They paid several land taxes, plus taxes on commodities, and also had to support the military. At the same time, Christian missionaries from the West were moving to the country and officials from Europe and other parts of Asia had come to develop commerce.

In the 1850s, a man named Choe Che-u (1824–64) began spreading a philosophy and religion called Tonghak, which means "eastern." He had failed the civil service exam and roamed the country pushing a concept that combined aspects of Confucianism, Buddhism, and Taoism with an emphasis on equality among all people. He put his ideas to song—which appealed to the peasants who were not well educated. He preached an end to the lavish lifestyles and power of the *yangban* and other elite groups, better treatment of the peasants, and a rejection of foreign influence.

The message was clear in one of the main slogans of the movement: "Drive out the Japanese dwarfs and the Western barbarians and praise righteousness." Peasant uprisings began in 1862 and the military was ill-equipped to respond. Choe was arrested in 1863 and executed the next year. That caused the movement to go underground for many years.

Meanwhile, the country opened up further to Japan and other nations, causing more hardships for the peasants, as rice was sold overseas. In the late 1880s, the uprisings resumed—mainly in the southwestern Chungcheong Province. Rebels then went to Seoul and protested outside Kyungbok Palace. They were dismissed by King Kojong. A corrupt and punishing official in Jeolla prompted a more passionate uprising that drew the ire of the palace, which dispatched soldiers to arrest the Tonghaks, as the rebels came to be known.

The arrests inflamed the rebellion, and the Tonghaks used sharpened bamboo sticks and farm tools to do battle. Soldiers deserted and joined the Tonghaks, who gained control of towns in Jeolla. In response, the king promised to fire corrupt officials in exchange for fair taxation and an end to rice exports to Japan. But that action further emboldened the rebels, who made more demands, including an end to the requirement that lower-class men must wear a certain hat. When the Korean military could not suppress the rebels, King

Kojong called in the Chinese and Japanese, who entered the country in 1894 and quickly destroyed the Tonghak rebellion. Chinese officials offered a mutual withdrawal, but Japan, taking advantage of the opportunity to exert its domination over the peninsula, forced a takeover of the palace, leading to the Sino-Japanese War. The Japanese easily defeated the Chinese and kept control of Korea.

The rebellion ended in 1895 with much bloodshed among the Tonghaks at the hands of the Japanese and the Korean royal forces. Ironically, the Japanese instituted many reforms in Korea that the Tonghaks wanted—better tax policies and an easing of class restrictions. But the broad ambitions of the Japanese, based on their imperialism and their belief that they were a superior people, brought deep troubles to Korea—much worse than had existed before the Tonghak Movement came to be.

CHAPTER 2

North Korea: A Distorted Mirror

IN JULY **2009,** North Korea launched seven Scud missiles into the Japan Sea. It wasn't the first incident of sword-shaking that the country had initiated in the recent past. It had launched a Taepodong 2, an intercontinental ballistic missile, into the chill of a quiet Sunday morning in April. It had—for the second time—tested a nuclear weapon underground in that same month. Across the globe, denunciations rang out as government ministers and United Nations officials warned of a new arms race. South Korean and Japanese anti-missile boats haunted the waters just offshore, ready to shoot down any new missiles if they wandered toward their territory. Once again, tensions were at sky-high levels on the Korean peninsula.

At the same time, a new famine threatened the countryside, endangering the lives of thousands of peasants. If not for cheap food imported from China and sold in local black market bazaars, rural North Korea could not feed itself. It is estimated that the same amount of money it took to launch the rocket in April, approximately $500 million, would have been enough to pay for food for half the population for a year.

If Oscar Wilde had written *The Picture of Dorian Gray* with a country in mind, modern Korea would be the ideal main character. In the course of its sixty-year history, the southern part of the Korean peninsula has grown by breathtaking leaps, seemingly becoming younger and stronger with every passing year. Meanwhile, a mirror country hidden in the attic regions of the peninsula—one that few people have ever visited—grows older, crueler, and more frail at the same pace. Yet it refuses to succumb.

South Koreans grow up, start families, and pursue careers under the menacing shadow of North Korean artillery. But the psychic impact goes beyond the military threat. South Koreans have a vivid sense that they are living only a segment of the national dream. They understand that half the country has been torn from them—and will eventually return.

For decades, that sense of division was fed by the fear that communists would overrun the South. That almost happened in 1950. Today, however, the overriding emotion most people have for North Korea is pity. The world understands that the communist regime cannot survive much longer, and that reunification will be costly for the South. But it will also be rewarding.

While there are certainly spiritual, familial, cultural, and humanitarian angles to the potential reunification of the peninsula, there is also a significant economic story. North Korea represents Asia's poorest and most unexploited hinterland. When unification does happen, it will bring a new chapter in development to the ancient country. But first, let's take a look back at the war that began Korea's division.

THE WAR TO BEGIN ALL WARS

All that's necessary to remind yourself that Korea is still in a state of war is to head north from Seoul for about forty-five minutes to the Gaeseong Cemetery. It's not really in Gaeseong, the former national capital of the peninsula that is now in North Korea. But the gravesites are strategically placed on low rolling hills that face the first set of border fences with the North. A few kilometers away in the foggy distance is North Korea. More specifically, it is the town of Gaeseong that these graves face. Most of the bones buried here belong to those who fled the North amidst the tumult of the Korean War. They longed their whole lives to be able to return. Even in death, their hopes are denied. But at least they can have the solace of gazing across at their beloved home ground, even if at a distance. Even if in death.

Not that there is much to see of Gaeseong. The only notable landmark is the fence itself. Actually, a half dozen different fences stretch across the country at the 38th parallel, cutting it like a surgeon's blunt scalpel. Beyond the fences are land mines and snipers. Beyond the no-man's-land is what appears to be a dreary and drab North Korea, a few stone houses visible amidst the fog that seems to perpetually settle here.

The visiting of grave sites is an important Korean tradition, as befits a Confucian nation. Family members bring food, spirits, and flowers as offerings to their departed ones. They usually lay out the gifts on the grave site and then commence to do *che-sa*, an elaborate bowing ceremony performed while facing the gravestone with their backs to Gaeseong. But even without looking directly at North Korea, the conflict with it intrudes. Faraway loudspeakers blast garish music and jauntily upbeat announcers spread Northern propaganda into the South. Battling loudspeakers on the Southern side broadcast loud renditions of Korean pop music and news updates. Pity the South Korean office worker who was hoping to visit his father's grave for a moment of lucidity and restfulness. Instead, he's treated to a fugue of loud and obnoxious propaganda emanating from both sides of the border.

It's not easy to forget the Korean conflict, neither the one that happened between 1950 and 1953 nor the one that has been frozen in time and space ever since. The Korean War is still with us physically, in the limbless survivors or the shrapnel-pocked walls that still grace some Seoul buildings. In the United States, it is remembered—when remembered at all—as "the Forgotten War." That despite the fact that more than 60,000 Americans died on Korean soil (more than died in Vietnam, a war that nobody has forgotten). In South Korea, it is referred to as "the Civil War." Somewhere between half a million and two million Korean civilians died in the mayhem. Another ten million became refugees—more than half the overall population of the country at the time. And all of them have scars that they have passed on to their children and grandchildren.

Not much is mysterious about that war. It started with a surprise attack by the Northern communists against Seoul. The attack went swimmingly. Within a few days, the defenders had collapsed and the communists were riding at full speed toward the tip of the Korean peninsula. The remaining South Korean fighters and millions of refugees gathered at Busan behind ten miles of fortifications for one last, vicious stand.

But then the United Nations decided to intervene. The first contingent was a group of U.S. Army soldiers who landed at Busan and proceeded to suffer nearly a 100 percent casualty rate in a few days. A Marine force soon reached Busan and helped defend the city. More troops arrived and began to enlarge the defenses, slowly pushing the Northerners back, a few yards at a time. Then, just three weeks after the first shots in the war were fired, General Douglas MacArthur, known affectionately as "Magadoo" (a mangled Korean transliteration of MacArthur) by South Koreans even today, launched a daring amphibious landing at Incheon, just southwest of Seoul. His commandos had four hours to capture the beach at Incheon and take the fortified embattlements that overlooked it, or else the high tide would sweep them away. They established a beachhead and then fought bitterly to keep it long enough for the second wave to arrive. Victorious at Incheon, the invading force then attacked an occupied Seoul from the communists' blind side.

The tables were turned. The North Koreans were now the ones fleeing at full speed, a few fellow traveling refugees joining them as they raced for refuge in the North. But there was no refuge. The U.N. armies went far beyond the 38th parallel—the original dividing line between the North and the South that was decided upon by the United States and Russia at the end of World War II—and soon set their sights on a complete victory. As U.S. and U.N. troops streamed northward in great haste to reach the Yalu River and the border with China, discipline started to disintegrate. Flanks were left unprotected. Units became more and more separated as they approached the Yalu.

Great Power politics came into play at that point. Some historians insist that MacArthur was intent on goading China into a fight to destroy the communist superpower with American war-fighting technology. Goad them he did, as the Chinese authorities viewed the U.N. assault past the 38th parallel as a direct attack on their own territory. Just before U.N. troops reached the Yalu, a massive counterattack of the Chinese People's Army units allied with North Korea began. The attacking role switched once again as the Chinese People's Liberation Army took on the role of the attacker and U.N. and South Korean forces waged a fighting retreat, pulling back to the original starting lines. In the midst of that retreat, millions of Northerners fled with the U.N. troops to the South and its promise of international support. The war finally reached a stalemate phase, with both sides trading artillery fire and commando raids for the next year and a half. A final armistice resulted in the border being drawn at the same 38th parallel from which the fighting had started.

There was never a peace treaty. Technically, the United States and South Korea are still at war with North Korea. The only difference is that—for the most part—the warfare is all psychological, with few bullets trading sides.

The war, and the ghosts of war that hang over the peninsula sixty years later, is very much still a part of life in Korea. But in some ways, it is strangely absent from the lifestyle and the discourse of the South. Few South Koreans will raise the subject of the war to visitors. Even discussion of North Korea, their neighbor and estranged co-nation, is considered unseemly in most circumstances. Yet North Korea exists, as much as some South Koreans wish it didn't.

OF BRIBES AND BRINKSMANSHIP

The history of inter-Korean contacts over the last sixty years has mainly been a narrative about diplomatic negotiations, whether over the end of the Korean War, arms reduction, nuclear weapons, or trade ties. So it's important to understand the North Korean and the South Korean approaches to negotiating strategy.

To grasp the basics of negotiating strategy on the Korean peninsula, let's imagine that it's all about haggling over the price of a used car. The first and most important cultural context that must be understood is that Koreans, Northerners and Southerners, recognize that any negotiation is part of a long cycle of negotiations. The goal is always the long-term end, not the immediate realization of the short-term end. Thus, the North Korean approach is to wait for the first move by the seller of the car, then to douse the car in gasoline, set it afire, and make a counteroffer. To people couched in conventional diplomacy, the kind that is most often practiced by most global governments, such an action is thought of as counterproductive, irrational, and borderline insane. Such negotiating tactics so thoroughly confuse American decision makers that it even led one of the masters of diplomacy, former assistant defense secretary Paul Wolfowitz, to say: "I'm more profoundly skeptical of North Korea than any other country—both how they think, which I don't understand, and the series of bizarre things they have done."

The South Korean view of negotiating with the North can be summarized this way: The buyer (South Korea) makes an initial offer publicly. Then it privately, through a back channel, offers to actually provide ten times the amount for the car and to throw in ten more free cars to make up for the seller's (North Korea's) loss. Such duplicitous bribery infuriates American negotiators, who see it as giving up the farm for the sake of the hog.

Both stances might seem irrational to the outside world, but remember the context of long-term negotiations. Both sides feel that they make better long-term progress when they take such stances, even if it leaves short-term negotiations over specific objectives in shambles. Scott Snyder, a foreign policy expert on the Korean peninsula, summed it up in his book, *Negotiating on the Edge: North Korean Negotiating Behavior,* as a cultural imperative for long-term cyclical negotiations and a lack of appreciation for short-term linear negotiations. " . . . [A]ccording to a cyclical conception of negotiations with North Korea," he wrote, "there is really no end game in the negotiating process."

Another important factor to take into account when analyzing North Korea's negotiating policies is to understand that the country has its feet firmly planted in the stream of Korean history. While many foreigners view the North Korean state as a bizarre historical mistake, Koreans themselves view it as a logical attenuation of previous Korean regimes.

North Korea, by all accounts, should have collapsed a decade ago. Or two decades ago. Or seven decades ago. The only thing that North

Korean "experts" can agree on is that it shouldn't be there—that its very existence defies rationality.

Many North Koreans would strongly disagree. They would, if given the chance to speak freely (a liberty they most certainly have never had), defend their country. And to some degree, they would be right, in that there is a historical legitimacy to the North Korean regime.

Go back 150 years to the time of gunboat diplomacy and you would have seen a country very similar to modern North Korea. The vast majority of people lived a ragged agricultural lifestyle overseen by a small number of ruling elites. For the peasants, if there was something stronger than their distaste for the *yangban* (the privileged upper class) it was their suspicion and fear of the outside world. When U.S. Admiral John Rodgers sailed his fleet up the Han River in 1871 and threatened to fire his guns if Korean ports weren't opened for trade, the response was one of nationalistic pride and zeal. The foreigners were politely told by messenger boat to go home (they were given several servings of rice, too—the Confucian rules of hospitality for strangers had to be respected, after all) while the people onshore turned their backs to the ships, hoping that the aliens would disappear. A few gunfights later and the Americans steamed home, having won a minor military victory but not achieving their diplomatic goals. Hence was born the term "the Hermit Kingdom," a sobriquet that can be aptly applied to modern-day North Korea as well.

The North Korean regime wants the world, with its notions of democracy, free trade, and globalization, to just go away. The country's search for nuclear weapons mastery is part of that desire. With nukes, North Korea has an ace-in-the-hole when the rest of the world demands change. Like a child holding a gun to its head, nobody will dare threaten a nuclear North Korea.

The problem for the rest of the world is that the logic of the North Koreans is correct. When North Korea first tested a nuclear weapon in 2006, there was tremendous debate among weapons of mass destruction (WMD) experts as to how successful the test really was. Some experts claimed that the only explosion was the dynamite wrapped around the nuclear core intended to spark a thermonuclear reaction, so the bomb was a dud. Others claimed that the evidence showed a small (very small) scale nuclear weapon did go off inside a mountain complex in the North on that cold November day. That debate became moot when the country tested its second bomb underground in April 2009. The second try was without doubt a successful nuclear explosion. North Korea must now be viewed as a nuclear state, with somewhere between four and ten plutonium-based bombs. The North Koreans do not yet have the technological ability to arm one of their missiles with a nuclear warhead, but few observers doubt that they won't eventually teach themselves that skill too.

Now that North Korea has nuclear weapons, there is little reason to believe that its negotiating posture will change its form. In fact, North Korea has always used extreme negotiating tactics in its dealings with the outside world. A prime example was the capture of the USS *Pueblo*, an American spy ship that was ambushed and taken over by North Korean marines in 1968. Even though the ship had been in international waters, and therefore the assault had been an act of piracy, the North Koreans held the crew for months and refused to back down in negotiating their release. When they finally did release the U.S. sailors, they kept the ship as a museum for their people to remember the "heroic" event. While the United States had one and only one objective in the negotiations over the *Pueblo* (the liberation of the sailors), North Korea saw the talks as part of a never-ending struggle against their hated American enemies.

Little has changed in North Korea's negotiating strategy since that time. The country's representatives always begin from positions of the farthest extreme and rarely back down from those positions. When concessions are made, and they sometimes are, they are usually matched with an equally ostentatious show of defiance and brinksmanship.

Sometimes, though, minor progress is made. Take the "break-through" of 2008. After two years of grueling negotiations, an agreement had seemingly been reached between the six parties (Russia, China, Japan, the United States, South Korea, and North Korea) in negotiations over the North Korean nuclear crisis. Suddenly, the North reversed course. It kicked all nuclear inspectors out of the country and broke the seals they had placed at the Yongbyon nuclear reactor. North Korean engineers began to fire the reactor back up. The problem, the North declared, was that the United States had welched on its agreement to remove North Korea from its list of terrorist states. Never mind that the United States was in the midst of doing so—the North, it seemed, was willing to go to the brink once again.

Then, just as suddenly, the crisis was over. U.S. negotiator Christopher Hill traveled to Pyongyang and worked out a proposal where the inspectors would be allowed back in and the North would be removed from the list of terrorist nations. Within days, both events occurred.

Does that mean it's time to start celebrating a new dawn of relations between the United States and North Korea? Not at all. Just a few months later, North Korea was launching ICBMs and detonating nuclear explosions in contravention of all the agreements it had signed.

Just as perplexing to the outside world are the strange negotiating stances taken by South Korea. During the administrations of Kim Dae-jung (1998–2003) and Roh Moo-hyun (2003–2008), the South pursued a tact known as "the Sunshine Policy." All dealings with the North would go toward the goal of opening that country up to the sunlight of the modern world. In actuality, the Sunshine Policy resulted in massive, large-scale bribery. Hyundai, one of the most powerful corporations in South Korea, spent more than $100 million on a resort for Southern tourists in the Kumkangsan region of North Korea. Very little was gained on the deal by Hyundai. In 1999, President Kim Dae-jung met North Korean leader

Kim Jong-il in Pyongyang for the first inter-Korean summit meeting. Seven years later, it was revealed that the only reason Kim Jong-il had agreed to the meeting was that Kim Dae-jung had secretly transferred half a billion dollars into secret North Korean bank accounts.

Does bribery pay? In this case, it certainly hasn't. The North continues to ignore the South and insists on making peace only with the United States (something U.S. officials have refused to do, out of respect for their South Korean allies).

To understand why the South is willing to demean itself in its relationship with the North, consider this: Many people in the South secretly admire their Northern brothers. Whatever else can be said about the North's history of famine and repression, nobody can question its willingness to sacrifice anything for the cause of Korean nationalism. The South, on the other hand, has made many concessions to archrival Japan, allows American soldiers on its land, and seems—to the jaded observer—to worship nothing besides money. Few Southerners will discuss this hypothesis openly, but catch them in their unguarded moments and many will betray an admiration for the North as the ultimate rebel brother who has given up everything else but has stayed true as a Korean patriot. When that's the inner attitude toward the North, there's little wonder that the South seems to think that bribery is the right way to handle affairs with its neighbor.

A BROKEN COUNTRY

When discussing what daily life is like in North Korea, it is important to first note that there are three North Koreas: the high officialdom, the Pyongyang elite, and everyone else.

The first North Korea revolves around the sheltered, opulent life of high officials of the regime. These lucky few live in palatial residences, watch South Korean broadcasts and CNN on their big-screen LCD TVs, and travel to Japan and China frequently on shopping and tourist jaunts. While numbering only a few hundred people, these aristocrats live a very different life from their compatriots. They consist of a few dozen former Manchurian freedom fighters who helped Kim Il-sung build the state after 1945 and somehow outlived him, along with a few dozen more of Kim's extended family members (including in-laws and their extended families) who control the different apparatuses of the state—the security services, the intelligence services, the army, and the senior ministries.

While they enjoy the same creature comforts as the average citizen of Seoul, these people spend their working lives overseeing one of the most brutal dictatorships the world has ever known. It's their job to make sure that the trains run on time, that the mines run by prison labor keep producing, and that any enemies of the state they might find get executed.

Working underneath the aristocracy is the second North Korea: the clerks, party workers, and apparatchiks who live in Pyongyang. This city's 3 million residents (those who don't belong to the aforementioned regime ruling class) are the favored elite of the Korean Workers Party, the military, and the regime. That means, for the most part, that they and their families are spared from starvation. Some of them even get some of the few perks available in North Korea, including washing machines, foreign clothing, and even hair salon appointments.

And then there is the rest of North Korea. Some 20 million strong, these people live in North Korea's other cities (Nampo and Hamhung are the other two largest cities in North Korea, followed by a handful of small cities that would probably be called towns in most countries) and—the vast majority of them—in the rural villages that dot the landscape of modern North Korea.

The exact number of North Koreans isn't known with confidence. The best we can do is to suggest a range of between 23 million and 25 million people. One of the reasons the numbers are unclear is because of the huge famine that rocked the country in 1996 and 1997. Starvation and misery were so extreme that some people ate grass to survive. Experts still disagree strongly over whether 250,000 people died (that's the official government death toll) or if the number is as high as 2 million, as some nongovernmental organizations claim.

However many North Koreans there are, we do know a few things about them. Most of them live in concrete housing structures built in the 1960s and 1970s. Each house tends to hold an entire extended family, where everyone sleeps on straw mats on the floor, just as was done throughout the peninsula until rising standards of living caused the Southerners to flee to urban apartments throughout the 1960s and onward (where they often still sleep on futon-like mats on the floor).

Each house tends to have a walled-in courtyard, where dwell a few chickens and maybe, if the family is lucky, a pig. Outside the house, and in any other available scrap of land nearby, the family cultivates a garden that supplies them with much of their own vegetables and cabbage for *kimchi*, the fundamental Korean food made out of pickled cabbage and eaten as an appetizer and in combination with the main course, as well as a little extra that can be sold in the nearest market towns for pocket change.

Most families belong to the local agricultural collective, which manages the rice fields throughout the country. This centralized farming apparatus is essentially owned by the state and requires the citizens of the countryside to spend a few days each month helping out with such labor-intensive processes as planting, flooding, and harvesting. The last process is a national event, bringing all the local people as well as army conscripts and Pyongyang citizens out into the countryside for a massive rice harvesting extravaganza. All members of the collective get a small portion of the harvest, which they store for use throughout the year.

In previous decades, almost every citizen's food was provided by the state in the form of monthly rations, called the Public Distribution System. However, in recent years, private gardening has become so successful that most North Koreans get the bulk of their nutrition from their own gardens or from produce bought at the free enterprise markets. A recent trend in gardening is to cultivate plots of land in the mountains (most North Koreans live in fertile valleys ringed by uninhabited mountain ranges) with barley, corn, and millet. The average North Korean now gets a daily nutrition load of approximately 1,100 kilocalories, which is one-third of the average calorie load of the American citizen, and roughly comparable to the calories consumed by the average sub-Saharan African or Indian.

To some degree, North Korea has become a welfare state in the sense that close to a third of its food comes in the form of free aid given to it by the United States, Japan, South Korea, and China, with the latter being the largest provider of aid. This aid comes in the form of cereals (used mostly as livestock feed), some rice, and large shipments of nitrogenous fertilizers.

A unique aspect of North Korean food consumption is the tradition of going into the mountains during the autumn to hunt for traditional foods such as wild mushrooms and roots. Although this practice magnified dramatically during the famines of the late 1990s, it is still commonly done, even by Pyongyang citizens, more as a cultural tradition (a tradition that used to be observed in the South also, before it was discontinued) than as a hunger-coping mechanism.

Besides food, most North Koreans receive almost all of their necessities from the state. Each citizen is issued two outfits (a summer version and a winter version made out of thicker material) and a pair of shoes, all of which are made out of Vinalon, a polyvinyl material that was claimed to have been invented in North Korea. In fact, it was discovered by a Korean scientist who lived in Japan in the 1930s. The material, most of which is made in an enormous factory in Hamhung, is stiff, shiny, and notoriously uncomfortable for anyone who has worn anything else.

North Korean children attend school from an early age and most children complete some form of secondary school. The nation's universities are the breeding ground for the elite of Pyongyang. Their most noticeable attribute is the perfectly equal number of females and males in the classes.

Although there are more than 1.2 million phone lines in North Korea, most of those are for strictly military or government office use. Cell phones were illegal until 2008, although many thousands of them were used illicitly in the northern part of the country, where callers roam on the nearby Chinese networks. In late 2008, the country's first cell phone network was launched by the Egyptian company Orascom, and it quickly garnered some 6,000 subscribers. Again, most of those users belonged to the Pyongyang elite. Several million people have black-and-white television sets that are locally produced and hardwired for the country's only channel—a twenty-four-hour news station, courtesy of the Korean Central Broadcasting Agency.

NORTH KOREANS IN SOUTH KOREA

Her long dark hair hangs in gentle waves, and her skin is fair and flawless. Yeh-nah wears black heels and a sweater dress—the fashion of the day in Seoul. She is tired from late nights studying for her graduate degree, but her eyes are bright and alert.

The thirty-year-old woman lives with her mother in a tiny apartment in Seoul. They have never lived so poorly—with barely enough money to eat.

Yeh-nah chose to flee Pyongyang in 2004 for political reasons. Two months before she left, Yeh-nah was brutally beaten by police for wearing pants in public. North Korean women can only wear skirts, and her transgression resulted in such severe injuries that she spent fifteen days in a hospital.

Yeh-nah is one of more than 15,000 North Korean refugees living in South Korea. She predicts that her homeland will collapse within the next two decades.

"Eventually it will be demolished," she said, "because North Korea is being influenced by South Korea."

Yeh-nah's mother worked as an actress, appearing in the political movies aired on North Korea's only TV channel. Occasionally, they produced nonpolitical movies, Yeh-nah said. Her mother did not belong to the Communist Party, but her father, an electrician, did. He died of cancer in 2001.

The family lived a comfortable life because her mother operated a business selling noodles in China and importing clothes and rice from China, then selling them on the black market in North Korea. She hid the operations from the government and gave food and goods to the army and government officials to keep them happy. At one point, the mother donated enough food to feed 600 soldiers.

After the "pants incident" that left her hospitalized, Yeh-nah fled North Korea by walking over the frozen Yalu River (Koreans refer to it as the Amnok River) into China. She is part of a growing tide of people who risk their lives in search of freedom. The secret journey for escapees like Yeh-nah begins at a river crossing. The entire 1,300-kilometer border of North Korea and China is bound by two swift-flowing rivers, the Yalu and the Tumen. The rivers divide more than two countries. They are a border between desolation and hope.

To cross the river, refugees must first choose between two methods of passage: bribery or the mad dash. The latter involves waiting until the border guards go on break and then running, then swimming, at full speed, in hopes that you won't be noticed. The penalty for getting your timing wrong is severe. Either you will be shot in the back by a North Korean border guard or shot in the face by a Chinese border guard. In some cases, the border guards choose to capture the refugee. That's not much of a reprieve, though. Capture by the North Korean guards usually means only that the hour of death is delayed so that the regime can hang you in front of your family. Capture by the Chinese results in repatriation to North Korea—a fate that often ends in hanging.

The other option, bribery, is the most common route taken. Most of the border guards are believed to be open to turning the other way at the appointed moment in return for relatively small sums (albeit large sums for the average North Korean worker) of cash. When they do, the race across the river has only one enemy: the Chinese border guards. If you have used contacts on the other side to bribe those guards too, then you are home free. The Chinese border guards, however, are much less numerous than their North Korean peers, and thus the ability to reach the Chinese shore is much less risky.

Setting foot on Chinese land is the beginning, not the end, of the flight. The North Koreans become illegal residents in a totalitarian state brimming with policemen and Communist Party apparatchiks who get decent bonuses for every illegally residing North Korean they capture. In the city of Yanbian, an ethnically Korean city of several hundred thousand people and one of the favorite destinations for North Korean refugees, a citizen can get a $100 honorarium for notifying the police of an illegal North Korean. Considering that $100 represents a month's wages, the temptation to do so must be very strong.

The next leg of the journey is by foot or train to Yanbian, Dalian, or one of the other northeastern Chinese cities that host legions of North Korean refugees (estimates range from 40,000 to 100,000 North Koreans residing illegally in northeastern China). There, refugees work as day laborers in the factories and construction sites of booming China. Many women are forced into sex operations—some of them are made to sit for hours in front of cameras for Internet porn sites. Others are sold to and forced to marry Chinese men.

The experience is terrifying. Refugees live in crowded apartments with a dozen or more roommates and only enough room to sleep on the floor. They hide and live in fear of being captured and sent back to North Korea to face death or brutal prison camps.

After a few months or, in some cases, years of this existence, it's time to start the process of flight once again. After having saved enough money to bribe policemen and pay for people smugglers, refugees begin the long journey to cross another Chinese border. One method is to hitch a ride to Mongolia, which is only a few days' journey from the cities of the coastal region. At a preordained spot a few miles from the border, smugglers drop the refugees off on the side of the road to begin the twelve-hour hike—best done in the middle of the night—to the nearest Mongolian town. Those who survive the freezing temperatures of winter or the scorching desert heat of summer can turn themselves into Mongolian authorities and be assured of not being sent back to North Korea.

A far more common path is to head southward and travel across the heartland of China by rail and autobus until reaching the border with Laos or Vietnam. Then smugglers guide refugees across that porous border. At that point, they must do the same trip across the length of Laos or Vietnam until they reach Thailand. Like Mongolia, Thailand is friendly to refugees and won't return them to North Korea. The entire trip can take weeks and is dependent upon a huge network of smugglers, some of whom might turn out to be government spies or might simply turn in their charges to the authorities to keep the refugees' payment. Although the border crossings are easier, the chances of getting caught on this long trip are just as great as the Mongolian option because of the numerous identity checks along the way. If a fake form of identification has been procured (another tremendous cost), the southern route is probably the best bet, but only if refugees have enough money.

Once in Thailand or Mongolia, the long wait begins. While both countries do send North Korean refugees to South Korea, they take their time in doing so. The main reason for the delay is fear of insulting China. If it were to become too easy for North Korean refugees to get to the South via their countries, China would become incensed at Thailand and Mongolia. It is in China's best interests, remember, to keep North Koreans in North Korea. So refugees are forced to wait in their new surroundings of Bangkok or Ulan Bator until their host governments approve exit visas to South Korea. These bureaucratic delays are the main reason that there are several hundred North Koreans in each of those capital cities at any given time.

Then, one lucky day, the exit permit and the ticket to Seoul arrive. The journey is over. Or not. In fact, one of the hardest parts of fleeing North Korea for the South starts upon arrival at Incheon International Airport. Imagine having spent your entire life in a closed, poverty-ridden totalitarian society where material goods are rare and even basic commodities like food and medical care are often nonexistent. Then transport yourself to one of the world's wealthiest societies, where grocery store shelves bulge with food and appliances, where everyone talks on cell phones, and where the purpose of life suddenly isn't just survival. And then imagine being told "Welcome Home."

The North Korean refugee's journey in the South always begins amid the rural foliage of Anseong at a place called Hanawon. It is the Republic of Korea's official resettlement center. Here, all North Korean refugees are required to attend a three-month program, during which they are taught things like how to make instant noodles, how to operate a cell phone, and why it's imperative to use public restrooms instead of the nearest alley. There are also rudimentary trade classes in carpentry, waitressing, and other low-skilled jobs. The Hanawon building is equipped to process 400 refugees at a time, each for the entire three-month period. Whereas most refugees traditionally began their Hanawon course immediately upon arrival in South Korea, many of them now have to join a backlist because the classes are oversubscribed as the trickle of refugees has turned into a steady stream arriving daily.

The number of North Korean refugees living in South Korea is expected to grow by about 2,000 per year over the next five years. If there is regime instability or collapse, the flood could become a tidal wave, with hundreds of thousands of new refugees seeking safety and shelter in the South. The South's government is eager to avoid that scenario and is thus lowering its threshold of openness to new refugees. The government used to offer, for instance, 36 million won (approximately $28,000) to each new refugee to pay for a down payment on an apartment. That number was decreased in 2006 to 25 million won. At the same time, rental prices in South Korea have nearly doubled. Refugees are also given a monthly stipend of 320,000 won (about $275), which is enough to pay for food and little else.

Once settled into an apartment and, if they are lucky, a job, refugees begin the struggle of adaptation. North Koreans are easily identified by South Korean residents. First, North Koreans are, on average, a few inches shorter than their Southern cousins, thanks to chronic malnutrition and periods of famine in the last decades in the communist country. They also have different accents and don't use English words.

North Koreans are often treated like an underclass by some Southerners, who feel an inherent superiority over their shorter fellow citizens. It's all very hard for Northerners to take, especially considering they were raised in an environment that constantly reinforced the message that North Korea was the apex of civilization. In addition, before 1950, North Korea was the industrial center of the country, where wages and education levels were much higher than in the agrarian South. For North Koreans, who are used to thinking of themselves as coming from the superior half of the peninsula, it's a difficult blow to learn otherwise.

It took Yeh-nah three years to complete her escape. She paid a broker to travel through China with her mother. They made it to a South Korean consulate in Shenyang, where she stayed for three years until she was flown to Seoul. Life in the consulate was monotonous. They sat in the building with nothing to do—just waiting.

Yeh-nah says that South Korea is much richer than she imagined. The lifestyle is difficult because of the stiff competition and fast-paced economy. She also struggles because money is so scarce. She is teaching piano to pay the bills. Her mother rarely leaves the apartment. They never eat out.

"Life in North Korea was much easier," she says. But she savors the freedom she has now and hopes for a brighter future.

PART TWO

ECONOMICS AND TRADE

CHAPTER 3

The IMF Crisis and
Its Impact on South Korea

LIKE PEOPLE, countries are shaped more by their traumas than their periods of stability. To understand modern South Korea, the full impact of the 1997–98 financial crisis that ravaged its financial standing must be understood. One part recession, one part currency disaster, and one part general hysteria, the crisis shook Korea to its core. But the tumult led to a broad restructuring of the economy, and today's vibrant, varied, and muscle-bound Korean financial system is a direct product of the confusion, uncertainty, and terror of those days in late 1997 when the whole country teetered on the precipice.

Although the event is known globally as the Asian financial crisis, or the "Asian contagion," in Korea it is known as the IMF crisis. Many a Western observer has commented on the use of that name as being part of a supposed trend of blaming Korea's faults on outsiders. But a close examination of the second half of the crisis—the second and third quarters of 1998—reveals that the International Monetary Fund (IMF) was just as capable of mismanaging an economy as were

South Korea's technocrats. The IMF's insistence on high interest rates nearly turned the recovery into a failure.

But once the IMF changed course and allowed the country to return to its tradition of low interest rates, the recovery did indeed occur—with a vengeance. By 2000, nearly all signs of the crisis had been sandblasted away and South Korea entered a new age of prosperity, one that continued until the global recession of 2008.

But the pain and scars are still ubiquitous. Every company that survived did so by reinventing itself and changing how it does business. The structure and culture of the entire economy is different today than it was prior to the crisis. One example is unemployment—a state of being that was once unknown in Korea. Because of the country's booming growth, nearly everyone who wanted a job had a job. And those jobs tended to be guaranteed for life. Being unemployed in today's Korea is still relatively rare—even during the global recession of 2008, unemployment didn't go above 5 percent. But the fact that it exists at all is testament to how much the country has changed in the last ten years.

THE LAST DOMINO

It was 1997, and it was, to put it mildly, a down year for the Asian markets. After years of breakneck growth throughout the continent, it was clear that some sort of drawdown had to occur. From China to Singapore to Indonesia and Korea, everything had become too overheated. Housing bubbles in almost every capital city gave an early indication that something was wrong. When you had to be a millionaire to own any apartment at all in cities like Taipei, Manila, and Jakarta, financial bureaucrats should have sniffed that something ill was in the wind.

But few people expected a dramatic crash. The region had experienced stellar growth for almost a full decade and, everyone assumed, it still had a long way to go. No matter how much real estate prices ballooned out of control, it seemed that the fundamental truth of the universe was that Asia grows. Black may be white and kettles may transform themselves into something else, but Asia grows and will always grow.

If locals were getting nervous about the continent's economic stability, all they had to do was look at the foreigners, who were pouring capital into the region. American and European financial managers had just begun to learn that the best way to get a bang for their investing buck was to diversify into Asian assets. Although the fundamentals of the stocks and bonds of the region were dizzyingly out of whack, it didn't matter.

Thailand was the first domino to fall. A glance at the economic fundamentals of the country would have told any even-keeled investor that the country was trying to maintain an unsustainable link between its currency and the U.S. dollar. Because of a flood of foreign capital into Bangkok, the central government had to keep buying the Thai baht on the open market to maintain its parity with the dollar. If that parity were broken and the baht were allowed to float, it would destroy that country's export industry—and those very companies whose shares the foreign investors were most interested in buying.

On June 30, 1997, the Thai government surrendered to multiple waves of attacks by currency speculators and broke the baht's peg to the dollar. The stock market collapsed, as did every other Thai asset class. The IMF rushed in to play the role of monetary peacekeeper and, in exchange for capital inflows, required the Thais to massively restructure their financial industry.

Indonesia was next, and it followed a similar pattern in the months of July through November 1997. Speculators attacked the country's currency, which the government was forced to float, and its markets imploded. The Indonesian spectacle was paired with political instability as the government was forced to resign because of violent street protests. The rest of Asia began to worry.

One country that felt relatively immune was South Korea. Its economic fundamentals were much healthier than those of the Southeast Asian countries. It had a relatively harmless debt-to-equity ratio. Its foreign currency reserves were comfortably in the multibillion-dollar levels. Its growth was still high-powered while inflation was kept at bay. The country might be on the same continent as Thailand and Indonesia, but its economic structure seemed to be on a different planet.

Not everyone there was so at ease, however. Kim Ki-hwan was, at the time, serving as an ambassador at large for the government of South Korea. "I was worried back in 1996 that the current account deficit was getting too large," he recalled during an interview from his Seoul office at Goldman Sachs (he has since been appointed the head of the Korean Development Institute). The "current account" is a nation's exports minus its imports. When imports are greater, it means that the nation is running a current account deficit, which in addition to causing economic difficulties can also play havoc with a nation's currency.

Kim spent the spring and summer of 2007 trying to get lines of credit established with international banks on behalf of the government, but he was having a hard time of it. "At the time, few people were worried about the state of the economy. But I was," he said. "I was having trouble convincing bankers that Korea was a worthwhile credit risk, and they weren't buying my argument. Clearly, something was not going right in the international markets."

What was going wrong was the fact that the Japanese yen was appreciating in value against the Korean won. After several massive swings downward in the previous few years, the yen was starting to climb back up. Since Korea's largest importing partner was Japan (i.e., it got most of its imports of raw materials from Japan), the country was sending more and more won to Japan for fewer and fewer goods as the yen increased in value. As a result, fewer won were circulating in Korea. To keep the won circulating at healthy levels, the government kept trading its foreign reserves (mostly dollars) for it. As a result, the amount of foreign reserves kept in the central bank as a weapon to fight speculative attacks against the won was quickly diminishing.

And that's exactly when the speculators attacked. In late October 1997, they started selling won in bulk on the Korean market. Its value plummeted. The government defended its value by buying won on the open market with its precious foreign reserves. But those foreign reserves weren't enough. The won went into free-fall.

A cheaper currency can sometimes be a boon for a country. For instance, if you want to attract a lot of tourists, you weaken your currency. But in a country that depends on exporting goods to other countries, a drop in the value of the national currency can be a lethal blow to the stability of the economy. The goods that you are exporting suddenly become less valuable, bringing in less real value to the exporting company. Thus, when the won faltered under the blows of foreign currency speculators in late 1997—and when the government couldn't defend it—a chain reaction began throughout the economy, starting with the stock market.

On November 7, the KOSPI (Korea Composite Stock Price Index), the main stock market index for the Seoul market, dropped 4 percent. It was a complete shock to long-time market participants, who couldn't understand why stocks were falling so dramatically when all the economic indicators were relatively strong. The bleeding wasn't over. The next day, the KOSPI fell another 7 percent. Sixteen days later, it dropped another 7 percent. There was no longer any denying the fact that Korea had caught the Asian contagion.

THEY DON'T EVALUATE, THEY JUST LEND: KOREA'S PRE-IMF STRUCTURAL FLAWS

While the crisis of 1997 is often referred to as a currency crisis, it could just as easily be termed a credit crisis. In fact, it was a two-headed beast. It couldn't have occurred if the Korean banking system and method of credit allocation had not been structured as it had. But the banking system wouldn't have collapsed in the way that it did if not for the sudden and massive depreciation of the won.

At the heart of the crisis was a structurally unsound method of lending money that was dominant at the time. To understand why that method was dominant, you must first fully understand the scope of the economic growth that occurred in South Korea for the previous three decades. And more important, you must grasp how that growth had become ingrained in the mind-set of Koreans.

Ever since the early 1960s, Korea had averaged between 6 percent and 8 percent annual growth. To fuel that growth, the country had settled on a system of massive, low-interest loans from the banking system to the industrial sector. The banks were able to support this system on a permanent basis because of guarantees provided by the government. Some of these guarantees were in written form and some were in unspoken understandings, but the government used the loan guarantees as a method to control and direct the manufacturing industry, via its tight ties with the banking industry.

In the years leading up to the crisis, primarily 1995 and 1996, interest rates rose in South Korea as part of a government strategy to avoid a flood of foreign capital into the country. South Korea was at the time in the process of joining the Organization for Economic Cooperation and Development (OECD), a club of the most developed nations in the world. It was an honor and a grand symbol for the once-poverty-ridden country to enter into such a group, and the government wanted it to go off without a hitch. There was one problem: One of the requirements of entry into the OECD was the relaxation of rules against cross-border capital flows. In other words, the government had to allow foreign money to come into South Korea—and in a big way.

The government was willing to make symbolic gestures toward allowing foreign money to flow into and out of Korea. But it didn't want to go all the way and allow foreign investors unhindered ability to invest (and disinvest) in Korean companies. So it figured out a half step: It would repeal laws against short-term capital flows, but at the same time it would raise long-term interest rates to ensure that Korean banks could lend to Korean companies and still make a tidy profit. The Korean companies, in the meantime, would still get the government loan guarantees, which would in turn make it palatable to them to pay high interest rates. The system guaranteed that the important business of lending money to Korean manufacturers would remain in Korean hands.

The system seemed to work in its first few years. Few foreign banks got into the business of lending money to Korean businesses. But there was a significant flaw. Along with the relaxation of rules that forbid transborder money flows came the end of restrictions on Korean banks borrowing money. Thus, a trend began in 1995 that had Korean merchant banks borrowing money from Hong Kong money-center banks as short-term loans. They would then take the dollar-denominated capital back to Korea and lend it to Korean businesses for the long term. The Korean banks made a fortune on realizing the spread between the low short-term interest rates they had to pay to borrow the money and the much higher long-term interest rates they got in return when they lent the money to Korean industrial borrowers. The risk they took, of course, was the fact that they were lending long money that they were borrowing short. Normally, that would make such a scheme impossible, but the Hong Kong banks were happy to continuously roll over the short-term loans, effectively transforming them into long-term loans.

The system worked so well, in fact, that the period starting in 1995 and ending (with the crisis) at the end of 1997 became one of the biggest boom periods of South Korean history. It was a period of cheap credit for anyone and anything. The banks were so flush with cash to lend that they became deeply irresponsible with their money. "They don't evaluate, they just lend," said one banker who avoided the disaster to come because he was stationed in Japan at the time. The banks, he said, were borrowing money to lend money. The only thing that kept them from making more money was the inability to find enough people and companies in Korea who wanted to borrow money. So they relaxed their lending rules and accepted lower and lower credit ratings from their borrowers.

As you can imagine, the arrangement couldn't last forever. When currency speculators attacked Hong Kong in the early fall of 1997, the Hong Kong banks needed cash stockpiles, in the form of dollars, to fight them off. Abruptly, the rollovers stopped and the Hong Kong bankers demanded their dollars back from their Korean peers. The Koreans obliged, but they were suddenly faced with a flood of demands. Not only did they have to pay back money that had been frozen in long-term loans, but they had to pay it back in dollars. Suddenly, Korean banks were draining their stockpile of dollars and desperately selling whatever won-denominated assets they could in return for dollars.

This rush for dollars in October and November of 1997—and the concordant desperation to sell anything won-related—was the root cause of the collapse of the Korean economy. At the time, there was much confusion as observers searched for a villain, as if something deep inside the character of Korea were to blame. In fact, it was a highly technical banking policy that was poorly designed and half-baked that caused the worst tumult in Korea's markets ever.

The good news was that the specific problem was easy to fix. All that needed to be done was to make the same rules apply for both Korean and foreign banks: Everybody lends and borrows under the same regulations and at the same interest rates. And that indeed was one of the first acts of the Korean government as it accepted the hard reforms upon which the International Monetary Fund insisted in exchange for $57 billion in bailout money. If only the "reforms" had stopped there.

BONE-CARVING PAIN:
THE IMF'S HAPHAZARD RESPONSE

In addition to confronting the agony and confusion of the financial crisis, the Korean nation was undergoing a presidential election in the fall of 1997. Kim Young-sam, the incumbent, had to fight against Kim Dae-jung, the long-time opposition leader who had run for president, and lost, twice before. In an effort to show the country that he was on top of the crisis and was aware how bad it was, Kim Young-sam addressed the nation on television on December 11, 1997, just a week before the election. "We are entering a period of bone-carving pain," he told citizens. He announced that the nation was about to enter a period of agonizing reforms that would right the ship, but he warned it wouldn't be easy to handle.

The reforms demanded of the IMF were mostly straightforward. Chief among them was opening up the financial services industry to a level playing field for foreign and domestic firms. But there were more. The Korean government had long had laws that prevented Korean employers from laying off workers during times of economic distress. Firing for cause was permissible, but even that move was rarely made. In South Korea, a job was a job for life. The only effective way of losing a job was to quit it.

During five decades of robust growth, such a policy never hurt the economy. When it was clear that the economy would continue to grow between 7 percent and 9 percent the next year, there was never much pressure to lay off workers for economic reasons.

But 1997 was different. As the economy shut down in response to the monetary crisis at the end of the year, factories and offices were dramatically oversaturated with salaried workers. The IMF demanded that the laws against layoffs, as well as the general cultural tradition of jobs-for-life, end. They did. Unemployment shot up from 2.1 percent in 1996 to 6 percent in 1998.

The change was startling to most Koreans. The idea of a breadwinner not being able to find a job was an alien problem for the country, and people weren't sure how to handle it. Kim Ki-hwan saw it as nothing short of a national crisis. "People simply didn't know how to deal with being unemployed," he says. "It was considered a disgrace, the mark of a lazy person. People had to change their mindset and realize that these were victims of an economy in recession. It wasn't an easy period." Kim himself established an organization to aid the children of unemployed workers, one of the first such organizations to be founded in Korea. It still exists today.

Another major "reform" demanded by the IMF was the adoption of a high-interest-rate policy by the government. South Korea, like the other Asian tiger economies of Hong Kong, Taiwan, and Singapore, had long favored relatively low interest rates as a method of fueling economic growth. As long as factories could borrow money cheaply, they would continue to ramp up capacity and expand their operations.

The IMF felt that it was a time for a change when it came to interest rates. The fundamental problem of the currency crisis was that dollar-denominated capital fled the country en masse. The only way to lure it back to South Korea was to increase interest rates—drastically—and thus recompense the foreign banks with a reward for taking on the risk of lending to a country in the midst of a financial catastrophe.

The problem was that the high-interest-rate policy simply didn't work. Faced with borrowing money at rates of as much as 40 percent, Korean industrialists simply decided not to borrow. With most

Asian nations recovering from their own crises, there was not much demand for Korea's exports in the first half of 1998, so there was little reason to expand capacity that was already too much for the given demand of products. Korean businesses, in other words, were cutting back, not ramping up.

Yet the IMF technocrats insisted that their policy would work, if given enough time. The dollars were sure to eventually come if only the interest rates were kept high enough, they explained.

But the capital flows simply didn't materialize. As a result, the Korean economy dipped deeper into recession. Gross domestic product (GDP) contracted by 6.7 percent in 1998. The rumbles of discontent among Korean business leaders started to grow stronger. But the IMF held its ground and stuck to its demands for high interest rates.

The IMF's argument was based on a currency-centric view of the crisis. The South Korean won had to be returned to its relatively high pre-crisis valuation (of around 800 won to the dollar, more than twice the value it held in the beginning of 1998). A top IMF official said the first order of business was to restore confidence in the currency, and that would be achieved through a country making it more attractive to hold domestic currency, which in turn requires increasing interest rates at least temporarily.

Banks, manufacturers, and service-sector companies started failing left and right. Samsung, for instance, had recently entered the automobile market and invested more than $10 billion in its Samsung Motors division. It now had to sell the venture to Renault at a fire-sale price in order to raise money to keep the parent company afloat. Kia, the country's second-largest car manufacturer, went bankrupt—its parts to be later bought by chief rival Hyundai.

But the biggest bomb to drop was Daewoo, which at the time was competing with Samsung for the right to be called the largest *chaebol* (the term for Korean conglomerates). CEO Kim Woo-choong responded to the crisis by trying to grow his way out of it. Despite the monetary collapse and the introduction of sky-high interest rates, he added capacity and borrowed extravagantly to capture market share in Daewoo's various businesses, including automobiles and appliances. Some analysts felt that he was operating under the assumption that Daewoo was "too big to fail" and that the Korean government would intervene and pay off its debts. But under the terms of the IMF deal, the government couldn't rescue failing businesses, no matter how big they were. Daewoo was doubly handicapped by the fact that its CEO had been a prominent supporter of former president Kim Young-sam. When Kim Dae-jung won the presidential election, his administration had little incentive to rescue the dying corporation. The death was a long, drawn-out affair, but Daewoo finally reached its end in the summer of 1999 and declared bankruptcy. Its parts were sold to foreign and domestic competitors.

It wasn't until respected international economists came to Korea and saw the damage wrought by the high-interest-rate policy that the IMF began to back down. Chief among those economists was Joseph Stiglitz, who at the time was the chief economist of the World Bank. After a 1998 visit to the country, Stiglitz made the argument that high interest rates were killing the country's economy. He even went so far as to suggest that the World Bank was deaf to a cultural difference—that low interest rates were a necessary part of the Asian economic structure and that forcing it to change was merely a misguided attempt at converting the continent to an "Anglo-Saxon" model of banking.

The criticism by Stiglitz and others made a difference. In the fall of 1998, the IMF reversed course and instituted a new policy of "normal" interest rates, allowing banks to lend cheaply to Korean businesses. The change had almost immediate results, with 1999 turning into a record year, with growth of 10.9 percent. The crisis, finally, was over. But its scars would remain for a long time.

The seeds for almost every one of the spectacularly successful policies of the last decade, a time during which the Korean GDP nearly tripled in size, were planted during the country's economic crisis. One was a decision by the government to push for a revolution in information technology. In 1998, exports of information technology were below $20 billion. By 2008, they had reached $100 billion. And most of that was not simple equipment construction or chip fabrication. It was value-added items like software or next-generation chipsets that required advanced manufacturing skills.

Another area of revolutionary change was in the automobile industry. Korea's automakers, once known only for being the lowest-cost manufacturers, had transformed into brands that had a reputation for high quality. The same phenomenon happened in other industries, from appliances to electronic goods. While the crisis was over by the end of 1998, its positive effects would continue to resonate for another ten years.

CRISIS REDUX? THE GLOBAL RECESSION OF 2008-2009

A collapse in the value of the won. Companies declaring bankruptcy. Banks shutting down. Credit ratings that were downwardly revised. Mass layoffs. The news of late 2008 and early 2009 was painfully familiar to most Koreans. The worldwide economic recession, which had begun with the collapse of the banking system in the United States, was being felt as strongly in Korea as anywhere else. But the disturbing news was especially hard to take because it was coming on the ten-year anniversary of the IMF crisis.

Some observers view this latest crisis as being more serious than what happened a decade ago. "The last time, it was a problem rooted in currency valuation," says Kim Jong-wook, a former senior vice president at Woori Finance, a major South Korean investment bank. "It had nothing to do with the economic fundamentals of the country.

This case is very gloomy. We are experiencing a global downturn due to the fundamental economic problems in the global economy. This is far more serious and will do far more damage."

It is hard to argue that South Korea itself was suffering from poor economic fundamentals in the months leading up to the current crisis. The country's GDP was growing at a relatively healthy clip of 5 percent. The overall debt-to-foreign-reserve balance was at 173 percent, compared to 1,957 percent in November 1997. The government had tremendous foreign currency reserves of $212 billion, something it was nearly bereft of ten years earlier. The economy, in general, was doing just fine.

But when your country's economic health depends on exports, the economic fundamentals of the countries to which you are exporting most of your goods are just as important as your own fundamentals. And when two out of your top-three export destinations (the United States and China) are experiencing near-depression-like conditions, you will certainly feel the effects.

The good news is that this time there is no need to bail out the government. Instead, the government of South Korea is bailing out the economy itself. In November 2008, it began pouring $120 billion into the currency and financial markets to support the won. Later, in December, the Bank of Korea, the country's central bank, executed a $30 billion currency swap with the U.S. Federal Reserve to help stabilize the won. Another $160 billion in government funds is expected to be spent by the end of 2010 to prop up the economy, create jobs, and increase liquidity in the credit markets. All of this government action resulted in an actual increase in the GDP in the first quarter of 2009—a sure sign that a turnaround has commenced.

Korea had little political reluctance in increasing its budget deficits to boost the economy, according to high-level government officials who designed the stimulus plan. They said Korea's national debt, currently at 33 percent of its GDP, is far below the average of OECD member nations (which is 75 percent). Korea, in other words, has a debt-to-equity ratio that is low enough to allow it to borrow heavily without damaging its credit rating.

There are plenty of other differences between this crisis and the crisis of 1997. A significant one is that the country has a much stronger, and more flexible, social safety net than it did ten years ago. Back then, it was up to the extended family of an unemployed person to support him and his family. Now there is a system of government unemployment benefits that makes it easier to survive without a job. One of the first government reactions to the global downturn was to loosen the restrictions on access to unemployment benefits, allowing a family to partake in them even if they had a modest savings account.

Money is pouring into other social welfare programs, including a job training program called JUMP, which stands for Job Upgrading and Maturing Program. It is meant to target temporary workers who can't find jobs and to train them in skills that will allow them to apply for full-time positions.

A novel Korean method of reducing unemployment is an emphasis on job sharing. This concept has been experimented with in European countries and the United States, but in South Korea, it has become a central tool for allowing companies to cut costs without firing people. The idea is to allow employees to take temporary unpaid furloughs while another employee assumes their tasks. In a similar arrangement, some workers will literally share a job on different days of the week, with an equivalent reduction in income. The government supports such corporate programs by offering tax credits and other financial incentives to companies that offer job sharing as an option.

Another hallmark of this crisis is that, unlike in 1997, there are bright spots in the economic map of the country. Shipbuilding, for instance, demands such long-term contracts that it hasn't been heavily affected by the recession yet. In addition, Korean shipbuilders increased their market share to 33 percent in 2008—at least a

25 percent increase from the previous year—due to the lower price of the won and to advances in technology that their Japanese and Chinese competitors haven't achieved yet. As an example, at Hyundai Heavy Industries, one of the country's largest shipbuilders, a modular assembly system was implemented that allows work to commence on a new ship while the previous holder of the berth is being launched. Previously, workers had to remove equipment from the berth from the old project and install new equipment for the new project, a process that could take months. Now the equipment is continuously being changed in and out, an improvement that reduces total shipbuilding time by up to 20 percent.

That's not to say that times have been easy for South Korea. Midway through 2008, experts expected the economy to grow by 5 percent in 2009. By February, those estimates had been revised down to a negative 4 percent contraction in GDP (the IMF's estimate) or a negative 2 percent contraction in the best case. Almost all of the slowdown can be traced to the dramatic drop in exports. In January 2009 alone, exports dropped by 37 percent from January 2008.

There is some reason to believe that things will improve relatively quickly. Chief among them is the won's battered valuation. The national currency lost nearly 25 percent of its value in 2008, which caused a tremendous loss of wealth for the country. But the good news is that a cheaper won today will make exports more competitive overseas. One very symbolic example came in January 2009, when Toyota announced that it would start purchasing Korean steel for the first time in its history. Toyota had proudly bought only Japanese-manufactured steel in the past, but the price disparity in 2009, thanks to the cheapness of the won, allowed Toyota to break a nationalistic taboo.

Yet another factor will play a bigger role in the near future, and that is the expectation that it will be harder and harder for China to keep the yuan so cheap against the dollar. Due to American domestic politics and the overall international financial climate, pressures are rising on Beijing to increase the value of its currency. If it does, even by a little, it will make Korean exports more price-competitive with Chinese exports to the United States. While Korean products will probably never be as cheap as Chinese products (because of the incredibly low labor costs in China), the difference in the spread between them is an important factor in consumers' buying behavior, especially in times of economic distress. "People will be more sensitive to the quality relative to the price," says Yang Eun-young, the deputy director of the Trade Promotion Strategy team at the Korea Trade Investment Promotion Agency. "So [they will be] seeking better-quality products at a reasonable price, as opposed to settling for something cheaper and risking having to buy another." In other words, Korean products are no longer known worldwide as the cheapest you can find. They are known for their quality. And that, more than anything else, will allow Korea to emerge from this crisis more quickly and less scathed than other countries.

CHAPTER 4

The Middle Nation:
How Korea Navigates
Between Japan and China

LIEUTENANT COLONEL YEO TAE-IK is a Korean hero. After graduating from South Korea's Air Force Academy in 1992, he went on to become an F-5 and F-16 pilot, eventually rising to vice commander of the 121st fighter squadron. In addition to flying practice defense sorties against North Korean Mig-23s, he helped organize the air defense plans for the 2002 World Cup games. He lived the dream of many Korean boys: to be a fighter pilot jockey.

Yeo lived temporarily in the Washington, D.C., area while participating in a fellowship program at the Center for Strategic and International Studies. He jumped at the chance to raise his eleven-year-old son in America, where the boy could benefit from immersion in an English-language environment and better understand American culture. His son is something of a prodigy, a student of American history who has a special fascination for the trivia of American presidents. That suits the elder Yeo just fine. He will forbid his son from entering the air force when it is his time to serve in the Korean military. He wants his son to be a historian. "I'm a fighter of the past," Yeo said when asked what he wants his son to become. "My son will fight for Korea's future. The battleground won't be hills or the sky. It will be who gets to write the history of our peninsula."

Yeo went on to describe the impact of one Chinese historian's academic paper that insisted that most of Korea belonged to China. Although it was published in an obscure journal and was never translated into another language, it infuriated Koreans after being mentioned in the nation's press. Korea, they insisted, belongs to Koreans, not to any other culture.

Looking to the East, Yeo then talked about the threat from Japan, which intermittently lays claim to Dokdo Island, a tiny collection of rock outcroppings that is under Korean sovereignty. The threat of a Japanese return to imperialism scares Koreans. It also brings them together to rally around a common cause. Scores of Koreans who operate dry cleaners in New York City wrap their clients' clothes in clear plastic bags on which are printed the words "Dokdo Island Is Korean Territory!"

What Lieutenant Colonel Yeo is really talking about is the fact that Korea has always had a tenuous position between the two great powers on the parameters of its territory: China and Japan. In fact, it is sometimes referred to as "the Middle Nation" because of this geography. From one perspective, Korean history has been a narrative of balancing the demands of its two larger neighbors. And Korea's future history, perhaps to be written by the younger Yeo, will probably be more of the same.

EMULATING JAPAN WHILE AVOIDING ITS FATE

To get a sense of how much competition there is between Korea and Japan, look no further than the World Baseball Classic of 2009. The international round-robin tournament of each country's all-star teams saw great performances all around, but the biggest shock occurred in the next-to-last round when Korea defeated Japan. Despite the presence of several major leaguers, including one of the greatest baseball players of all time—Ichiro Suzuki—Korea beat the Japanese team and advanced to the final round. Koreans gathered around television sets everywhere. City streets, bars, and homes erupted into a frenzy of victorious cheering. The Korean team, by defeating their neighboring nemesis, was going to the finals.

And the final round played itself out just like a TV script. Korea advanced to the championship game and who else would they face off against for the title but . . . Japan. The game was held in Los Angeles in a stadium packed with Korean expatriates and emigrants. Some Korean fans waved banners that said "Dokdo Island is our land!"

The game itself was a nail-biter. It ended up a tie at the end of nine innings and stretched into extra innings. In the tenth inning, Japan was threatening to score with men on first and third. And then who comes to bat but Ichiro.

Now, any baseball manager would say that there should have been only one option in this situation. You walk one of the world's greatest hitters, load the bases, and then go up against the next hitter, who is several levels below Ichiro in terms of his ability to get on base. Instead, Korean pitcher Lim Chang-yong pitched directly to Ichiro. After two strikes, two balls, and multiple fouls, Ichiro singled to left field, bringing in the winning run from third. Japan won the game.

Despite the loss, Lim was treated like a hero back home. He showed Korean pride by avoiding the humiliation of intentionally walking Ichiro. He showed that no Korean pitcher bows down to Japan.

Whether it is baseball or cell phone sales, the competition between Korea and Japan is fierce. That's partially due to the history of Japan's ruthless colonial rule over Korea in the first half of the twentieth century. But that's only half the story of the relationship between the two countries. In addition to the sense of rivalry and competition, there is a sense of a shared future. Korea, after all, partially emulated the Japanese model to grow its economy in the second half of the last century. It relied as well on loans and grants from the Japanese government (which it received in return for mutual diplomatic recognition in 1965) to boost its early industrial growth. And Japanese corporations often provided the technical know-how that Korean companies required to build new factories and design centers across the Korean peninsula.

Now that South Korea has transformed itself from a third-world country into a developed industrial powerhouse, in part by following the Japanese model, its challenge today is to avoid Japan's fate once reaching the same level of development. Japan also rose out of the ashes of World War II, rebuilt its factories, and was the economic success story of the 1960s and 1970s. By the 1980s, there were fears in the United States that Japan would one day be the world's sole superpower.

Instead, Japan followed a path of extreme caution in its economic policies. The Japanese people were encouraged to save all of their extra income rather than spend it, a tact that reduced the ability of the consumer to feed more economic growth. Even more harmful was the fact that most Japanese chose to save their money in low-interest-bearing accounts in the bank of the country's post office. Trillions of dollars worth of savings were kept in the post office's bank, essentially removing all that money from circulating in the economy. Japan's growth slowed to a trickle and then stopped altogether. The 1990s are known in Japan as the "lost decade," but the 2000s haven't been much better to the country. It has essentially had zero growth since the 1980s.

Another element of the zero-growth period in Japan was an over-reliance on the *keiretsu* companies—the mammoth conglomerates that rule the country's economic landscape. Instead of trying to break them up, the Japanese government encouraged their continuing dominance, even though their ultraconservative management policies contributed to the low growth of the economy. Unlike the chaebol in Korea, the huge conglomerate corporations that sprouted up during or shortly after the Korean War, the keiretsu of Japan date back to the Meiji period of the 1800s. Most of them were founded as rice traders during the shogun period and went on to become conglomerates with the backing of the imperial government. It is much harder to force the creative destruction of a 200-year-old company that is part of national lore than it is to confront one that is only a few decades old.

Korea is currently in the position that Japan was thirty years ago. As the 1980s dawned, Japan had catapulted itself into the cozy group of the world's economic leaders. Likewise, in 2010, Korea has established itself as the world's fifteenth-largest economy. So, how can Korea continue to grow and avoid the lost decades that Japan experienced?

Part of the answer to that question lies in the very same problems that dogged Japan for the last twenty years: emphasizing safety in economic policy over growth and supporting large multinational conglomerates that, by their very nature, don't grow very fast. If Korea can avoid those two mistakes, it has a good shot at renewing growth after the end of the current global recession.

Korea is already far ahead of Japan in one area: The fact is that for the last ten years, Korea has discontinued its official policy of favoring large conglomerates over other companies. The chaebol of Korea have lessened in influence and scope since the International

Monetary Fund (IMF) crisis of 1997–98. One of the biggest conglomerates, Daewoo, was even allowed to fail. Most of the others were forced to deleverage and consolidate their fortunes into fewer businesses. Samsung, for instance, is now primarily an electronics company with a few other subsidiaries. There is always pressure coming from the powerful chaebol to reverse this policy, something the Korean government must avoid if it is to escape Japan's fate.

The other fundamental challenge before Korea is to avoid adding too much public debt. The Japanese government has boosted its economy for the last few decades by borrowing heavily. The total amount of public debt now equals 172 percent of GDP—not a healthy place to be. South Korea's debt-to-GDP ratio is much lower—only 33 percent—and must be kept near that level to prevent government borrowing from strangling the economy.

Above all else, however, Korea must avoid trying to conserve its gains and instead always push for new growth. When looking at the example of Japan, Koreans should know that in safety is decline.

THE YELLOW CLOUD TO THE WEST

Koreans are obsessed with appearances. They like fancy clothes and shiny shoes, and they drive immaculately clean cars. But many Koreans will go out in public wearing something that goes completely against the goal of looking good. It's an accessory that clashes with any outfit: a large white cotton mask.

The masks attach to the face with strings that wrap around the ears. They cover the nose, mouth, and even the chin. In the spring, these masks are especially prevalent because of one major health concern: yellow dust.

Yellow dust, known in Korean as *hwangsa*, is exactly what it says: a yellow-colored dust that blows in from Inner Mongolia—a palpable reminder of China's dismal record at environmental cleanliness. It is caused by the devegetation of the Mongolian highlands, which over the last few decades have transformed from pasture land to desert. The dust is primarily composed of minerals like quartz and feldspar, but it picks up heavy metals and carcinogens like dioxin as it passes over the industrialized areas of China before reaching Korea.

The dust storms hit in the late winter and throughout the spring in Korea. On the worst days, schools close and people are urged to avoid spending too much time outside. The yellow dust is blamed for some deaths, especially among elderly people with respiratory problems. The economic and environmental damage in Korea is also high, estimated at more than $5 billion a year.

The Korean government has proposed a number of initiatives to combat the problem. One proposal is to build a forest in the Kubuqi Desert. The plan is sponsored by the Gyeonggi Province government, which is pledging one billion won through a private organization to plant trees in China. The Korea Forest Service and other groups have already been developing green zones in the Kubuqi Desert.

The problem with yellow dust is emblematic of the two countries' relationship. Korea has grown rich off China's growth, exporting industrial tools and parts that are then made into finished products in Chinese factories. But Korea would choose to ignore China's rapid growth and change if it could. In 2007, Chinese imports to Korea outweighed exports going in the other direction. That's not how it's supposed to be. Korea had planned to slowly transition from low-wage manufacturing jobs to higher-end service and executive-level jobs while China outcompeted for cheap factories. Instead, China has grown so quickly that it is already starting to compete in the white-collar industries. But China's rise, like the yellow dust it sends to Seoul every spring, is very hard to ignore.

China commands one-fifth of the world population and attracts more foreign direct investment than any other country, and its economy is growing faster than any other large economy. But per capita income still is less than $4,000 a year, while South Korea's income is more than $20,000. Despite explosive economic growth since the 1980s, China remains a relatively poor nation.

Compared to the Asian tigers of Taiwan, Singapore, and Hong Kong, which quickly modernized in the decades after World War II, China suffered from decades of political unrest followed by strict, radical communist rule that put ideology above everything else, including economic health.

When Mao Zedong established the People's Republic of China in 1949, the Chinese people had suffered through decades of military oppression and an internal battle over political leadership. The Communist Party, with help from the Russians, prevailed over weakened Nationalist leaders and the country underwent some level of industrial development with the building of roads and schools. Mao's early years showed some progress, but his focus on creating a radical socialist society ultimately caused economic disaster.

Mao's so-called Great Leap Forward (1958–61) should be more aptly named the Great Leap Backward. As part of his radical attempt to re-create society and isolate China from the rest of the world, Mao established a centrally controlled and planned economy that was based on huge farming communes. The government owned virtually all the land. And Mao lacked the well-educated technocrat advisers that in South Korea surrounded President Park Chung-hee during the same time period.

Therefore, Mao's vision of pushing China toward an ideal, socialist society took shape at a time when the Chinese had little knowledge about how to create a successful modern economy. Based on flawed information, Mao launched a massive attempt to manufacture steel using primitive stoves on the communes. People cut down trees to fuel the furnaces and put their pots and pans and anything with steel into these furnaces, furthering their poverty. And local officials lied about the production to make the central office happy.

On top of that, poor decisions, mismanagement, and weather problems led to famine in the countryside because of orders to send food to the cities. An estimated 20 million to 30 million people, mostly children and the elderly, starved to death in the early 1960s. At the same time, Russia abruptly pulled its aid because of ideological differences with Mao.

When it became clear that the Great Leap Forward had ruined the country, Mao stepped down in 1959, but he continued to control the country. From 1966 to 1969, he pushed another disastrous campaign, called the Cultural Revolution, which, among other things, sought to eliminate wage and class differences between urban and rural people and encouraged violence against the government bureaucracy as a way of perpetuating revolution among Chinese youths organized in the Red Guard.

It wasn't until after Mao's death in 1976 that the country began moving toward economic growth. Deng Xiaoping abolished the communes and loosened the government's control to allow for more market-driven reforms. Farms were privatized to increase production.

China's economic modernization officially began in 1978—almost two decades after Park Chung-hee had launched his aggressive push for Korean industrialization and export-based growth.

When Deng began loosening China's economic policies in 1978, one percent of national output came from private businesses. Now private industry produces roughly 70 percent of national output. The Chinese economy has grown more than seventy times larger and the poverty rate dropped from 53 percent in 1981 to 8 percent in 2001.

Leaders in both Korea and China used the strong arm of the military and centralized government to push their agendas. President

Park's policies weren't universally liked, and he and other military dictators showed little tolerance for political opposition. On the whole, however, the economic reforms in Korea were far more visionary and effective.

Under Deng and his successors, China opened up again to the world, welcomed foreign investment, instituted the one-child-per-family policy to control population growth, and encouraged its oppressed intellectuals to join the economic recovery. The Open Door program, which welcomed foreign capital and businesses, infused life into the hobbled economy—and yet the people learned that political change would not be tolerated. In what became known as the Tiananmen Square massacre in 1989, Deng ruthlessly quashed pro-democracy protests that had gone on for months. The pictures of army tanks rolling into the square and shooting down scores of protesters were seen across the world on television.

Korea also had its own massacre—a military crackdown on pro-democracy protesters and students in Kwangju in May 1980. Scores of demonstrators were killed by soldiers ordered to quash the uprising by Chun Doo-hwan, Korea's president and army general. The birth of the Kwangju uprising, like the Tiananmen Square protest, was more complex than simply a push for democracy. But the response was similar in both cases. The military came in and used force to end the rebellion. In both cases, hundreds of protesters died.

The important difference between Kwangju and Tiananmen is that democracy did come to Korea afterward—namely, with Roh Tae-woo, who became president in 1988. China remains a communist country that shows little tolerance for political opposition. And unlike Korea, the Chinese government still owns a good deal of the business operations in the country.

KOREANS IN JAPAN AND CHINA

Today, two of the largest concentrations of Koreans living outside the peninsula are in China and Japan. The third major community is in the United States. The immigrant journey to the United States is a much different story than the migration of Koreans to their Asian neighbors—Japan and China—which occurred, for the most part, during one of the most desperate times in the country's history: the Japanese occupation.

By the 1920s, most Koreans suffered terribly under Japanese rule. As part of the occupation, the Japanese confiscated land and farms from Koreans, forcing them into desperately poor living conditions. The economic hardship drove many Koreans to leave the country to look for work. Those living in the northern part of the peninsula generally traveled across the Yalu River into Manchuria and other parts of China. Those living in the south and on Jeju Island generally went to Japan.

For the most part, neither community gained the level of economic success that Korean immigrants reached in the United States. Koreans in China, known as *Chosenjok* ("Chosen" is a historical name for Korea), couldn't prosper because of the overall economic troubles there under Mao Zedong. And Koreans in Japan, often referred to as *Zainichi* (which means "staying in Japan"), faced significant discrimination from the Japanese, and many of them were forced into hard labor during World War II. Koreans in Japan also went down an unusual political path, with a high percentage of the population actively supporting North Korea and communism.

In China, some Koreans organized politically against the Japanese, and many later fought on the communist side during the Chinese Civil War. After Mao Zedong came to power, tens of thousands of Koreans chose to go back to their homeland. But most Koreans decided to stay in China and obtained Chinese citizenship.

Today, several generations of Koreans continue to live in China, mostly in the northeast tip of the country. The Korean population in China, which stands at more than 2 million, is the largest outside of the peninsula. Still, Koreans are not among the largest ethnic minorities in the country. The highest concentrations are in three provinces that are closest to the North Korean border: Heilongjiang, Jilin, and Liaoning. Part of that area, the Yanbian area in Jilin Province, is a Korean autonomous region that had been majority Korean but has lost Korean population since the 1990s.

Ah Jong is a third-generation Korean immigrant in China. She doesn't know all the details of her family history, but said her father's father came to China during the Japanese occupation from Jeolla Province in the southern part of the peninsula. Her mother's parents came from what is today North Korea. Her grandparents were very poor.

Both her parents, who are ethnic Koreans, were born in China. Her father grew up on a farm and was very poor. Both parents attended school until middle school, and then their education was stopped during the Cultural Revolution. Her father continued his education later and earned two college degrees in Beijing. He is the president of an oil company, and her mother works in the pharmaceutical industry.

Ah Jong was born in 1981 and lived in a city in the Yanbian area. Although Koreans in China are allowed to have two children, she is an only child. Her parents, she said, chose to have one child so that she could have the money and means to get a better education. Unlike most Koreans in Yanbian, who attend Korean schools, Ah Jong went to a Chinese school.

Growing up in Yanbian, Ah Jong lived better than most of her peers because of her father's job. She said she didn't experience discrimination because Korean culture is accepted and dominant in her area. Still, the area is generally poor. Only 10 percent of people have cars, and there is a major trend for young Koreans, as well as

Chinese living in the area, to move to the big cities like Beijing and Shanghai, where there is better economic opportunity. At the same time, South Korean companies are opening up many businesses and factories in Yanbian and other parts of China and employing many ethnic Koreans from those areas. There also is a growing population of South Koreans choosing to move permanently to China.

While South Koreans are seeing great economic opportunities in China, ethnic Koreans in China are also trying to come to South Korea. The population loss in Yanbian is partially due to the migration of many Koreans—often illegally—to South Korea.

Ah Jong obtained a student visa and has been studying in Seoul since 2006. She would like to stay. "Most of the Koreans want to come here," she said. "So many students who have higher educations go to Shanghai and Beijing, and others who want to make money come here[to Seoul]. It's a big problem for people in China, but we have no way to solve this problem."

The Korean community in Yanbian could become nonexistent in ten or twenty years because of the migration trends, Ah Jong said. At that point, the Chinese government could take over the region and any remaining Koreans will likely move to other parts of China.

Like the Chosenjok of China, the Korean community in Japan is also undergoing significant transition. But theirs is more political.

The Korean population in Japan was established through two main groups: poor Koreans from the peninsula who chose to move to Japan to look for work, and tens of thousands of Koreans who were forced to move to Japan to work in mines and factories to support the Japanese during World War II. Both groups lived difficult lives, often sleeping in shacks and ghettos.

At the end of World War II, about 2 million Koreans lived in Japan. After the war, most returned to Korea, but 600,000 stayed behind. Among those who stayed, the Koreans in Japan divided largely into two groups: *Chongryon*, whose members supported the North Korean communists, and *Mindan*, who backed South Korea. (Both names are shortened versions of the groups' full names.)

Chongryon came from a group that previously belonged to the Japanese Communist Party (called Minjon). Before that, another leftist group, the League of Koreans, had operated for a time before being severely suppressed by the Japanese government.

Chongryon focused its efforts on supporting North Korea and explicitly did not get involved in Japanese domestic politics, thereby avoiding interference from the government. The organization grew to become a dominant force in the Korean community in Japan and operated a sophisticated school system to teach Korean and communist ideology. At its peak, Chongryon ran 180 schools across Japan. The group also had close ties to the North Korean regime and even pushed its members to "repatriate" to North Korea.

In the decade or so after the Korean War, many Koreans in Japan saw North Korea as a successful country, in part because North Korea was sending money to Japan for schools. And for decades since late 1959, North Korea sent a Soviet-built ship to and from Niigata, Japan, for trade goods. At the same time, South Korea was undergoing political upheaval under the Rhee Syng-man administration. Many Koreans in Japan thought the peninsula would be unified quickly and under the communists.

Soon, people began boarding ships to North Korea. By 1967, more than 88,000 Koreans from Japan had moved to North Korea. And more continued to go. By 1976, more than 92,000 had gone to the North.

In 1965, with the signing of normalized relations between South Korea and Japan, Koreans in Japan also began moving to South Korea. By the late 1970s, the migration to North Korea had slowed considerably—in part due to word trickling back that those who had gone to North Korea couldn't come back.

Despite efforts by Chongryon leadership and schoolteachers to paint North Korea as a utopia, Chongryon members began to hear otherwise. They learned of famine there. They learned that their relatives were struggling to survive, and that many had been sent to labor camps because of political suspicions.

Still, loyalty to North Korea and Kim Il-sung remained fairly strong for many years. But that loyalty suffered a huge blow in 2002, when Kim Jong-il admitted to Japanese officials that his country had abducted more than a dozen Japanese citizens. The abductions from Japan occurred between 1977 and 1983 and were conducted by North Korean spies. Allegations of the abductions swirled for years, but North Korean officials denied responsibility until 2002.

North Korea claimed that its spies abducted thirteen people, but other reports put the number much higher. The story has taken many twists and turns and has caused a huge uproar in Japan. It also shocked North Korean sympathizers in the Korean community in Japan.

The power of Chongryon has been fading in recent years, while Mindan is growing in membership and status. At the same time, second- and third-generation Koreans in Japan—most of whom don't speak Korean—are becoming increasingly assimilated in the country. In 1986, 86 percent of Korean students attended Japanese schools, 13 percent attended Chongryon schools, and one percent South Korean schools. Only a small percentage of Koreans in Japan use only Korean names.

Over the years, Koreans in Japan faced deep discrimination by the Japanese government and people. They have had to be fingerprinted. Very few enter the government or hold positions of power. And Koreans who don't take Japanese citizenship still don't have the right to vote in many areas of Japan.

Koreans in Japan are bitter about many tragic episodes in their history, notwithstanding the occupation of the Korean peninsula. In

1923, mobs of Japanese vigilantes massacred hundreds of Koreans after false rumors were spread that Koreans had taken advantage of the damage caused by a huge earthquake in Kanto, as well as allegations that Koreans had poisoned the drinking wells.

During World War II, tens of thousands of young Korean women were forced to become sex slaves. They were taken from their homes across the Korean peninsula and forced to have sex with dozens of Japanese soldiers each day in so-called "comfort stations" across Asia. The women endured horrible suffering and were ostracized from society, and their plight was not recognized publicly until many decades later, when a few "comfort women" came forward to tell their stories.

Still, ethnic Koreans living in Japan and in China have developed a strong sense of loyalty to their new homes, choosing to stay even when they could have left, and choosing Japanese and Chinese land as their burial places.

CHAPTER 5

So Long, Uncle Sam:
The Korean–U.S. Relationship

THE RELATIONSHIP BETWEEN South Korea and the United States is clearly in a state of drawdown. U.S. forces based in Korea are reducing their numbers. American investment in the country is falling from the highs of the early 1990s. Korea-America trade is sliding in importance as both countries concentrate on China as their primary trade partner. Every facet of the relationship between the United States and Korea is going through a period of diminishment.

This development may be viewed as a reason for melancholy. Or it may be seen as a singular triumph of the alliance between the two countries. For many decades, South Korea depended on the United States for its defense and its economic stability, as well as for psychological support as it grew in size and strength. The main reason the United States is considered less important today is because South Korea has reached maturity. The two countries are now going through an awkward stage, not unlike a parent sending a child off to college, a bittersweet but necessary moment.

What will not end, however, is the special place that Koreans have in their heart for America. "This is the only foreign power that came to Korea in arms and never tried to steal territory," says Park Sun-won, a former official in the South Korean national security apparatus and a visiting fellow at the Brookings Institution in Washington, D.C. He points out that while Korean anti-Americanism is real and fierce, it also is only skin-deep. "Ask any Korean who complains about America where they would most like their children to grow up, and they will say America," he says. In other words, the United States is like that obnoxious uncle. Koreans may always have something negative to say about him, but deep in their hearts they still love him.

The reason Koreans are so contradictory and seemingly confused in their feelings about America is that the relationship itself is so often contradictory and confused. It is based on two pillars: defense and trade. The defense side is undergoing a transition period as it has become obvious that the forces of the Republic of Korea (ROK) are more than able to handle the challenge of a feeble and deteriorating North Korean military. The trade side is simultaneously undergoing an upgrade, with the hoped-for ratification of a free trade agreement between the two countries, and a downgrade, as both the United States and South Korea focus on trade elsewhere.

FROM GINSENG TO SUVs: THE KOREAN–U.S. TRADE RELATIONSHIP

From above ground, the ginseng plant is easily noticed in a wild forest. Its red shoots and bright crimson berries stand out amidst the brown and green of the rest of the setting. Even when not bearing fruit, the plant's three prominent leaves would catch the eye of an astute observer because of their resemblance to another forest plant: poison ivy. But look more closely and you'll notice two smaller leaves at the base of the leaf stem, and you would be reminded of the Latin name for the North American version of the plant, *Panax quinquefolius* (medicine with five leaves).

The early fur trappers in eighteenth-century Canada knew to look for the five leaves and the red berries. They also knew that it was neither the leaves nor the berries that they were looking for, but the root. Ginseng root had been known for its medicinal properties in Europe for centuries, and in China for a few millennia before that. But it wasn't found in Europe or China. It was found in the wild and grown agriculturally in only one place in the world: Korea. The country, in fact, had a global monopoly on the market for ginseng on which its economy depended. Korean ginseng farmers knew how to cultivate it, harvest it, and then dry it in the sun to preserve its active chemicals. And they carefully guarded those secrets. Dried ginseng root—which takes at least five years to grow—was highly valued throughout China and Europe, and it was thought to be grown only in Korea.

That is, until those fur trappers noticed it growing in the wild in the northern forests of Canada. Soon, they discovered that local Indian tribes would search the forests for the relatively rare plant to create wound poultices and herbal broths for those recovering from illnesses. The trappers would employ Indian scouts to gather ginseng roots from the forest floor, which they would bundle and dry over fires and then ship back to Europe along with their packages of beaver and mink fur.

The trappers soon found that they were receiving far more return on investment for the ginseng than for the furs. Thus began the great ginseng bubble of the eighteenth century. Nearly everyone in the colonies got into the game of searching for and trading in ginseng—even George Washington's family made its initial fortune from the root. With the appearance of a new, cheap source of the root, demand exploded in Europe as ginseng became common to use as a tea and coffee supplement. Even China began importing large quantities.

Meanwhile, back in Korea, a financial disaster erupted. The Korean farmers who had lived off ginseng profits for centuries suddenly saw a massive decline in the value of their product. The royal treasury also saw tax revenues plummet. It was hard times for all.

The story didn't end there, though. In China, medicinal distributors noticed that the North American ginseng wasn't getting the same results as the old-fashioned Korean ginseng. Perhaps the two plants were different, after all. After a time it was determined that the Korean ginseng kept its good qualities because it was sun-dried on specially made racks over the course of several days. The North American ginseng was fire-dried. The value of Korean ginseng increased again, although it never reached the levels it had been at prior to the invasion of North American ginseng. The Americans would eventually lure some Korean ginseng farmers to their shores who taught the Americans the art of drying ginseng, again turning the market bipolar. As for Korea, it was forced for the first time in centuries to build new businesses and grow new crops. Global trade, the country learned, was not very kind to you if you didn't have a diversified economy.

The ginseng bubble and its implosion of the seventeenth and early-eighteenth centuries was not the first example of global trade and its fickle personality. But it was the first trade-related contact between what would later become the United States and what would later become the ROK. Little did those ginseng farmers and gatherers know back then, but their respective lands would still be linked closely by trade 200 years later.

The United States was, until a few years ago, South Korea's largest export market. South Korea, a trillion-dollar economy, is the seventh-largest importer of U.S. products. It has been that way for several decades and doesn't appear to be changing any time soon.

That's not to say that both countries don't still put trade tariffs on most goods that pass between them. But that is set to end. In April 2007, then Korean and U.S. presidents Roh Moo-hyun and George W.

Bush signed the KORUS Free Trade Agreement (KORUS FTA), which slashed tariffs on most products, including food, cars, and electronics. The KORUS FTA was supposed to be the dawn of a new era in free trade across the Pacific. South Korea would be the first country besides Mexico to sign such a wide-ranging pact with the United States.

But the treaty has not been ratified in either country. With the election of Barack Obama in America, it appeared that the KORUS FTA might be stillborn. Obama promised during his campaign for the presidency to "renegotiate" the treaty, especially its provisions dealing with the automotive industry. The prospects of renegotiating such a tightly argued agreement, which took more than a decade to reach, are very dim. When Obama called for a renegotiation, he was really calling for the treaty to be canceled.

The details of the telephone-book-size pact are numerous and intricate, but the most important elements revolve around food, cars, and services. Korea agreed to fully open its market to most U.S. foodstuffs, including corn and soybeans. Agreeing to this provision was a tremendous sacrifice on the Korean side because the country has long held a protectionist stance against food imports.

In the automotive section of the agreement, Korea agreed to reduce a number of taxes and laws that made it difficult for American car companies to compete in Korea. Most of these obstacles taxed cars by vehicle weight or size, which disadvantaged the U.S. car companies (who tend to make larger vehicles than Korean and Japanese automobile manufacturers). The elimination of such vehicle size–based taxes and rules should give American companies a better competitive footing in Korea. However, Obama, the U.S. labor unions, and many U.S. legislators believe that American cars still won't sell well in Korea. "The American manufacturers want regulated trade," says Tami Overby, president and CEO of the American Chamber of Commerce in Korea, an organization that has been pushing both countries to ratify the FTA. "They want a rule that says if you sell one car in Korea, then we get to sell one car in

Korea. They just don't understand that this is a 'free' trade pact, not a 'regulated' trade pact."

Nevertheless, Overby admits that if the United States requires changes to the agreement, such changes can be made in a more diplomatically palatable manner, such as a letter of amendment or an affiliated memorandum of understanding. "Reopening the negotiations is an absolute nonstarter. Everyone understands that," she says.

The KORUS FTA changes the playing field in Korea in a number of other arenas, too. It opens the Korean market to American-made electronic goods. It allows U.S. companies to buy Korean telecom firms and brokerage houses. It allows Korean-made clothes to come to the United States duty-free as long as they use American or Korean-made fabric. It even ends the taxation of U.S.–produced animated movies.

The biggest question is what happens next for the KORUS FTA. In light of the problems that the U.S. automobile industry has endured in the second half of 2008 and 2009, there might be enough political backwind for the Koreans to allow the reopening of that section of the pact. Meanwhile, Korea itself hasn't had an easy time ratifying the treaty. After the cabinet of President Lee Myung-bak sent the treaty to parliament, it should have been a simple process to get committee approval followed by a legislative vote. But opposition politicians declared that stopping the legislative process was imperative in order to delay, if not cancel, the ratification of the bill. To keep opposition legislators from disrupting the committee meeting, committee members barricaded themselves into a meeting room in the capitol building. Angry opposition legislators took a sledgehammer to the doors of the room, smashing it to splinters. They were disheartened to find that their opponents had piled furniture against the doorframe, still restricting their access. After smashing their way through that obstacle, an old-fashioned fistfight ensued, albeit one with fire extinguishers and sledgehammers.

Even if Korea ratifies the bill, it will still be meaningless without U.S. ratification. Thus, the chances are that the KORUS FTA will die a slow and lonely death, ignored by both U.S. legislators and President Obama.

WHERE'S THE BEEF? WHAT THE BEEF CRISIS DID AND DIDN'T MEAN

The sordid tale of Korea's relationship with U.S. beef started in 2003, with a downer. That's what American slaughterhouse employees call a steer that can't lift itself off the ground. In this case, the downer wasn't budging from the floor of the delivery chute that led to the killing floor of a slaughterhouse in Washington State. No matter how hard the attendants tried to push, bully, and cajole the lame steer, it wouldn't rise. The supervisor had the animal pushed aside and slaughtered on the spot. But he also sent samples of its brain to the local office of the Food and Drug Administration for testing, to make sure that the animal wasn't too sick for its beef to be marketed.

What the technicians at the laboratory found horrified them. It also set off alarm bells around the world. The brain tissue of the dead steer looked like someone had poked holes throughout it. Instead of a healthy network of neurons, the tissue looked like Swiss cheese intermixed with large agglomerations of plaque-like material. Immediately the technicians recognized what they were looking at. This steer had bovine spongiform encephalopathy, otherwise known as "mad cow disease."

Prior to this incident, there had never been a confirmed case of mad cow disease in North America. The world's worst outbreak of the disease was in the mid-1990s in England, when thousands of cattle were put to death after several dozen people came down with a human cousin to mad cow disease, called Creutzfeldt-Jakob disease. Creutzfeldt-Jakob is a horrifying way to die: It takes several years from the onset of symptoms to mortality, and the journey along the way is what you would expect of something that eats your brain away from the inside out. First, the victim becomes relatively immobile as the body's motor functions cease to operate. Then each of the body's subsystems fails until the heart finally stops. Family members of Creutzfeldt-Jakob victims spend years nursing their slowly deteriorating loved ones, who descend deeper into the painful depths of the disease.

Shortly after word leaked out that there had been a positive identification of mad cow disease in the United States, food safety organizations throughout the world immediately took action. Within days, more than eighty countries shut their doors to American beef imports. It was a crippling blow to an industry that is critical to the U.S. economy. During the next few years, more than half the countries that imposed a ban on U.S. beef lifted their closures. But almost forty countries kept the closure in place five years after the discovery of the single sick cow, even though no further cattle tested positive. South Korea was one of them.

A trip to the neighborhood grocery store in Seoul or any other Korean city would quickly show the aftereffect of the U.S. beef ban on the average Korean consumer. The only available cuts of beef were Australian, which cost from $8 to $10 per pound, and Korean, which could cost as much as $30 per pound. Korea, after all, has little grassland for cattle to graze on, and most beef producers are small family farms with only a few head of cattle. That's a far cry from the factory farming system in the United States.

Congressional leaders were irritated by countries like South Korea for refusing to lift the ban on American beef even after it was clear that there was no epidemic of mad cow disease. They accused foreign governments of hyping a health scare as a tactic to avoid opening their markets to free trade. During trade negotiations, the United States pushed for an end to the ban on beef. But the South

Korean administration of Roh Moo-hyun resisted the requests, saying the food security of his people was more important than pleasing a foreign ally.

That changed in April 2008. The new South Korean president, Lee Myung-bak, was visiting President Bush at Camp David when he mentioned in an offhand way that South Korea was once again going to allow beef imports from the United States. His message was well received by Bush, who spent more than the usual amount of time strolling the grounds of the wooded presidential retreat with Lee.

When he returned home, Lee's reception was much gloomier. A handful of protesters met him at the airport with placards claiming that he was responsible for the future death of thousands of Korean children, thanks to his beef diplomacy. Lee ignored them. A month later, the protests were still happening. They moved from the airport to Seoul's central municipal park and were occurring every day. Demonstrators shouted slogans and waved signs calling for President Lee's resignation. The number of protesters grew into the thousands.

The protests transformed from a simple traffic inconvenience matter to a national sensation when the Munhwa Broadcasting Corporation (MBC), one of the major television networks, ran a documentary that claimed that American cattle-raising practices encouraged the transmission of mad cow disease. The program also claimed, without any scientific evidence, that Korean people had a specific gene that exposed them more than others to the ravages of mad cow disease.

The shoddy journalism and its claims soon took on a life of their own on the Internet as websites, e-mails, and instant messages proliferated, making more and more outrageous claims. Suddenly, the protests in the center of Seoul swelled. Now tens of thousands of people were cramming into the main square of Seoul's central municipal park. And the types of people attending the protests bloomed from professional activists to parents, housewives, schoolchildren, and representatives from all strata of Korean society.

The demonstrations themselves took two personas. The first was during the daytime and evening, when parents and children attended. The park had a feel of a 1960s counterculture sit-in, with guitar players strumming and strangers joining together to sing folk songs. There was also a bit of performance art going on, with demonstrators dressed as Holstein cows handing out pamphlets and others dressed as a menacing Uncle Sam walking on stilts among the protesters.

But once night fell, and the children and their middle-class parents left, the demonstrations took on a completely different air. Suddenly student leftists and labor unionists started to hurl bricks and bottles at the riot police stationed nearby. Cars and buses and buildings were vandalized as street battles between the police and the hardcore protesters lasted throughout the night.

This daily replay went on throughout the late spring and early summer of 2008. President Lee, who had at first purposely ignored the demonstrations, struggled with how to respond. At first he demanded an end to the demonstrations for the sake of public order. Nobody left. Then he issued an apology for making the beef decision unilaterally. Nobody left. Lee's approval ratings plummeted to below 20 percent.

Finally, in early June, Lee appeared on national television to apologize publicly. He announced that his entire senior advisory staff had resigned in disgrace. He also declared that Korea would limit its beef imports to only cattle that were thirty months of age or younger, which supposedly made them less prone to mad cow disease. At first, nobody left. But the enthusiasm and excitement of the earlier demonstrations did seem to dissipate. Then slowly, over the course of the summer, the crowds got smaller and smaller and the nightly battles with the police got tamer and tamer. By the end of the summer, the entire affair was over.

But what were the beef protests really about? The first answer is that they weren't really about the beef. It's true that the nation endured a sudden and massive hysteria about the safety of American beef, but most Koreans admit that they didn't really believe the hyped stories.

The protests also weren't necessarily about the United States at all. There was certainly an anti-American theme to them, but that was more of a sideshow.

What the protests centered on was President Lee Myung-bak.

To understand the beef protests, one must have a reasonably sound knowledge of Korean politics. For six years, the left-leaning side of the national polity flourished under President Roh Moo-hyun, a former labor activist and civil rights lawyer. When Lee Myung-bak and his conservative Grand National Party won the 2007 elections, it served as a warning siren to the political left. Images of right-leaning authoritarian presidents from South Korea's recent past emerged in the fevered dreams of the leftists. The country absolutely had to find a way to get rid of Lee, under any circumstances, they decided. The beef issue presented an opportunity.

"Although it might seem from overseas that the demonstrations were against America, up close it was clear to me that they weren't," says Park Sun-won, the Brookings Institution fellow. "Most of the signs and slogans said 'Lee Must Resign.' The people there didn't really care about the U.S. or food safety. But they all wanted to send a message to the president."

Jeffrey Jones, a prominent Seoul attorney and former president of the American Chamber of Commerce in Korea, echoes that sentiment. "The two months of demonstrations that ensued really became political in nature—about the president and the fact that the left had lost power," he said. "Suddenly the conservatives, with Lee Myung-bak, came into power. The left-leaning powers felt out in the cold and they saw an opportunity to regain political strength. It was more a demonstration of politics and trying to get rid of Lee Myung-bak than it was about Korean beef."

In the end, the beef protests of 2008 might be viewed as a strange but unimportant chapter in the history of U.S.–Korean relations. Korean consumers apparently think so. At the end of the holiday season of the same year, grocery giant E-mart announced that it had sold 46,000 gift sets of American short ribs—more than the total number of Korean beef packages.

NO LONGER A TRIPWIRE

Peel away the diplomacy, the cultural allegiance, the mutual love of baseball, and the countless other layers of the U.S.–Korean relationship and you will find, at its innermost heart, a military alliance. Forged in the fight against Japan in World War II and then steeled in the Korean War, it is one of the strongest and most conjoined military alliances on earth.

During the Second World War, a determined, if tiny, band of Korean communist partisans rebelled against the Japanese colonial occupation of their country. The net effect of this uprising was negligible—a few hundred dead and a minor headache for the Japanese military machine. Far more worrisome to the Japanese were dozens of Korean independence activists in the United States. This band of lawyers and businessmen were to follow the U.S. forces into the Korean peninsula at the end of the war and would go on to establish the new government of the Republic of Korea. Led by Rhee Syng-man, this group of fiercely anticommunist leaders was nurtured by the American occupation army that controlled the South from 1945 to 1948.

When North Korea invaded the South in the summer of 1950, President Harry Truman wavered over whether to withdraw U.S. troops and write off Korea or to defend America's Asian ally. After a few days of high-level discussions, the Truman administration decided it would not allow South Korea to fall, under any circumstances. Over the course of the three-year war, more than a million American soldiers served in Korea and more than 50,000 of them fell in battle. The South Korean military, cut to ribbons in the first days of the war, recovered with U.S. military assistance and proved to be a viable and fierce fighting force.

With the end of the war, it was clear that U.S. forces would not leave South Korea to the whims of its northern neighbor ever again. Ever since the drawdown of combat troops in the immediate aftermath of the war, there has consistently been between 30,000 and 40,000 American troops stationed in Korea to defend that country in case of further aggression from the North. Today, the number of troops is roughly 28,000.

The underlying strategic premise of the American troop presence is that they will serve as a "tripwire" in case of a surprise attack from North Korea. Fewer than 30,000 soldiers, after all, aren't enough to fend off a military onslaught of several million enemy soldiers. Still, American troops are stationed there to slow down an attack long enough to allow several hundred thousand U.S. reinforcements to arrive, push back the advance, and then counterattack into North Korea.

Meanwhile, some 600,000 South Korean active duty troops are charged with conducting most of the fighting in the case of such an attack. According to post–Korean War rules, the alliance has officially been under United Nations command. But in reality it has been under U.S. Forces Korea command. In 1994, the South Korean army was released from U.S. command during peacetime, but in the event of war, it would immediately return to American leadership.

The tripwire strategy remained in effect for more than fifty years. Then, in 2003, Secretary of Defense Donald Rumsfeld called for a top-to-bottom review of the U.S. ROK defense relationship. This was partially in response to the needs of U.S. forces as they geared up for the invasion of Iraq. But it was also due to a long-held sense that the tripwire strategy was outdated and no longer needed.

A new operational plan was put forward and approved that called for a gradual drawdown of U.S. forces in Korea from 38,000 to 24,000. In addition, the U.S. troops would be resituated and garrisoned below the Han River, south of Seoul. South Korean forces would take control of each of the ten strategic missions that were until then performed by Americans, starting with complete control of the demilitarized zone. By 2012, according to the plan, the wartime command of ROK forces would fall under Korean leadership. Two allied armies fighting the same war separately. Tripwire no more.

While the plan appeared to meet the needs of the United States by reducing its footprint in South Korea, the Koreans weren't too happy about it. Korean defense officials lobbied U.S. policymakers to overturn the plan or at least deaden its impact. Some Korean officials feared that North Korea would interpret the move as a victory and thus increase tensions on the peninsula. Others simply worried about the economic impact of the potential drawdown: The U.S. military presence brings $2 billion in revenues each year to the South Korean economy.

But the plan has proceeded regardless. The big question is whether it means that the U.S. commitment to South Korea has diminished. U.S. officials claim that it doesn't. "This alliance has a reason for being that far exceeds the specific command-and-control structures," General B. B. Bell, the commander of U.S. Forces Korea, said in February 2008.

Meanwhile, Korea has its own military transformation to busy itself with. Until recently, the ROK military had one mission: to fight a war with North Korea. Now it is being asked to participate in multiple missions, with broadly varying needs and equipment requirements. For instance, in the aftermath of the U.S. invasion of Iraq, South Korea sent a brigade of combat engineers to the Kurdish-region city of Dohuk for rebuilding purposes. Although not a single Korean soldier was killed or wounded—in fact, they saw no combat at all in the relatively peaceful region of Iraqi Kurdistan—it was the first large-scale deployment of Korean military forces in a foreign theater since the Vietnam War (in which 50,000 combat and logistics soldiers served).

In addition, the Korean Air Force provided planes and crew for resupply missions in Afghanistan. That mission was much smaller in scope, but stretched the resources of the nation's tiny air force.

As the world becomes more globalized and as threats from nonconventional sources multiply, the South Korean military will need to expand its mission list, and its flexibility. First on the list is to diversify its spending into all three arms of the military. Currently, the government spends 80 percent of its military budget on the army, with the air force, navy, and special forces left to scrap it out over the remaining 20 percent. "In order to meet the emerging threats to Korean security, there needs to be a better balance of spending," said a military source who requested to remain anonymous. "A future Korean military will resemble the U.S. military, which evenly splits its spending between ground, air, and naval forces."

The reason for such a change is that nobody knows what the next threats will be and where they will come from. The South Korean military has just as much chance of being called on to protect sea-lanes in the Gulf of Aden or to rescue hostages in Latin America as it does to fight off North Korean tanks. The more flexible the military, the more chance it has to respond successfully to unknown threats.

KOREATOWNS

Koreatown in Los Angeles was relatively unknown to most Americans until the 1992 race riots, when television cameras took footage of gun-toting Korean businessmen perched on top of buildings and their angry confrontations with black residents. Today, the downtown neighborhood bears little resemblance to that time. The community is flush with new condo high-rises, office buildings, and clear symbols of an immigrant community that has, to a large extent, made it.

Koreatown has become a mecca for those who don't need to work fifteen-hour days at a dry cleaner or corner convenience store. It's a place full of coffeehouses and day spas, where the well-to-do can while away their days and nights chatting, sipping tea, and getting massages.

That evolution can be seen at a growing number of day spas, like the well-known Olympic Spa on Olympic Boulevard. On the outside, the place looks like a typical day spa frequented by women looking to spend a relaxing, luxurious afternoon. And some areas of the sprawling spa offer such pampering. But on the bottom floor, the scene is much different. This is where women from all walks of life wander from bath to sauna to scrubbing bench. This is where the Korean virtue of cleansing comes to life.

The ritual isn't pampering. It can actually be painful to have sandpaper rubbed vigorously over every inch of your skin. It is a form of exfoliation unlike anything offered elsewhere in the United States, where a rough hand mitt removes piles of dark-colored dead skin in one sitting.

In Los Angeles, New York, suburban Washington, D.C., and other major cities with the largest concentrations of Korean immigrants, these places are called spas. In Korea, they are known as a *jim-jil-bang*—a communal bathhouse.

In Korea, more spartan bathhouses are located within walking distance of most city neighborhoods and in villages. Seniors—men and women who go into gender-segregated sections—are the most common visitors. Many people go at the same time every day. The bathhouse is a prime location for socializing, escaping the stresses of the world, and gathering energy for the remainder of the day.

The traditions of bathhouses are among many that Koreans have brought to the United States in recent decades. Today, some 1.6 million Koreans live in the country—mostly in the largest cities like L.A. and New York. But they also can be found in the smallest towns, often operating convenience stores, Japanese restaurants, and dry cleaners.

Koreans began coming in small numbers to the United States in the late 1800s. There were a small number of political dissidents then, and about 7,000 workers sent to Hawaii to work as strikebreakers on sugar plantations to replace Japanese workers who were walking the picket lines. But those workers quickly left the fields in search of better work. The second wave came after the Korean War and was dominated by students seeking graduate studies. The third wave began in earnest in 1965, after immigration laws were loosened, and in that wave came a range of generally well educated Koreans seeking economic prosperity.

The U.S. population of Koreans is the second largest concentration living outside of the homeland. There are more than 2 million Koreans in China. The third largest population is the Korean population in Japan, called the *Zainichi*, which numbers 600,000.

Korean immigrants in the United States are among the better-educated immigrant groups. Nearly 50 percent of all Korean immigrants have a college degree or better, compared to 26.8 percent of all Americans. Despite their high level of education, many Korean immigrants lacked fluency in English and therefore turned to small businesses as a way to make a living. They devoted long hours to building their businesses into successful enterprises. The children of Korean immigrants are much more likely than the general U.S. population to get a college education and gain professional employment.

The success of Koreans in general can be attributed to social and professional networking done through churches. The Korean immigrant community has a higher rate of Christians than the overall population in Korea. Decades ago, churches became the primary place for new immigrants to seek trustworthy advice and connections with other Koreans in America. Thus, many new Korean immigrants first sought out a Korean congregation for practical reasons, and then ended up becoming Christian.

The number of Korean churches is staggering. In the Los Angeles area, there are more than 700 Korean congregations—mostly Protestant denominations. One Korean sociologist found twelve zip codes in the area that have more than ten Korean churches each. Two of the largest and oldest Korean churches are Oriental Mission Church (OMC) and Young Nak Presbyterian Church. They either originated or continue to be located in Koreatown. The growth of these two congregations is eye-popping. In 1973, both OMC and Young Nak had a weekly following of about 450 people. By 2000, the weekly worshippers at each numbered around 5,000 every Sunday. Both churches also have huge budgets. OMC's annual budget stood at about $4 million in 2000, and Young Nak's was $7 million.

While church life has become a critical part of life for Korean immigrants, there are other traditions brought over from the homeland that are important for immigrants, too. Many Korean communities participate in a system called "gye"—where a group of people put their money into a pot and then lend it out to one person at a time. It's a loan system—run separately from banks—that has helped Koreans open businesses and pay for homes, college tuition, and other large expenses.

Economic experts have studied the impact of Korean immigrants on the U.S. economy and have seen a benefit. Since Koreans dispro-portionately open and expand small businesses and their median income is higher than the national average, they are credited with raising the overall per capita income in the states where they live.

Just as other aspects of the Korea–U.S. relationship are drawing down, the interest among Koreans to come to the United States has also begun to fall. Korean immigration peaked in 1987, when nearly 36,000 Koreans entered the United States, and then dropped sharply in the 1990s—attributable in large part to improving economic con-ditions in the homeland. Nevertheless, the presence of Koreans in the United States is expected to remain high for years to come.

PART THREE

INDUSTRIES

CHAPTER 6

Korea in the Driver's Seat: A Short History of the Korean Car

THE KOREAN CAR hit a new milestone in 2009. For the first time since Koreans started making cars, they won the coveted North American Car of the Year Award, presented by a group of fifty prominent automotive journalists. The recipient of the award was the new Hyundai Genesis, a relatively cheap ($40,000) entrant in the lucrative luxury car market to compete with Lexus, Mercedes, and BMW. The Genesis comes with a six-cylinder engine (there also is a four-cylinder model) that can go from zero to sixty miles per hour in 5.7 seconds. The built-in navigation system can also play movies, and every vehicle comes with leather seats.

No Korean car had ever won any major awards in North America since Hyundai started selling cars on that continent in 1994. It would have been quite an achievement for the company to have won any award. But to win the crown prize of North American Car of the Year was a true triumph.

The Genesis beat out vehicles made by all the other major manufacturers, including Ford, Volkswagen, Audi, and Toyota. The reviews are not perfect. The car gets knocks for bumpy suspension and a slow response to voice commands, among other things. But critics praised it for overall quality and handling. And the $40,000 price tag is about $20,000 less than the comparable Lexus model.

As the car website Edmunds.com puts it: "If ever an automaker deserved a 'Most Improved' award, it would be Hyundai. Within the last decade or so, the Korean company has gone from building cars that were the butt of cruel jokes to competent vehicles that just might be the cause of some sleepless nights for Honda and Toyota executives."

Hyundai is barreling ahead to gain global market share in the automobile industry, and it is following a textbook business model established by the Japanese makers: Start with small economy cars, move up to midsize cars, and then enter the luxury market. Hyundai also is developing alternative fuel vehicles, including the Elantra LPI Hybrid Electric Vehicle. The compact sedan, unveiled in April 2009 at the Seoul International Motor Show, will be powered with a liquefied petroleum injected (LPI) engine and advanced lithium-polymer batteries.

But even with the critically acclaimed Genesis, the company understands its brand problem. Whereas the Mercedes-Benz has its three-pointed star and Ford has the famous blue oval, you won't find any company logo on the front of the Hyundai Genesis. Nevertheless, the story of the Korean car encapsulates the history of the country's economic growth and development.

When General Park Chung-hee was elected president in 1963, he decided that his country would make cars and become a world economic leader. To the American diplomats in Seoul, and even to naysayers among his own economic advisers who claimed Korea could not move away from a farming economy, Park's dream was a fantasy. One diplomatic cable sent back to Washington shortly after the 1961 military coup referred to Korea's economy as "a basket case" that will always require U.S. aid to keep its people from choosing communism. Yet Park persevered. Over several decades, and through several administrations, Seoul pursued—and attained—the car dream.

Yet the journey was far more turbulent than Park had envisioned. To him, it was simple. Build the steel industry to supply the raw product. Build the road system and then build the cars. But even after Korean companies accomplished all that, they still had to survive in the vicious world of consumer sales and brand management. Not all of them did survive. One that did, Hyundai Motor Corporation, did so by changing its own culture and rules. That's why the story of how Korea went from being a land of few roads in 1953 to having a successful car manufacturing industry, with modern Hyundai claiming a competitive spot in the world marketplace, reveals so much about what the Korean economy used to be and what it is today.

THE STEEL

Park Tae-joon sat on Waikiki Beach in Honolulu, staring blankly out at the tourists rising and bobbing in the waves. He wasn't supposed to be on vacation. In fact, the former army general hadn't taken a day off work for more than a year. But here he was, a former poor villager feeling the weight of his country's future on his shoulders. His dreams of building Korea's largest industrial project—a modern integrated steel mill—were about to disappear. He thought of walking straight into the ocean, too ashamed to return to his family and to his former mentor, President Park Chung-hee.

At that point, in 1969, a group of Western corporations that had previously pledged financing for the construction of the steel mill had turned their backs on him. International groups, including the

International Monetary Fund (IMF), also withdrew their support. Park had just made a last-ditch effort to change the opinion of key company leaders, only to leave empty-handed.

Now he was on an unscheduled detour, staying in a condo owned by a U.S. steel executive who urged Park to take a few days rest. His mind wandered to past points in his life, including his years studying and working as a diplomat in Japan. That's when the idea hit him. He quickly threw his clothes into his suitcase and got on the next plane to Japan. After a few days of meetings with old colleagues, he flew to Seoul and went directly to see President Park.

Four years later, with a big hand from the president, Park Tae-joon and his dedicated army of workers transformed the fishing and rice farming town of Pohang on the eastern coast of Korea into a two-mile stretch of gleaming industrial might. That year, the first sheets of cold steel rolled off the factory floor at Pohang Iron and Steel Company, now officially known as POSCO. From then on, the company and the country never looked back.

The success of POSCO and other Korean steel companies was a critical reason for the country's rise in another industry—carmaking. President Park decided early on during his sixteen-year rule of Korea to build an integrated steel factory. That was a centerpiece of his economic plan. Just as he stubbornly remained dedicated to the Busan-Seoul highway plan, despite a chorus of naysayers, President Park also committed himself completely to the steel plan—which would be a much more difficult mountain to climb.

One of the astonishing facts about POSCO is that the founder and the first employees had no experience or expertise in steelmaking. They learned it all from others, while making many visits to Japanese steel plants, which at that time were considered among the world's best.

The steel factory's success was made possible by President Park's protégé, Park Tae-joon. He grew up in a small village near the southern tip of Korea and was the oldest of six children in a peasant family. He studied engineering and science at a Japanese university and then entered the military.

The two Parks met in the army, where both quickly rose through the ranks to become generals. President Park was impressed with his military colleague's management, engineering, and political skills. So he tapped Park Tae-joon in 1967 to lead his steel project and gave staunch support from then on.

Always serious and focused on efficiency and lowering cost, Park Tae-joon decided immediately to do away with the usual shenanigans of Korea's business culture. He jotted down three demands on a piece of paper and took it to President Park for approval. The POSCO founder said he wouldn't take on the project unless he could avoid the tacit rule of donating large sums of money to the ruling political party, having to bend to political pressure on hires, and going through government bureaucracy to purchase products and services. Park Tae-joon wanted full control to develop the project on his own and without the burdens of politics and red tape. The president quickly gave his blessing and signed his initials to the paper. For years after that, Park Tae-joon carried the paper with the president's initials in his pocket to show to any politicians or government officials whom he angered when he refused to contribute to a political party or to give other political favors.

In those early years, "Chairman Park," as POSCO's founder was known, often slept on the floor of a makeshift office on the grounds of what would become a two-mile stretch of factories in the town of Pohang, on the eastern coast of the Sea of Japan. He was soft-spoken and had an uncanny ability to root out problems that could have spelled disaster without intervention. He tended to the smallest detail and the most ambitious expansion plans.

Long before the first plant was built, the project encountered huge hurdles, including negative reports from world economic organizations, including the IMF, and the collapse of funding from U.S. and European partner companies. Chairman Park saved the project by persuading the president and the Japanese government and steel industry to allow reparations funds from the Japanese occupation of Korea to go to the steel mill. Japanese steelmakers also lent a great deal of technical expertise to the Koreans.

In 1973, the first section of the ambitious plant churned out one million tons of crude steel. The company charged ahead, pushing toward bigger and bigger dreams.

A decade later, POSCO factories produced 9.1 million tons of crude steel. By 1992, the capacity had grown to almost 21 million tons a year. Two years later, the company was listed on the New York Stock Exchange.

Back in the early days, POSCO quickly became a prime supplier of cold-rolled steel sheets for automobiles and the hot coils that are needed to make the sheets. Partly because of its support from the government, POSCO quickly became profitable and a key player in Korea's growing economy. The company sold steel at prices lower than overseas competitors to Hyundai and Daewoo, the country's largest automakers.

POSCO also made many other types of steel, including steel used to make refrigerator doors, appliances, bridges, and transformers. Three-quarters of its sales today are to Korean companies, and the rest is shipped to about sixty other countries. Today, POSCO dominates and supplies about 60 percent of Korea's steel needs. It produces enough steel to make thousands of automobiles a day.

The company's plants are considered among the most efficient and modern in the world and can produce steel at $100 less per ton than the largest U.S. steel firms. The company also invests millions of dollars a year in education efforts to find more modern and environmentally friendly ways of producing steel.

With almost 20,000 employees in offices spread across a dozen countries, POSCO is one of the top five steel producers in the world and has factories in China, India, and Japan. Its net profit in 2007 was $3 billion (3.68 trillion won). And it is still pushing ahead.

THE ROAD

To fully appreciate the story of Korea's roads, it helps to become familiar with another Korean farming peasant named Chung Ju-yung. As the eldest son, he was expected to stay in the small village of Asan and keep the farm productive and the extended family well-fed. But he had a habit of running off to nearby towns to find day-labor work. It was better, he felt, to earn cash than to risk a whole year's worth of work with the hope of a bountiful crop.

His father disagreed. Every time the younger Chung ran away, his father would track him down and bring him home. It wasn't until his fourth try, when he made it all the way to Seoul and started working in a rice shop, that he gained freedom. He did so well at the shop that the owner gave it to Chung, confident that the young man could manage the operation better. Unfortunately, the Japanese colonial authorities decided that rice distribution was too important to be run by Koreans. So they confiscated the store.

Chung tried again. This time, he managed to get a loan to buy a small auto mechanic shop. He knew nothing about cars, but he was sure he could learn. Soon, he had turned the store into the only place where the Japanese officials (who were the only people who could own cars then) knew their Japanese-made autos would be fixed quickly. Chung made a lot of money and expanded the business. Within a few years, the one-man operation had grown to more than fifty people.

But then World War II interfered. Japanese authorities again decided that they should own all auto mechanic shops, and Chung was left penniless a second time. At the end of the war—and the defeat of Japan—Chung tried his hand at a new business: construction. He built a new contracting enterprise from nothing and called it Hyundai, which in Korean means "modern." He wanted his company to be at the forefront of a new and vibrant Korea. Then, on June 25, 1950, the North Koreans invaded. Chung abandoned his business and fled, along with everyone else, southward.

When the North Korean Army crossed the border, they met only minor resistance. The South Korean Army, along with most civilians, simply melted away and retreated south. Nevertheless, it took nearly ten days for the North's tanks to reach Busan, Korea's southernmost city. By the time they did, newly landed American Marines stopped them on the outskirts of the city long enough for a major counteroffensive.

The fact that the U.S. Marines could travel in boats from America to Busan faster than the North Koreans could get there by land (today it's a five-hour drive, if you can somehow avoid the traffic jams) tells you all you need to know about South Korea's road system in 1950: There wasn't one. Outside of a few dirt paths and one railroad line, Korea simply didn't have paved roads. Ask any U.S. veteran of the Korean War what it was like to be transported by vehicle and he'll surely tell you some colorful stories of the mobile infantryman's nemesis: mud.

According to development economists, the quickest way to pull an undeveloped, rural society out of poverty is to build roads. And that was President Park's biggest goal in the early 1970s. He wanted roads, and he wanted them built quickly. The crown jewel of that plan was the Busan-Seoul highway, an eight-lane, 266-mile-long expressway that he envisioned after visiting West Germany and traveling the autobahn. It was to be called, officially, the Kyungbu Expressway, and by cutting a diagonal line across the peninsula, it would be the spine for all the other roads that were still to be built.

The problem was that a couple of mountain ranges stood in the way. Park's initial vision was a dauntingly difficult engineering challenge. He wanted long tunnels through the mountains in some places. In other places, he wanted mountainsides blasted away by dynamite. When Korean and Japanese companies placed bids on the project, they were as high as $1.4 billion in today's money.

Except for one bid. Chung Ju-yung offered to do it for only $649 million, but with an altered route. The war years and the decade afterward had been good to Chung. He had launched a construction company that soon was building bases for the U.S. Eighth Army. He transformed the enterprise into an international engineering firm, building roads, factories, and hospitals throughout the world.

When Chung and his executives decided to bid on the Kyungbu project, they spent weeks surveying the route. Since they were one of the only Korean companies that had road-building experience, they knew how important the route design was. Chung knew that if he could make the road much more serpentine, enabling him to reduce the difficulties of mountain-crossing points, he could drastically cut the cost of the project.

Hyundai won the contract and began construction in February 1968. In other countries, a project of this magnitude would typically take five years, maybe three at the least. Hyundai got two years and two months to complete the task.

The building of the Kyungbu Expressway is now a piece of nation-building lore in South Korea. Engineers worked triple shifts, the amount of construction equipment in South Korea more than doubled, and the entire country breathlessly awaited and read reports about the previous day's progress in the morning newspapers.

It wasn't all smooth and steady for Hyundai. The mountains still had to be crossed, and one tunnel, called the Tangjae tunnel, proved to be a monster. Repeated cave-ins delayed progress and injured and killed some workers. At one point, crews became convinced that ancient spirits were being disturbed and were causing the accidents. Absenteeism—nearly unheard of in Korean workplaces then and now—became a significant problem.

Chung persevered. He threw more machinery and more crews at the Tangjae tunnel. He doubled wages for those workers who did show up at the site. And it worked. In June 1970, the tunnel and Highway 1 were complete.

At the opening ceremony for the road, Chung Ju-yung stood next to President Park and his wife as they cut the ribbon to open the road. Afterward, Park gazed silently out at the long, black, empty expanse of roadway with Chung at his side. All of the cars in Korea, both men knew, would barely fill up a portion of this new highway. Park turned to Chung, the probably apocryphal story goes, and asked: "What do you know about making cars?"

With visions of his youthful days spent in the auto repair shop probably running through his mind, Chung is said to have simply replied: "I can do it."

THE PONY

Chung's response was more than self-indulgent confidence. He knew a lot about cars because his company had been building them for two years. But in the car industry, "building" can be a relative term.

What Hyundai was really doing was assembling a kit of car parts that had already been manufactured in the United States by Ford. The Korean workers merely assembled the kits for the Ford Cortina, compact cars that were then sold in Korea.

But both President Park and Chung wanted to do much more. They didn't want to subcontract for Ford. They wanted to compete with Ford. The Cortina assembly plant gave the company a nucleus around which to build a real car company. So in 1970, Hyundai pulled out of the partnership with Ford and went looking for a partner that would help it build the kind of car company Chung wanted.

It wasn't easy. There were discussions with Toyota, General Motors, and Volkswagen, but nobody offered the Koreans a chance to simply license their technology. They all wanted a Korean partnership to resemble something like the Ford deal: a Korean-branded subsidiary of the mother company.

Chung had more success with Mitsubishi. The Japanese industrial giant had a fledgling car business that was learning to crawl under the shadow of Toyota and Nissan. Mitsubishi offered technical assistance and technology licensing, but it didn't have the wherewithal to offer complete car designs for a Korean car.

The negotiations should have ended there. In fact, they did for another Korean company that was trying to enter the car business. Daewoo (which means "great universe" in Korean) had a hauntingly similar corporate biography to Hyundai's. Its founder, Kim Woochoong, was born to a privileged family in southern Korea. The Korean War ended those privileges: Kim's father, a regional governor in the Rhee Syng-man administration, was captured during the North's invasion and executed.

With his father dead, Kim became the family's sole provider. He earned a living in a very traditional way—delivering newspapers. Although it was a good way to make a few coins, it couldn't feed the family. So Kim got into the habit of delivering his papers earlier than any other delivery boy and then returning in the afternoon to collect his money. He soon cornered the town's newspaper delivery market.

Kim later established a construction business that built American military bases. After the war, Daewoo diversified into multiple business lines and was soon a full-fledged conglomerate.

Kim also wanted desperately to get into the automobile business. But he lacked Chung's desire to do so on Korean terms. Instead, he stopped his search after establishing a partnership with General Motors. By the early 1970s, Daewoo was producing GM car kits in its Korean factory.

Chung, meanwhile, was doing it the hard way. With Mitsubishi's technical help, he began building a car company from the ground up. He found designers in Italy and a British car executive named George Turnbull to oversee the construction of the new factory in Ulsan. Turnbull requested four years to build the plant. Chung gave him two.

Chung managed to finance the new company on highly desirable terms, thanks to government loan guarantees (courtesy of President Park, who was still beaming about his new highway). A consortium of American banks joined Korean and Japanese partners to underwrite the loans for Hyundai Motor Corporation—the first time that private foreign capital was used to finance a major Korean industrial project.

In 1976, the first Hyundai car rolled off the assembly line in Ulsan. Dubbed the Pony (the first of many Old West–themed car names—Koreans have always had a weakness for American Westerns), it wasn't much to look at. Boxy and with noticeable gaps in the frame, it also boasted what journalist Richard Steers referred to in his biography of Chung, *Made in Korea: Chung Ju Yung and the Rise of Hyundai*, as "the worst paint job of all time. . . . "

But it was all Korean, and it was a moment of great pride for the nation. It soon became the most common car on the Kyungbu Expressway. Chung used that road as part of his quality-control strategy. He ordered his driver to take him up and down the Kyungbu so that he could personally count the number of Ponys that were broken down on the shoulder. He then compared those numbers to the market share of the Pony to determine the quality of the car. It turned out that his car held up to such scrutiny.

With the success of the Pony in Korea, Hyundai aimed for the all-important export market. Chung's advisers recommended a half-decade-long preparatory plan that involved significant market research and a brand-new design that could be customized for each country's conditions. Chung overruled them and instead ordered that exports commence immediately in thirty countries simultaneously.

The result was again a smashing success. Although the number of cars being exported was minimal, they were snapped up upon arrival at African, Middle Eastern, and South American ports. The quality was abhorrent, but nobody else offered such a cheap car. Chung then ordered his managers to travel with the cars and take careful note of how they held up in different countries. The cars in Saudi Arabia, for instance, lost their paint within a few days under the oppressive sun. Thereafter, a special paint formulation was applied to all Saudi-bound cars. Likewise, the cars in Brazil suffered from significant suspension damage due to the country's poor roads—soon a reinforced suspension system was placed in all cars headed for Brazil.

The export strategy worked. By 1985, Hyundai was selling as many cars overseas as it was in Korea. It had now introduced multiple models, with all of them selling well.

Daewoo, meanwhile, was achieving success selling its GM cars. It had done so well in its partnership that GM had approved a new Daewoo brand of cars to be sold in Korea.

Both companies now eyed the greatest export market of them all: North America. In 1986, Hyundai launched its "Cars That Make Sense" marketing campaign for that region. Just a few years earlier, such a plan would have been ridiculed. But the communist regime of Yugoslavia had proved that cheap cars could sell in America—its Yugo had been a mild success that year.

Hyundai's strategy was simple: Undersell everyone else. The Hyundai Excel hatchback was priced below $6,000, far less than its Japanese competitors. And it worked. A protean network of seventy-five dealers quickly sold more than the 100,000 car target for the company's first year in America. In 1987, Hyundai sold almost 300,000 cars in the United States, Canada, and Mexico.

Chung Ju-yung had done it. From abject poverty—and after multiple bankruptcies—he built a successful construction and engineering giant. Then he transformed that company of broad-shouldered construction workers into a successful automobile manufacturer. He had come in first, with Daewoo close behind, in the race to build the first Korean car that could sell on the international markets. And just as important, Korea was now recognized as the industrial giant that it had somehow willed itself to become.

THE MOTHER OF ALL WARRANTIES

The story should have ended there, with Korean determination and cleverness spurring worldwide success. But in business, stories rarely end. They just enter another stage.

In the car business, both Hyundai and Daewoo were chagrined to discover, the next stage after a successful product launch is building brand loyalty. That was easy in the developing countries where these companies first exported cars. When you are the only business that sells a car cheap enough for a certain portion of the population to buy, that portion tends to remain loyal.

But the market was different in North America. Americans and Canadians who couldn't otherwise buy cars were happy to buy a cheap car, but the agreement came with one important condition. The car had to be a value for the money. Nobody was willing to spend even $6,000 if oil leaked on their shoes every time they tapped their brakes or if their monthly repair bills trumped their loan payments.

The core of the problem could be seen on the factory floor at Ulsan. Economist Alice Amsden wrote about what she saw there in her 1989 book *Asia's Next Giant*. At the time, Hyundai had two identical plants—one in Ulsan and one in Japan, where the same cars were produced by Japanese workers who had been trained by Mitsubishi. The Japanese plant could produce four cars in the same time it took the Ulsan plant to produce one.

Amsden learned, however, that ethnicity itself had nothing to do with the difference in productivity. The Korean workers were just as motivated, well-trained, and compensated as their Japanese colleagues. The problem, Amsden discovered, had to do with the parts. In the Japanese plant, one line manager who had worked in both factories found that it took five seconds to attach a specific screw. In Ulsan, it took twenty seconds. The difference wasn't in the person doing the screwing, and it wasn't in the floor layout, either. It was the screw. "Ulsan uses Korean parts and Japanese parts are used in Japan," the line manager told Amsden. "The Korean screws barely have a thread, and you have to slowly ease it into the hole or it will break apart. We end up throwing away five screws for every one that works. In Japan, we didn't throw any screws away."

The very reason automobile manufacturing was so appealing to Korea's economic planners in the 1960s was the same reason that Hyundai was having quality problems. At the time, subcontractors made 40 percent of the car parts. And those subcontractors had also built their businesses from scratch in coordination with Hyundai's car business creation. They had done so in exchange for guaranteed contracts. So they produced substandard parts either because of a lack of incentive (the Hyundai contract was guaranteed, anyway) or a lack of ability.

And North American consumers were starting to notice. The Hyundai Excel became known as having the worst repair record of any car. Owning an Excel wasn't a badge of honor for someone who could otherwise not afford a car. It became a badge of shame. In Korea, people bought Hyundais anyway out of a sense of patriotism. American car buyers had no such loyalties.

American Hyundai executives and dealers understood this and tried desperately to communicate their concerns to headquarters in Seoul. But the message never got to the top. As a result, Hyundai's sales slipped throughout the second half of the 1990s. The brand was clearly dead in the water, and most of the original American executives had left by 1999.

Things were even worse for Daewoo. It had launched its first Daewoo-branded luxury sedans in America two years earlier and failed miserably. Meanwhile, the financial crisis of 1997 had pushed the company toward death's door. When the government of Kim Young-sam ordered all the chaebol to sell off their nonperforming assets and consolidate business lines, the Daewoo CEO took the biggest risk of his career: He expanded operations and plowed what little cash the company had into new divisions of the company (the car export business to America being one such example).

The move didn't pay off. The Korean government refused to guarantee new loans to Daewoo and the company officially entered bankruptcy in 1999. CEO Kim Woo-choong fled to France with the few million dollars that were left in Daewoo's bank account. Daewoo would go down in history as the biggest Korean chaebol to fail.

Meanwhile, things weren't much better for Hyundai America. In 1999, Finbarr O'Neill, a Hyundai corporate counsel who had no auto industry experience, received the unenviable task of overseeing the burial of the company. While waiting for the Seoul headquarters to send another Korean executive, O'Neill started to do something that no Hyundai America executive had done in a decade: He visited dealerships.

What he found surprised him. Despite the horrible quality reputation of the cars, the Hyundai dealers' repair bays were empty. The cars, he found out, had undergone a spectacular improvement in quality in recent years. Underperforming subcontractors were fired and quality control among suppliers was improved with Hyundai's help. Suddenly, the Hyundai cars weren't breaking down. The dealers assailed him with the message: These cars aren't lemons anymore, but we're the only ones who know that.

For the first time, O'Neill knew that there was a way for Hyundai America to survive. He then did something that every American executive who works for an Asian company is told to never, ever do: He went to Seoul and told his bosses that they were wrong. He even had a plan for how to fix their mistakes.

And that's when a miracle occurred. The Hyundai executives (Chung Ju-yung was by now retired and dabbling in politics) listened and agreed. It was a singular moment in Korean business history—and is probably the most emblematic event of the new, post-IMF Korean economy. Hyundai headquarters granted O'Neill's request to stay on as CEO of Hyundai America and even approved his audacious plan.

Upon his return, O'Neill set into motion a strategy that was quickly ridiculed by the automotive press and demeaned by other car company executives. Hyundai offered a ten-year, 100,000-mile warranty for every car. The industry standard at the time was a three-year, 30,000-mile warranty. After that three-year period, or by the time the owner had driven the car more than 30,000 miles, the manufacturer no longer guaranteed to fix—at its own cost— any faulty car parts, including the fundamental parts (engine, frame, axles) of the drivetrain system.

Hyundai boldly declared that it had fixed its quality problem. And it went several steps further. It was willing to guarantee, with its own pocketbook, that its cars weren't going to break down. To a public that was used to slick-talking salesmen and marketing doubletalk, this "mother of all warranties" was something special. People returned to Hyundai showrooms out of curiosity. Once there, they saw a whole range of models, including the popular Santa Fe SUV. The cars were attractive and cheap. And once the worry over quality was taken away by the warranty, shoppers started pulling out their checkbooks.

O'Neill's plan didn't just increase sales. It tripled them. And it saved the Hyundai brand in America. Today, Hyundai is the world's fourth best-selling car brand, and the company annually sells more than 500,000 cars in the United States alone. Hyundai is exactly what President Park and Chung Ju-yung envisioned while looking out over their empty highway thirty years ago: a competitive player in the global automobile marketplace.

CHAPTER 7

Samsung Eternal: From Rice Trading to $174 Billion in Sales

EVERY JANUARY, the electronics industry moves en masse to Las Vegas for what is probably the world's biggest trade fair: the Consumer Electronics Show (CES). Hundreds of thousands of executives, salespeople, designers, programmers, and even hand models descend on the Vegas convention center, coming from Helsinki, Tokyo, Chicago, and other places, near and far, for the event. The show is traditionally dominated by the major electronics, telecommunications, and computer companies, including Sony, Nokia, and HP, which host enormous press conferences that fill auditoriums to announce new products.

January 2009 was no different. Even in the midst of a recession, the hotels were filled with CES-goers. But anyone who had attended the show in a previous decade would have been stunned to find that the Sonys and HPs of the world weren't the leading attention-getters.

Instead, it was a Korean company, Samsung, that drew the biggest crowds and generated the biggest buzz.

Ten years earlier, Samsung's presence at CES was so small and insignificant that its booth was relegated to the far reaches of the convention hall. But by 2009, it had the largest booth and was the talk of Las Vegas. Samsung's new product lineup dominated the several thousand square feet of booth space. A 300-foot-long wall of TVs played Samsung commercials on endless loop; among them was a sliver of a plasma display big-screen television that came in at just over one inch thick. Another display highlighted Samsung's new auto-focus camera technology. When a G.I. Joe doll was robotically moved in front of the camera, the auto-focus lens recognized his human-like face and instantly focused on it; when a flower bouquet was then moved in front of the lens, the camera duly focused on it in close-up mode.

How did this Korean company transform itself from being a bit player in the electronics business to an international powerhouse, employing more than 250,000 employees worldwide and boasting revenue amounting to more than 20 percent of South Korea's GDP? How did Samsung change from being a parts supplier into a major global brand?

It all began in 1938, when an ambitious trader in the rice business set audacious goals for his newly formed company.

SAMSUNG'S EARLY HISTORY

Lee Byung-chull had an idea that none of his employers would take seriously. The young rice trader thought that Korea—then an impoverished province of Japan—could not only export food to China and

Manchuria, but could also become a regional trade powerhouse. Most food trade in those days went in one direction—from other countries into Korea. But Lee felt that products like dried seaweed and pickled fish would be well received in other parts of Asia.

Acting on his idea, in 1938 he started his own company, which he called Samsung. In Korean, the name means "three stars." An interpretation of the name with deeper meaning is that the company should aim to be "big, strong, and eternal."

His new enterprise, based in the southern Korean mountain city of Daegu, quickly found success as both an exporter and an importer. However, his newfound wealth was completely wiped out by the end of World War II and the chaos that followed the end of the Japanese occupation. But Lee rebuilt his company, this time headquartered in Seoul. The Korean War then reduced the company to scratch once more, leaving Lee penniless. But again he reformed his company amidst the rubble of postwar Seoul.

Had Lee remained a food trader, his company probably would never have grown much larger than it had been in its early days. But he recognized that a good business prospect is a good business prospect, regardless of the industry. So, in 1954, he established a textile mill. Soon, his cloths were able to beat any imported cloth on price, making his product popular among clothes makers. After he had established a foothold in the market, advisers urged him to expand quickly with new factories. Instead, he poured his profits into improving the quality of his fabric, and within a few years the textile arm of Samsung, called Cheil Industries, dominated the Korean market and began to export its product overseas.

Lee continued to build new businesses, investing in insurance and financial services, construction and real estate, and even shipbuilding. Along the way to building one of Korea's largest companies, he also pioneered modern business practices in the country—such as creating Korea's first human resources department. Unlike other firms that hired and fired according to each manager's whim, Samsung centralized those tasks so that each business unit could focus on pursuing its market.

Lee's most propitious move came in 1969, when he formed Samsung Electronics. Lee had come to the conclusion that the production of electronic appliances would be well suited to Korea's abundant and educated labor force and that there would be enough domestic demand for such products. He envisaged also that the products could eventually be exported, once production became efficient. He established the company despite the concerns of the federal government, which saw the move as a duplication of resources. A firm called Lucky Goldstar was the recognized leader in domestic appliances and, government bureaucrats worried, having another chaebol compete with it could not be good for business. But Lee was sure that there was enough room for more than one electronics manufacturer in the country.

Samsung Electronics' first product was a fan that was known to break under the lightest mistreatment. However, the next year's model was noted for its ruggedness and durability. The company's relatively simple black-and-white television sets also had trouble gaining traction because of their poor quality, but Lee soon found that the cheap sets sold like hotcakes in Southeast Asia, so he built the television division with an emphasis on exports.

By 1974, Samsung Electronics was standing on its own feet. Four years later, it had developed and started production of microwave ovens. Within a few years, Samsung became the world's largest producer of microwave ovens, although most U.S. and European customers rarely saw the Samsung brand. The ovens would be built by Samsung and then a domestic brand name would be added on just before shipment to lead customers to believe the product was homemade.

As Samsung Electronics grew, Lee noted that the company was somewhere between a parts maker and an original equipment manufacturer (OEM). While many consultants suggested that he choose one identity or the other, Lee persevered in maintaining and growing both aspects of his company. That strategy, more than any other, would lay the foundation for the powerhouse that Samsung is today.

In 1974, still early in the electronics company's history, Samsung purchased a nearly bankrupt semiconductor manufacturer called Korea Semiconductor. Although there was much internal dissent regarding the purchase, Lee was adamant that it was a good move. At the time, semiconductors were high-tech toys with little real-world value. But Lee knew that someday all appliances would have chips built into them, and he wanted his company to know that industry, too.

Lee emphasized the semiconductor business within the hierarchy of Samsung Electronics. In the early 1980s, he declared that the company would invest heavily in the dynamic random access memory (DRAM) industry. At the time, the 64-kilobyte chip was the industry's reigning king, manufactured by the American company Micron Technology as well as some Japanese firms. Samsung plotted to make its mark with a 256-kilobyte chip. A massive research and development investment followed, with Samsung luring Japanese engineers and Korean-American designers to the company.

By 1987, the early investments and Lee's grand vision started to pay off. The computer industry had gone through two cycles since Samsung's entry into the market, and by that point the company had a 256-kilobyte chip ready to sell before Micron and other competitors were ready. Several Japanese chipmakers tried to leapfrog Samsung by concentrating on the next generation, a one-megabyte chip, but technological hurdles couldn't be quickly overcome. Samsung was practically alone in the market. By 1988, Samsung had made so much profit from its 256-kilobyte chip that it had offset all of its previous losses in the semiconductor division. From that point on, the company dominated the DRAM market and grew furiously as demand increased with the PC revolution.

By this time, Samsung had become an enormous conglomerate, with a large engineering division, massive real estate holdings, sports teams, Korea's largest amusement park, and a big shipbuilding business. But the crown jewel of the brand was Samsung Electronics.

In addition to its chip business, it was still producing large amounts of household appliances and electronics products for domestic consumption and, increasingly, for export. As was the case with virtually all Korean conglomerates at the time, the ownership structure involved not only Lee's personal holdings, but also significant amounts of cross-holding of shares between companies within the group. However, cross-holdings have been outlawed in Korea since the Asian financial crisis of 1997–98.

By 1987, Lee had retreated to his mansion on the outskirts of Seoul, where he spent most of his time gardening and reading Korean classical poetry. He had three sons, each one of whom wanted to take the reins in his stead. When it came time to choose, Lee disregarded traditional Confucian practices and chose the youngest, Lee Kun-hee, for the job. The youngest Lee had been educated in Japan and the United States and had a clear grasp of what the elder had built and ideas on how to build an even bigger business.

When Lee Byung-chull died in 1987 and Lee Kun-hee took his place, it was an important time in South Korea. The Seoul Olympics were only one year away and the games would be Korea's coming-out party, announcing that it was now a major force in the world, politically and economically. The several dozen chaebol that dominated the country were eager to display their power and prowess on this world stage. But Samsung was the only one to be an official sponsor of the Olympics—an expensive marketing technique, but one that Lee Kun-hee was adamant about. As the world watched the opening ceremonies, Samsung took its place as Korea's leading company, run by a dynamic and cosmopolitan young chairman, emblematic of this young country's ambitions.

CHANGE EVERYTHING BUT
YOUR WIFE AND CHILDREN

The company that Lee Kun-hee inherited was enormous and would have been a headache for any leader. Lee knew that one single person could not possibly manage the entire conglomerate by himself. But he also worried that if each subsidiary operated independently, then competition for corporate resources would become the primary focus of its various managers. So Lee relied on the staff of the office of the chairman, which was commonly referred to within the company as the Office of the Secretaries. The main function of this staff was to coordinate investment and other business activities between the various group subsidiaries, to avoid duplication of effort, and to ensure the efficient allocation of group resources. In 2008, the staff was disbanded when Lee stepped down from office.

After taking over the reins from his father, the younger Lee wanted to take his group to new heights. He knew that the only way to do that was to make an investment in a new industry in much the same way that Samsung had placed such a big bet on DRAM in the early 1980s. Samsung wasn't geared to creating new markets in the way that Sony had created the market for portable music players with its Walkman and that Apple would later remake with its iPod. Up to this point, Samsung had entered preexisting markets that were due for a big jump in growth, and then used its deep pockets and determination to dominate those markets. After exploring several options, Lee decided that Samsung would enter the television and automobile markets.

The latter choice would turn out to be one of the biggest missteps in the company's history. Lee took an enormous amount of internal and external criticism when he announced in 1996 that Samsung would become an automobile manufacturer. The auto industry was a relatively low-growth, low-margin, capital-intensive business that was rife with competition. Lee, however, felt that automobiles fit the Samsung model (that model being initial massive capital investment, a tolerance for low-quality early models, followed by a rigorous pursuit of quality in later models). He also considered the move into cars as his patriotic duty. "I agonized over many days and nights over whether to move into the automobile industry," he wrote in a 1997 essay. "Many were opposed, saying that there was no reason to enter such a complex business . . . there is no reason to take such pains, if I think just of Samsung and myself. But considering our economy, in which exports are so essential . . . , I thought that someone had to enter and upgrade the entire industry."

Regardless of how well-thought-out his reasons, Lee's foray into automobiles was a failure. Perhaps if the 1997 currency crisis hadn't happened, Samsung could have kept the investment going until it gained traction. But the crisis and its financial aftermath required the company to call it quits in 1999, and Samsung Motors was sold to Renault at little profit.

The assault on the television and computer display industry paid off much more handsomely. Samsung had produced televisions since the 1970s, when its black-and-white exports were a success. But the world's undisputed leader was Sony, with its patent-protected Trinitron technology. Lee prophetically foretold of a major change in the industry and wanted Samsung to dominate it. At the heart of that change was a move from old cathode ray tube (CRT) technology to larger, thinner devices that would have more high-tech innards. Although many within the electronics industry saw big-screen TVs as the future, few companies were leading the charge because of the dizzying array of potential successors to the CRT: plasma displays, light emitting diodes (LEDs), organic light-emitting diodes (OLEDs), liquid crystal displays (LCDs). Most of the television leaders, including Sony, decided to wait on the sidelines until a clear winner among the many technology choices emerged.

Samsung took a different tact. It invested heavily in all of the emerging technologies and soon dominated each one. Eventually it would be the LCD TV that dominated the industry, but the others remained in important niches. By the end of the 1990s, Samsung had become the world's leading television manufacturer. It even has a joint venture with Sony to make LCD panels for use in Sony TVs.

By 1993, as Samsung began its penetration into the big-screen television markets, Lee Kun-hee had been running the company for seven years. By then, he had the respect and allegiance of his managers and executives. It was time, he felt, to shake things up in order for the company to make the next leap forward.

In June 1993, he called a meeting of all of Samsung's top executives, held at a retreat near Frankfurt, and forced them to watch a video of how poorly Samsung's washing machines were made. He then launched his Frankfurt Manifesto: Samsung would no longer be a follower; it was time to take the company to the next level and become the leading consumer electronics and appliance brand in the world. Not in Korea. The world. To do that, Samsung had to become known for high-quality, attractively designed products that led the way instead of following in the footsteps of others. Lee said that it was time for Samsung to reconfigure itself from top to bottom. "Change everything," he exhorted his employees, "but your wife and children."

And change is what Samsung did. By 2003, it had become the world's largest electronics company, boasting higher sales than even the legendary Sony. It entered into the mobile phone market with a splash in the early 2000s and soon dominated that market too, with so many handset options that consumers could surely find the perfect one for their taste and budget.

Not everything went smoothly, however. The financial crisis of 1997 caused Samsung, like all chaebol, to downsize and make dramatic cuts. The company fired thousands of workers and massively reduced its debt-to-equity ratio from 370 percent in 1996 to a more manageable 193 percent in 1999. As a result of its cost-cutting, the company was able to endure the 2001 dot.com collapse relatively unscathed.

But Lee Kun-hee and Samsung could not escape scandals so easily. In 2007, the former chief counsel of the company, Kim Yong-chul, supposedly had a religious epiphany. He approached government investigators with the internal accounting books of the company, which he claimed showed several allegedly illegal transactions. In April 2008, Lee Kun-hee resigned the chairman's post and opened the door for new blood to lead the company.

Samsung in the post-Lee years is still recognized as the behemoth of the Korean economy. In 2007, Samsung Group (the overarching conglomerate) produced $174 billion in revenue and $13.9 billion in profits. It accounted for more than 15 percent of South Korea's gross domestic product for that year.

THE SAMSUNG WAY: DIGITAL SASHIMI

To the confused outsider, Samsung Electronics appears to be a hodgepodge of businesses crammed under one corporate roof. From semiconductors to LCD TVs to mobile phone handsets, there seems to be little rhyme or reason behind the businesses Samsung has chosen to be a part of. How did such a company rise to be the world's leading consumer electronics company and one of the world's most recognizable brands?

To understand how Samsung got to be where it is today, it's necessary to first understand the realities of its first great electronics success: the DRAM market. Every computer (and every other electronic gadget, too) uses two devices to do its "thinking": the central processing unit (CPU), which consists of trillions of tiny gates that are moved between the on and off positions to represent logic, and some DRAM, on which the computer does its active "thinking." The CPU (or processor) controls the fundamental logical operations of the computer and executes the computer programs, whereas the

DRAM is where the inputs you make on the keyboard or using a mouse are fashioned into a change on the screen.

CPU design is extremely challenging and is dominated by one company: Intel Corporation. Each generation of CPUs is approximately twice as fast and powerful as the previous generation, which means that Intel is always ahead of everyone else by a mile.

Designing the DRAM units, however, is much more simple and straightforward. DRAM consists of a series of logic gates tightly compressed onto a chip. That means that the manufacturer that can keep its costs down the most will win the biggest slice of market share.

But DRAM, because of its simplicity, also has a much more unrelenting march of progress. While CPUs tend to double in power every eighteen months, DRAM tends to double in power every twelve months. So the DRAM business is dominated by equipment design: The company that can build the newest factory with the newest chips the fastest and the cheapest is the one that wins.

The DRAM market is dominated by Samsung and has been since 1987. It is a cutthroat business that has razor-thin margins and is constantly in the process of changing to the next generation of chips. There is no room for mistakes in preparing for the next cycle of chips—if you stumble in the design room, the manufacturing process will get hammered just a few months later. The only way to survive in such a breakneck market is to stay ahead of the competition both in new chip design and in manufacturing efficiency.

That philosophy has crept beyond Samsung's DRAM business and into its consumer electronics product development process. The best summarization is from a speech given in 2003 by Samsung Electronics CEO Yun Jong-yong, in which he said: "Speed is the key to all perishable commodities from sashimi to mobile phones. Even expensive fish becomes cheap in a day or two. For both the sashimi shop and the digital industry, inventory is detrimental and speed is everything."

A mobile phone is like a dead fish? If you don't get the analogy, then you are in good company. The executives at Sony and the other electronics giants of yesteryear didn't, either. But Yun is right. The purchase of an electronics device is based more on status and symbolism than it used to be. The desire to have the newest, flashiest, and most impressive phone is what drives us to make our purchases. Thus the electronics company must be there with multiple products, each of which will appeal to some buyer. That's a significantly different approach from the Sony method of product development, where huge resources are put into R&D to create a single, monolithic product (the Trinitron, the Walkman, the PlayStation) that is so far ahead of the curve that everyone wants one. If companies like Sony and Apple kill with one fell swoop to the head, then Samsung kills with a thousand paper cuts, each one drawing a little blood.

While no single company appears to threaten Samsung's approach and mastery, there is one looming cloud to the East: China. Dozens of innovative and hungry Chinese companies are now competing to be the next Samsung, copying the Korean company's "digital sashimi" methodology. None of those companies are anywhere near Samsung's size, but they all hope to get there one day.

THE ROAD AHEAD FOR SAMSUNG

When Lee Kun-hee resigned from his post as chairman of Samsung in April 2008, it was supposedly the beginning of a new era for the company. But the new era actually started during the financial crisis of 1997 and 1998.

Just before the crisis, Samsung was basking in its newfound role of leader of the pack of chaebol that dominated the Korean economy. The top thirty chaebol, combined, accounted for more than 40 percent of South Korea's GDP. Samsung alone accounted for fifteen of those percentage points.

But the entire chaebol system was under attack during the financial crisis. Critics pointed out that the byzantine accounting, the under-the-table deal making between government officials and executives, and the persistent corruption—all hallmarks of the Korean way of doing business, chaebol-style—contributed to the crisis. The time had come, many legislators, journalists, and civil society activists proclaimed, to put an end to the chaebol.

Some of the big ones were allowed to fail. As explained in chapter 3, Daewoo went bankrupt in 1999. Other chaebol were forced to massively cut staff and sell divisions. The new economy that emerged during the crisis had no place for the legacy ownership structure and confusing chain of command that most chaebol had used. Legal changes in the aftermath of the currency crisis required a broad-based simplification of company structure in Korea, including the elimination of cross-holdings (the practice of one subsidiary owning shares in another subsidiary of the same parent company).

Samsung felt those pressures too, and underwent a painful restructuring. The number of employees was reduced by more than 20 percent. This restructuring was the most painful period of the group's history. That said, the group still comprises more than forty-five affiliated companies.

At the heart of it all is Samsung Electronics, the anchor brand of the company. The other key divisions of the company are Samsung Life Insurance (Korea's largest life insurance company), Samsung Construction and Trading (a large engineering and construction company), and Samsung Heavy Industries (primarily a shipbuilder). Then there are fifty-nine other divisions. Some are niche businesses and some are joint ventures with other multinational companies. The company is involved in almost every conceivable industry. As has often been pointed out, it's not inconceivable for a Korean to be born in a Samsung hospital, go to a school built by Samsung, live in a housing complex owned by Samsung, and then to be buried in a coffin made by Samsung.

Conglomerates can sometimes succeed (it's hard to criticize General Electric for its mishmash of subunits, considering that they all usually deliver excellent earnings), but it's not easy. Samsung has an excellent track record of reform over the last ten years. It started that process with the cuts made after the financial crisis and the elimination of cross-ownership. It continued its reforms with the establishment of a more conventional style of corporate leadership in 2008. In January 2009, there was a major reorganization of Samsung Electronics—the many subdivisions were combined into two units: one that makes parts (e.g., semiconductors, LCD screens, chipsets) and one that makes branded devices (e.g., mobile phones, appliances). Most company observers expect more changes to be made. Some subsidiaries will be sold off, others merged. Meanwhile, a more professional and traditional chain of command, including a Samsung Group–wide CEO, will probably be implemented sometime in the near future. It's inevitable that more changes are coming.

CHAPTER 8

LG's Rebirth: Lak Hui Learns to Create Its Own Luck

BEFORE ITS ASCENT to the heights of the global electronics industry, LG was known throughout the world as a manufacturer of cheap commodity goods, if it was known at all. In Korea, it was recognized as a prominent household brand. Its most famous product was "Lucky" toothpaste. To Koreans the name Lucky became a synonym for toothpaste, much like facial tissues are known as Kleenex in North America. What a long way it has come since then.

Today, LG is known as a high-end producer of premium electronics and appliances, including washing machines, air purifiers, mobile phones, and air conditioners. Its $4,000 top-of-the-line refrigerator with built-in television gained fame when Oprah Winfrey told viewers that it "is one of my favorite things." LG phone handsets garner a richer price than others with similar features. Even its air conditioners are crème de la crème. The LG Art Cool model is as thin as an LCD screen and has a front panel that doubles as a picture frame;

you can even purchase models with copies of classic pieces of art already installed in the frame or customize the product by adding your own artwork or photography.

But LG is no Fendi or Gucci. Its products are available to the masses, albeit at costlier prices than similar items, and its market share indicates just that. In 2008, the company surpassed Sony Ericsson as the fourth-largest distributor of mobile phone handsets in the world (Nokia is number one, Samsung number two, and Motorola number three). Its appliance division has been growing by leaps and bounds, primarily because of its now-recognized and appreciated brand name. A 2007 survey by J. D. Power and Associates ranked LG appliance customers as being more loyal to their brand when it came to washing machines and dryers than any other company's customers.

How did a company that started out as a bulk plastics manufacturer transform itself into one of the world's most valuable brands? It began with a focus on quality. But that was quickly followed by masterful marketing. Few companies in the history of global business have reinvented themselves the way LG did. This is how LG did it.

THE VALUE OF A BRAND

When the clock ticked past 11:59 on December 31, 2008, a group of LG executives held their breath. The company had become the first-ever corporate sponsor of London's world-renowned New Year's Eve fireworks show. By attaching their brand to the annual event, LG executives hoped to further penetrate the consumer consciousness of the United Kingdom, one of the most valuable electronics markets in the world.

The clock struck midnight. The first rockets rose lazily into the sky, spiraling and emitting a shower of white sparks. A second fusillade of rockets took off, trailing red sparks behind them. The display was underway. Massive booms of thunderous explosions echoed throughout London. Dizzying, twirling, luminescent fireworks arced across the sky in a steady rhythm.

What was missing from the show was any attempt to write the letters "LG" with the fireworks. Unlike similar pyrotechnic displays in the United States that are sponsored by corporate donors and littered with gaudy attempts at brand imaging, this one was about the fireworks alone. The LG honchos had requested only one thing in exchange for their million-dollar sponsorship deal—that the fireworks display use explosive bursts of red and white (the LG corporate colors).

It was a mark of subtlety and taste that many Korean companies lack. In fact, it was a brilliantly successful move. The LG brand mavens didn't want to bash the millions of London viewers over their heads with their brand image. They just wanted to create a mood of festivity and excellence, and then, almost subconsciously, drape their brand over that mood.

Branding has never been the strong point of Korean companies. Samsung, for instance, first became known in North America and Europe in the 1980s as "that microwave company whose ovens barely ever work." It would spend billions of dollars in marketing and advertising in the last two decades to overcome the perception that it was a manufacturer of cheap products. Hyundai's first attempt at selling cars in the United States in the early 1990s was a dramatic failure because of shoddy workmanship. It would take more than two decades of incessant advertising to convince Americans that Hyundai vehicles were well made and reliable.

LG struggled with branding as well. In 1947, the company's first product was a popular face cream. Then the company determined that it could save money and improve quality by manufacturing its own plastic containers rather than importing jars from China. Thus was born Korea's first plastics and chemicals company, dubbed

Lak Hui Chemical Industrial Corporation (*lak* and *hui* being the Chinese root words for happiness and joy). At the time, the country had almost no manufacturing base, especially in the southern part of the peninsula. Koo In-hwoi, who founded the company, saw it as his patriotic duty to establish a chemicals company and capture the new market for plastics. Koo stressed that creating harmony between people was the path to a success. Hence, one of his first products was a cosmetic facial cream meant to make women look and feel more attractive.

Lak Hui soon became the leading maker of industrial resins for plastics manufacture in Korea. When the Korean War hit in 1950, the company's products were in great demand and Koo was able to build several factories throughout the country. One of its earliest successful products—a comb—said as much about the low state of the Korean economy as it did about Lak Hui's manufacturing abilities. The comb was called the Oriental, and you could buy it in a range of colors and sizes. And everybody in South Korea wanted one. Even the country's first president, Rhee Syng-man, placed a special order for the combs.

Koo quickly resolved to prevent his company from being stuck with the image of a low-cost manufacturer of a basic industrial commodity. He wanted to capture the higher-end products that were being made out of his plastic resins. So in 1958, Lak Hui formed a sister company, called Goldstar, to start producing plastic radios, which were hard to find in the desolate postwar economy of Korea. Goldstar radios were a big hit. They were far cheaper than the Japanese-produced Sonys that were about the only other option, yet they were of sufficient quality to work—most of the time. The company got a big boost from the government, which launched a national campaign to get companies and wealthier individuals to buy the Goldstar radios for villagers so that they could keep up with the news and developments in the country.

By the 1960s, the new company was commonly referred to as Lucky Goldstar (with "lucky" being an Anglicization of *lak hui*).

Both business divisions became leaders in their industries. Lucky was now a diversified chemical company, producing everything from household detergents (and toothpaste) to advanced polymers for industrial customers. Meanwhile, Goldstar had branched into all types of electronics goods and practically owned the domestic market for refrigerators, air conditioners, washing machines, and other household appliances.

The 1970s and 1980s saw the company expand its operations into exports. Wherever it went (mostly into the developing world), its products became known as the cheapest available solution. While Goldstar fans and air conditioners may have not worked very well, or for very long, they were cheap enough for the emerging middle classes of such countries as India, Brazil, and Mexico to afford.

Although the company worked hard at improving the quality of its manufacturing processes and products, it was still held back by a major obstacle: its name. Lucky Goldstar seemed to be a perfect fit for a company that saw great success as Korea worked its way out of poverty and the ravages of war. But the name hardly applied well to a top-tier manufacturer of quality goods. "Just try saying 'Lucky-Goldstar' without laughing," wrote electronics maven Seth Porges in his CrunchGear.com blog in 2007. "It's an almost hilariously Asian-sounding name and it sounds like a warning label on a box of detergent."

The company wanted to expand its overseas electronics business but "couldn't get shelf space abroad," said Paul Chung, an LG corporate branding executive based in Seoul. Its products would be relegated to the bottom of the displays. "We were treated as a cheap brand. We were only in Kmart and other low-end retailers," Chung said. "We needed a different name."

Corporate executives decided to rebrand the company in 1995. But there was resistance to bringing in a completely new name among some leaders who felt that such a move would hurt the corporate legacy. So they settled on the initials "LG." But there was a further stroke of genius in the renaming. When the company launched the new brand, it gave no official guidance as to what the "LG" stands for. Yet the tagline that followed all marketing and advertising literature was "Life's Good." With this move, the company could stay true to its roots while suggesting to consumers that it stood for a positive, life-affirming lifestyle.

The new name stuck hard and fast. And since it was linked to a complete redesign of most of the company's products, it could garner a completely new brand identity. "They ditched all the negative stereotypes of Asian electronics (cheap, generic, poorly made)," wrote Porges about LG, "and replaced them with all the good ones (well-designed, compact, simple)."

But LG's branding efforts didn't stop there. As the company gained market share in the global television, handset, and household appliance markets, it also invested heavily in advertising and marketing. Whereas Samsung and Sony tend to spend 6.5 percent to 7 percent of their revenue on advertising, LG usually doesn't dip below 8 percent. And much of that money falls on the marketing side, rather than on simple advertising. The company has invested heavily in providing promotional material to electronics stores and telecom companies that will help those firms sell their products. And it continues to find creative ways and new venues, like the London fireworks show, to get its subtle brand message into the consumer's consciousness.

IF IT AIN'T BROKE, TEAR IT DOWN AND REBUILD IT

Things weren't going so well in the appliance industry in South Korea in 1994. An increase in the value of the won, the national currency of South Korea, had reduced the competitiveness of exports. And the domestic market was the scene of a fight-to-the-death for the three giants of the business: LG, Samsung, and Daewoo. Each one was trying to steal market share from the others through a strategy of underpricing, in hopes of making profit on volume. "These guys were slashing prices all over the place, and it led to price erosion for everyone," said Chung.

The situation seemed to be worsening. According to an LG internal projection, the price of the won was about to appreciate even higher, which would in turn increase export inventory. For the CEO of LG Appliances, Kim Ssang-soo, a burly man who had clawed his way to the corporate headquarters through creative leadership and a stunning work ethic, it was a trying time.

What needed to be done, he finally decided, was to tear apart every preconception and assumption about the business and rebuild the company, its products, and the workforce from the ground up. So he launched his company's first TDR, "Tear Down and Redesign," team. But rather than hire a group of consultants to reenvision the company, Kim insisted that the TDR team be composed of employees from all parts of the company, including designers, engineers, assembly-line workers, and senior executives. He pulled together a team of forty employees, took them off their usual jobs, and placed them in a room with LG's best-selling washing machine. Take this thing apart, he told them, and examine every screw and bolt and determine if it deserves to be there. Then rebuild it from scratch. But don't rebuild the same machine. Rebuild it as the best washing machine anyone could ever want.

The team went to work. Their task wasn't just to design a new washing machine. It was to create a new process for building such a machine. That meant supply chains had to be designed and set up for each part. The layout of the factory floor had to be drawn out in every detail, and every motion of each worker had to be choreographed in advance. Shipping routes, in-store marketing material, and after-market warranty servicing work had to be planned in advance.

The other job of the team was to reconceive what a washing machine should be. A truly revolutionary device, they decided, wouldn't simply wash clothes but would centralize the care and maintenance of clothing. Thus was born the idea of the steam-cleaning washing machine. After a load is done, the team members mused, wouldn't it be nice to ensure that the clothes didn't get wrinkled while they sat in the machine waiting for the owner to put them in the dryer? So every few minutes, the drum would rotate while nozzles sprayed a fine mist of boiling steam at the clothes to keep them fluffed and wrinkle-free. It was a relatively simple solution to a vexing problem for anyone who forgets to put clothes in the dryer right away.

That's how the Tromm Steam Washing Machine came into being. Later versions would use steam throughout the entire washing process, including a prewash, which would allow detergent to soak into stained areas. A bonus aspect of washing with steam, LG would soon find out, is that it saved on water usage and energy, making the machines marketable as "green" appliances. The clever engineering of the device, along with its elegant design, also allowed the appliance division to market the machines as high-end products. It was the first case of LG moving from a mass-market line to the premium end of the buying chain. And it was wildly successful. Today, the Tromm machines are still big sellers throughout the world, selling for about $1,500 at home appliance stores.

The design process also remains an important part of the vast enterprises within LG. After his stint as CEO of LG Appliances, Kim Ssang-soo was appointed CEO of LG Electronics in 2003 and established the TDR process firmly everywhere in the larger organization (in 2007, he left the company to become CEO of Korea Electric Power). "What happened first with appliances later spread to LG Electronics and even to LG Chem," said LG's Chung. "Today, TDR teams are a part of the way we do business throughout the company." At any given time, as much as 40 percent of the workforce of the company is involved in TDR projects.

DESIGN AS JOB ONE

It used to be that the world had two types of mobile phones: bar phones (so-called because they resembled a chocolate bar) and clamshell phones (the ones that flip open on a hinge). And the flip phones, pioneered by Motorola, were winning.

It was early 2005 and LG, which was a small-time manufacturer of cell phones, wanted to join the big boys' league. To do so, it needed to create a revolutionary product that would lure consumers to pay a premium for it. Just one product was all it needed. Once the company made a name for itself, carriers would fight to sell its phones.

What the company did to create a blockbuster new phone says a great deal about its new direction: It put a designer in charge of the process from day one. Not an engineer. Not a marketing maestro. Not a sales executive. A designer.

In the electronics industry, product designers are typically aligned somewhere between packaging experts and the janitorial staff on the corporate totem pole. They are usually brought in late in the process, long after the fundamental shape and dimensions of a new product have been decided upon by electrical and mechanical engineers. It is typical for designers to get the last-moment directive to "make this hunk of wires and metal visually appealing."

But LG decided to do things differently with its new phone. The mission was to design a device that was so sleek and attractive, and also so filled with techie features, that middle-class consumers would covet it enough to pay extra. This was not meant to be the type of phone that came free with a two-year contract. It needed to be so enticing that consumers would fork over an extra $200 or so to possess it.

The designer that LG put in charge of the project, Cha Kang-hee, was told to create a bar phone that broke the boundaries of bar phones and made them popular again. He examined a group of typical bar phones and realized quickly what was holding them back visually: the antenna. If the phone could be a true rectangular bar, it could be designed around lines and sharp corners. But bar phones weren't really bars. They had a knobby antenna growing off one corner, ruining all symmetry and interrupting the visual lines that the eye would normally follow as it appraised the device. The mission, Cha decided, was to eliminate the antenna.

When his team brought in engineers, he approached them with his new idea. Impossible, ranted the engineers, a phone needed an antenna and it had to extend outside the device in order to pick up the radio waves. There must be some way to hide the antenna inside the device, Cha mused aloud. Absolutely not, the engineers responded, the metals inside the phone would interfere too much with the signal. An internal antenna might make a prettier phone, they argued, but it wouldn't matter if the customer couldn't get reception on it.

Cha probed one more time: What if you rearranged the innards of the phone so that the other parts didn't interfere with the antenna's ability to pick up a signal? It couldn't work, the engineers said, a little less vehemently. Then they started throwing out ideas that would make it work. Cha knew at that point that his battle was mostly won.

What emerged from the design project was a fully functioning bar phone that had no visible antenna. It was a revelation to consumers in North America who had fled their bar phones for flip phones. The new phone, dubbed the Chocolate, went on sale in 2006 and reached sales of one million units faster than any other phone that had come before it. Since then, LG has sold more than 13 million Chocolates, a spectacular figure for such a high-end phone. In January 2009, propelled by the success of the Chocolate and its follow-on products, LG became the world's third largest seller of cell phones, behind only Nokia and Samsung and skipping past Motorola, whose flip phones have long since gone out of style.

The electronics industry is as cutthroat as any these days. Manufacturers from China to Mexico create essentially the same products with the same parts, with only a few tiny elements to differentiate a product. It has become increasingly difficult to stand out in the crowd.

Some companies try to stay ahead of the technological curve and lure buyers with slightly advanced features that nobody else has. Sony was long known for this approach. Sony's PlayStation gaming console was usually slightly more powerful than the products of its competitors, Microsoft and Nintendo (although by 2006, the PlayStation was losing its edge). Others, like Samsung and Taiwan's Acer, try to flood every niche of the market with multiple products in hopes of winning the quantity game. Still others, General Electric most famously, attempt to stand out by ensuring that their products are known for being of the highest quality, even if they cost more.

LG has taken a novel path toward differentiating itself from the masses: emphasizing design. Of course, all electronics companies want to have good product design and are willing to pay designers top dollar to deliver it. But LG takes the notion of design to the extreme. In a typical company, engineers or marketing executives tend to lead product teams. At LG, designers are often the team leaders. They get to have veto power over everything, from the choice of interior parts to the shape of the boxes in which the item is packaged.

LG backs up its emphasis on design with a four-pronged design philosophy. Every product, the philosophy dictates, must have these four qualities: It must visually stand out from the crowd of competitors; it must feel sleek and sophisticated; it must have a pleasurable aura to it; and it has to fit into the customer's lifestyle (in other words, it should have the right features that people want, not the most features and, most assuredly, not lack a necessary feature).

The focus on design goes beyond changes to the process of product development. One fundamental decision the company made early on was to go all out to develop its own cadre of designers, rather than simply hire designers from other companies. LG wanted to overhaul its design hiring process from the ground up. So it instituted a push to hire the top design graduates just out of school. Then it created a program that pushed those hires as hard as possible to immediately contribute to the company. But it also established a separate system of promotion of designers that avoided the typical requirements of seniority. Today, successful designers at LG can reach the level of senior vice president by their early thirties, whereas that achievement was traditionally reachable only by someone ten years older.

LG's products, from its appliances to its mobile phones to its air conditioners, show the effects of the design-oriented approach to electronics. They all stand out from the crowd and therefore fetch a higher price than their competitors. Design, after all the hard work, has been very good indeed for LG.

THE BATTERY THAT WILL CHANGE THE WORLD

It was supposed to be a fixed competition. Two companies had been selected to vie for the chance to produce the batteries for General Motors' Chevy Volt, the world's first mass-produced plug-in hybrid electric vehicle (PHEV). One of the companies was a start-up whose technology was based on breakthrough research from the Massachusetts Institute of Technology (MIT). This company had raised more than $100 million from investors to build its next-generation battery. Most telling was the fact that one of those investors was none other than General Motors. GM liked the battery so much that it decided to buy the company.

Nevertheless, when the winner of the "bake-off" was announced on January 12, 2009, it was LG Chem that was standing on the victor's podium. How did this scrappy foreign company win the most-watched auto-parts competition in decades? How did it beat another company that everyone assumed had first place in the bag even before the competition started?

LG Chem was the precursor company to what is now known as LG Group. Founded in 1947 as Lak Hui Chemicals, its purpose was to provide a plastics manufacturing industry for a nascent South Korean economy. It would go on to diversify into multiple lines of business while expanding to more than twenty countries. In 2009, the company had more than 14,000 employees and produced more than $14 billion in annual revenues. Yet a decade before, it was still primarily focused on products that came in rolls: plastic film and plastic polymers that were used as the precursor material for finished plastic products. The story of the battery that would go on to change the world, however, was grounded in the IMF crisis of 1997 and 1998.

LG, like most Korean companies at the time, was desperate for cash to stave off imminent bankruptcy. It sold off a number of its smaller businesses and even considered selling its appliance division—one of its most profitable businesses. At the same time, every LG office was going through a back-to-basics process. Every employee was urged to discuss one question: What products would pull LG out of the crisis and fuel future growth? The company couldn't just focus on the immediate financial disaster within and around it. It had to be thinking of life after the crisis as well.

The company's executives took the directive from above with gravity. They ordered the research and development division to report on the most promising scientific and engineering work they were working on. When the report came back, one idea stood out from the rest: In 1995, some researchers had started to look at lithium-ion batteries. These batteries could hold three times the energy of nickel metal hydride batteries, their closest competitors, but they were expensive and potentially dangerous. If the batteries were not kept cool, they could endure something called "thermal runaway," otherwise known as catching on fire. The LG researchers thought they had a packaging solution that could keep thermal runaway from happening. If specially designed ceramic plates were used as buffers between each cell of the battery module, any overheating problems could be isolated and kept from spreading to other cells. If successful, the system would significantly improve the safety profile of lithium-ion batteries. The LG Chem executives liked the project and saw its promise. In the early 1990s, laptop computers were just starting to shift over to lithium-ion batteries; a demonstrably safer battery would allow LG to move into that soon-to-be billion-dollar market with a superior product. With permission to infuse the project with a large increase of funds, and with the backing of headquarters, LG Chem was ready to transform the concept from a scientific query into a full-fledged product.

Fast-forward to 2007. LG Chem had successfully entered the lithium-ion battery market for laptops and established itself as one of the world's largest suppliers. But its core technology for making the batteries safer wasn't a great fit for the laptop market. The tiny space allowed for the battery in a laptop was too small for the packaging system to work to its full potential. Nevertheless, LG made a good business out of making lithium-ion batteries, although margins were being squeezed by Chinese manufacturers who could crank out cheaper versions, thanks to significantly lower labor costs.

Then the news of the Chevy Volt contract came over the transom. The American auto giant was going to develop a car that could travel forty miles on electric power alone. If the driver wanted to go further, an onboard gasoline engine would kick in to recharge the batteries. At night, the car could be plugged into a wall socket to recharge the battery with electricity from the grid. It was a revolutionary approach to powering an automobile. If the world could push its cars with electricity and use gasoline merely as a backup, it would effectively take oil out of the transportation equation.

There was just one problem with the idea: Nobody had designed a battery that could hold that much energy and still fit inside a car.

LG Chem knew its chemistry and packaging design were ideal for the Volt's needs. But it was at a supreme disadvantage because it wasn't an American company, and the first electric car from the American carmaker had politically charged implications. The LG battery would therefore have to be head and shoulders above everyone else's for GM to be willing to pick it.

LG gave GM a demonstration battery pack to begin testing in its labs. The experimental protocol was rigorous. GM's battery testers didn't just want to know if the battery could hold the requisite amount of energy. They wanted to make sure the battery would work when the weather was extremely cold and extremely hot. They wanted to make sure that even if the battery fully discharged it could recharge again overnight. They wanted to be confident that repeated use wouldn't cause safety problems. They wanted to guarantee that the battery would perform as promised for the lifetime of the car—that it would still hold all its rated energy ten years after purchase. And, most important, they wanted to guarantee that the battery pack wouldn't explode into flames under any conditions.

In early 2008, GM announced that it was down to two potential battery providers: LG Chem (represented by its U.S. subsidiary, Compact Power) and A123Systems, the MIT-based start-up. A123 was famous in the battery world for producing a revolutionary battery that could keep a power tool running for hours longer than any competitor's battery. The company had secured more than $100 million in financing from some of the sharpest venture capital players and also from key industrial partners, including GM. They were the hands-down favorite to win the contract.

Yet when the winner was announced, it was LG Chem. It was a tremendous upset for such an important contract. The battery pack is rumored to be worth somewhere around $10,000. Even if only 200,000 Chevy Volts are produced, the contract will be worth some $2 billion. And if the car is successful, millions of them will probably be sold. Not only that, but every car manufacturer is in the process of designing its own PHEV to compete with the Volt, and LG Chem has won the first major contract in this new market. It probably won't be its last.

What made the big difference between LG Chem and A123? In the end, it was safety that led GM to choose the Korean company. The original packaging concept the LG R&D team had designed turned out to work very well in an automotive battery pack, and it ensured that the batteries would be safer and less prone to thermal runaway. A123 batteries, while relatively safe, couldn't match the safety profile of the LG Chem batteries. And that's what makes LG Chem a safe bet to dominate the new world of electric vehicles.

CHAPTER 9

Technology Nirvana: Korea's Wired and Wireless Leadership

IT USED TO BE that Japan was the place to find the newest and coolest gadgets. Sometime in the last decade, the global gadget headquarters switched from Tokyo to Seoul. Part of the move was due to the emergence of global giants like Samsung and LG. Part of it was due to visionary leadership from the South Korean government, which subsidized and supported next-generation software protocols and wireless technologies. But the Korean people played a part, too. South Korea is only one generation removed from abject poverty. Koreans still relate to technological advances with a youthful "wow" as opposed to the tired "so what?" that has become common in North America and Europe. When everything is new, there is a fascination with and an embrace of all things fresh and young. "Koreans tend to follow trends and show great interest in what is new, which leads them to be highly adaptable," an executive at SK Telecom, the country's largest wireless provider, explained.

That's why a visitor to Korea is almost always astonished at the number of people watching their cell phones on the subways, the number of PCs in each home, and the number of schoolboys flocking to a PC baang (or PC room, the Korean name for an Internet café) in the late afternoon. Technology is a national obsession. A Korean owning the latest cell phone is the equivalent of an Italian wearing the latest fashion from the Milan runways or a German driving the newest car on the autobahn.

Some Koreans criticize the nation's love affair with technology, calling it more of a religion than a healthy obsession. Between gaming, e-mailing, texting, and watching portable TV on their handsets, Koreans spend an enormous amount of time interacting with technology—sometimes, it seems, more than interacting with fellow humans.

Whether it's a good thing or not, the strong relationship with technology is a fundamental part of what Korea is today.

THE ROOTS OF THE BOOM

Korea has long been a country at the technological edge. Admiral Yi Sun-shin's invention of the ironclad boat (dubbed turtle ships) helped to defeat the Japanese naval invasion of the late 1500s. A few years later, when Japanese forces invaded by land from the North, they stormed Korean defenses in tightly packed bunches of heavily armored infantry, overwhelming the defenders at the point of attack. An anonymous Korean inventor created the *hwacha*, one of the first pieces of antipersonnel artillery. It consisted of a wooden box filled with tubes. An arrow was placed in each tube with a gunpowder rocket at its end. After lighting a common fuse, the hwacha fired as many as a hundred arrows, all of which landed in a precise spot. If aimed correctly, the hwacha could take out an entire Japanese offensive formation. In a trend that would be oft-repeated, Korean technology helped to save the country from what might have otherwise been a successful Japanese invasion.

During the Joseon Dynasty, when most Koreans lived in stifling poverty, technological innovation was not an overriding priority. But when Korea gained independence from Japan at the end of World War II, many Korean leaders saw it as a means to leapfrog back into the orbit of developed nations. It wasn't until 1965, when President Park Chung-hee signed a treaty of recognition with Japan, that things started to move forward. In addition to loans worth $5 billion that Japan agreed to give South Korea, the pact also gave the emerging Korean companies access to Japanese industrial know-how. Many soon-to-be chaebol recruited Japanese engineers and scientists at above-market rates. Sometimes these Japanese knowledge workers were hired as employees. At other times they were hired as weekend consultants. Friday-night flights from Japan to Seoul were often packed with these moonlighting workers, who would then return by plane late on Sunday night and spend the workweek at their "regular" jobs.

Thanks in part to Japanese know-how, Korean companies like Samsung, Hyundai, and the steelmaker POSCO became leaders in their fields. As Korea advanced economically throughout the 1960s and 1970s, it kept pace technologically with the rest of the world, too. In the 1980s, the Korean telecommunications industry became known as one of the most technically advanced in the world after it installed a nationwide network of digital electronic switches for phone service. In the run-up to the Olympics of 1988, the government spearheaded an effort to bring landline phones to more than half of all homes, a dramatic increase for a country that, just a decade before, had been ranked with countries like China and Vietnam in per capita phone installations.

With the arrival of the Internet in the 1990s, South Korea found its groove. While the United States took the lead with dial-up access, the South Korean government decided to leapfrog to the next level by officially endorsing and subsidizing broadband access to all Korean homes. The government chose digital subscriber line (DSL) technology as the de facto standard for the entire country. By the late 1990s, the country began to adopt broadband Internet access in a big way. While other countries also made broadband a technology goal, Korea had a distinct advantage: apartment buildings. More than 60 percent of Koreans live in urban multistory apartment buildings, the highest rate in the world for a non-city-state. Because of the density of these buildings, wiring costs were much more affordable than in places like North America, where most people live in unattached single-family homes. By 2000, more than 90 percent of Korean homes had broadband connections.

But the Internet drive didn't stop there. In addition to wiring homes, the government also subsidized classes for every citizen who wanted them. The classes taught housewives, senior citizens, and schoolchildren how to navigate the World Wide Web. Thus Korea, in addition to having the highest rate of broadband access in the world, also has one of the highest computer literacy rates.

The national Internet push included a subsidized computer as well. The government provided citizens with a basic PC (at a subsidized price) designed for web browsing and word processing. The computers were distributed through the national postal service, so citizens didn't even have to leave home to pick them up.

By 2004, South Korea had become a technological nirvana. While the United States and Europe struggled to reach more than 50 percent broadband penetration, Korea had near-universal broadband access. And Koreans were using the high-speed network in unique ways. Gaming became (and still is) a national obsession. Other features of what we now call Web 2.0, such as social networking, avatars, music downloading, and multimedia sharing, became a normal part of daily Korean digital life in the early 2000s.

That's when Silicon Valley and other technology hubs began noticing Korea's position in the digital universe. The country has become the most popular testing ground for new technologies and products. Microsoft, HP, Sony, and Philips, among others, all use Korea as the initial launching pad for many of their products. As the saying goes, if it plays in Busan, it will play anywhere.

Another important and related development is that South Korea now has a raging information technology (IT) industry. Before the 1997–98 financial crisis, IT exports from Korea totaled less than $20 billion per year. By 2005, IT exports reached $79 billion. In addition to DRAM semiconductors and mobile handsets (traditionally strong sectors), Korean companies export PCs, software, computer games, servers, and displays. Much of the growth in those exports leveled off by 2004. Then, once again, the government stepped in.

In the fall of that year, the South Korean government announced its IT 839 policy. The policymakers had selected eight services, three infrastructures, and nine products on which to concentrate. The eight services were HSDPA (an upgraded version of CDMA cell phone service, which is the protocol used in South Korea), WiBro (wireless broadband), broadband convergence, DMB (digital multimedia broadband, or television on your mobile phone), u-home service (multimedia home networking), location-based services (mobile GPS applications), RFID (radio frequency identification chips or tags), and IT service (namely, upgrading the national level of IT services). All of these technologies were considered cutting edge in 2004. Some of them still are.

The three infrastructures were broadband convergence (getting every device, whether mobile or stationary, to be able to access the Internet at broadband speeds), u-Sensor (the use of RFID chips to tag everything), and software (increasing Korea's capabilities in all types of software). Finally, there were nine products that the entire country's IT industry was to focus on: mobile telecom devices, broadband home devices, digital TV, next-generation PCs, intelligent robots, system-on-a-chip integrated circuits, RFID devices, embedded software, and digital content.

Such a long laundry list might seem like wishful thinking, but there is serious money behind the IT 839 plan. All told, some $70 billion will be spent by the government and private partners by 2010 to implement the vision. The program is already five years old and, in two specific areas, some of the returns are in: digital mobile television and robotics.

A TELEVISION IN EVERY PALM

The Korean way of developing new markets is different from other countries. In North America and Europe, for instance, new technologies are introduced by private companies. If the public adopts the new technology, the government might step in to tax it and ensure that a single standard of interconnection is maintained. But the private markets take the first step toward legitimizing the technology through public acceptance.

In South Korea, the government is often involved with technological development from day one. The government selects a promising technology, provides funding for research and development, and then works to get company buy-in.

In some cases, that model has worked well. In the early 1980s, for example, when the country was establishing a mobile phone industry, the government selected the CDMA (code-division multiple access) standard for coding wireless signals, even though 85 percent of other countries selected the competing GSM (global system for mobile communication) standard. That's why, even today, most handsets from other countries won't work in South Korea. Yet the move accomplished its primary goal: the preservation of Korean handset makers using the domestic market. Both Samsung and LG dominated the domestic market because their goliath competitors (Nokia and Sony Ericsson) didn't bother to make CDMA phones. While Samsung and LG cut their teeth on the domestic CDMA market, they went on to compete strongly in the global GSM market, too, and today they are giants in the global industry. Thus the government-sponsored adoption of CDMA worked well: It helped foster a domestic manufacturing industry that might not have otherwise existed.

But many of South Korea's forays into state-sponsored technologies have not worked out as well. Take, for instance, the DMB project, otherwise known as digital multimedia broadband. In layman's terms, that's mobile television. In other words, watching TV on your mobile phone.

The idea itself is relatively simple: Set aside a portion of the radio spectrum for mobile television broadcasting and mass-manufacture handsets that can receive the signals. Then build a network of repeaters throughout the country that can send the broadcast signals everywhere. Put the repeaters everywhere, including subway tunnels, to make sure the signals are ubiquitous. Then launch a satellite that will cover rural and mountainous areas where it is otherwise too expensive to place repeaters. Once those steps are complete, the entire country will have a constant broadcasting signal that everyone will pick up everywhere.

That's exactly what South Korea did. By 2005, its network and satellite were in place and the nation readied for mass rollout of the new service. Handset makers added chips to their new phones to receive the new television signals, and a host of broadcasters prepared special versions of their programs for the very small screen. And then, with much fanfare, the service launched.

One year later, the two largest broadcasters had a grand total of 1,015 paying subscribers. Four years later, that number increased considerably, though not enough to make the broadcasting companies profitable. By spring 2009, the Seoul metropolitan transit service, which operates the city's subways, was threatening to rip out the subterranean repeaters because technology providers couldn't pay the placement fees established in contracts.

So what went wrong? The government and the mobile phone industry had selected an emerging technology and made it a priority to adopt the technology. They had thrown all their chips on the table, and they came up empty. Meanwhile, countries that delayed rollout of DMB are now glad they did: It's a money-losing proposition, not worth the significant expense of establishing an elaborate network.

The key mistake made by the DMB boosters was that they failed to consider the fact that most Koreans already had broadband connections at home and on their phones. If Koreans wanted to watch television on the Internet, they had plenty of opportunities. Just about the only place where they couldn't watch TV was on the subway, and most Korean consumers decided that it wasn't worth an extra $15 a month to pay for the luxury of doing that.

The broadcasters, meanwhile, had chosen en masse to adopt the new technology, and invested heavily to create new programming for the service. That investment has been an enormous money-loser for the seven broadcasting companies that entered the DMB market after 2005.

Nevertheless, almost every telephone sold in South Korea includes a chipset that allows DMB viewing. And millions of commuters watch the few free broadcasts, such as the nightly news, during their trips on the train. But very few Koreans have selected the option to pay for more programming.

In hindsight, many of the reasons for the failure of the DMB experiment seemed obvious: Korea was already too wired. The cost was too expensive. But the real problem had to do with the origins of the program. It was born in a government office, where bureaucrats chose it from a field of competing technologies for sending TV to mobile phones and then forced it upon the country. Instead of letting the market pick the technology, the government selected one and tried to foist it on the market.

Most of the other technologies chosen in the IT 839 plan aren't doing much better than DMB. WiBro, which allows high-speed data connectivity for phones and laptops, has been successfully adopted by the Korean public, but Korea's rush to institute WiBro didn't lead to other countries choosing it: Most other countries have selected the competing WiMax standard, which is a similar wireless broadband system. RFID chips, likewise, haven't had a higher market adoption in Korea than anywhere else, despite the fact that the government poured funds into projects encouraging its adoption. And none of the other government-selected IT 839 technologies can be considered to be a raging success.

South Korea's IT industry, which barely existed fifteen years ago, has grown like wildfire, partially because of the government's role as an active supporter of emerging technologies. But that approach no longer fits today's IT industry. The industry should learn to please the market, both in Korea and in export markets, to compete on the global stage. The sooner the government decides to exit the technology selection business, the better off the country's IT industry will be.

A ROBOT IN EVERY HOME

In 2007, the South Korean legislature backed a new law that laid the foundation for any future laws related to the treatment and programming of robots. The Korean press heralded the event. Even some foreign newspapers picked up the odd item and congratulated the country for being so forward-thinking.

Nobody stopped to ask why the government was passing laws for machines that haven't even been created yet, and might never be. If they had, the answer would give a fascinating peek into a changing Korea.

As mentioned previously, intelligent robots are among the technologies that the Korean government chose to emphasize and support in its IT 839 program of 2004. The Ministry of Knowledge Economy has gone even further, calling for a robot in every home by 2020. The legislature was, then, just doing its part to create public awareness for the hoped-for coming age of robotics.

While such government support is welcomed by the robotics community, it has not yet made much of a difference for the industry. So far, the best demonstration projects involve lumbering robots programmed to do a few neat tricks and then shut down. There's the dancing robot, or the robot that recognizes its creator's face, but that's hardly what the Korean government means when it promotes its vision of a future robot-assisted society.

The motivation for such a vision isn't hard to figure out. Korea's population is aging quickly and its workforce has gentrified to the point where it's difficult to find Koreans willing to do society's difficult, dangerous, or dirty jobs. One response to this problem has been to allow migrant workers into the country, a trend that has become more prevalent in the last ten years. Another response has been to push for the creation of advanced robotics. Robots can lift elderly citizens if they fall in their apartments. Robots can change dirty diapers. Robots can clean the streets.

Other countries face the same dilemma as Korea, but they haven't all turned to robotics to solve the problems of an aging population and a need for a lower-class workforce. There is something uniquely Korean that allows the country to embrace a robotic future and view it as a deliverance from modern problems, whereas other countries fear such a future. Koreans' love of technology and their willingness to follow geek fashion trends certainly play a part, too. Technological innovation, to the Korean consciousness, is what brought South Korea out of the grip of poverty and transformed the country into an industrial powerhouse. Technology, therefore, must be the answer to creating the next leap in productivity and prosperity.

And then there's Japan, Korea's age-old nemesis and the one other country that has identified robotics as "the next big thing." Japan also has an aging population, a mass vacancy at the bottom rung of the class system, and an overarching love of technology. Japanese factories perfected the use and manufacture of industrial robots for applications such as welding, lifting, and riveting. Sony created the first robot, the AIBO, for the mass market. It is a robotic toy dog which barks, wags its tail, and responds to some limited commands. Japan's Honda has created the most advanced robot—the ASIMO—which can dance a jig and play the violin, though not at the same time. Such achievements leave a hollow spot in the hearts of many Koreans. Thus, the ancient rivalry between the two countries contributes to Korea's rush to robotica.

While the motivations are clear, the technology isn't. Engineers have been working on robots for more than a hundred years, and the field hasn't advanced much beyond what was accomplished a hundred years ago. True, ASIMO can play the violin, but that's only because it has been programmed to do so. If it could be taught the basics of violin playing and then learn to play a piece just by reading the sheet music, that would be a breakthrough. But we are far from achieving the expertise in the fields of software, sensors, and artificial intelligence that is required for that to happen.

There is no doubt that the Korean government and society have the willpower and determination to realize the official goal of having a robot in every home by 2020. The question is this: What will that robot do? We already have vacuum cleaner bots that essentially replace the need for anyone to do that odious task. But can Korean researchers design robots that water the plants, wash the dishes, clear the table, and cook dinner? And can it be done in ten years?

A more reasonable government-initiated project is the plan to build a billion-dollar robot theme park and science center in Incheon by 2013. The idea is to combine a Disney World–type amusement park centered on robotica with a science and technology park, using robots that are designed and manufactured on site. The central government is investing approximately $100 million and hopes to find private investors to pay the rest. It's hard to say whether the concept will survive the current financial crisis and find the requisite investors, but one can't accuse the Korean techno-governmental complex of thinking small.

A NATION OF GAMERS

Most foreigners would assume that the national sport of Korea is golf, considering how many Koreans populate the Ladies Professional Golf Association. Those who are more familiar with Korean culture understand that archery is the heritage sport of Korea, a piece of the national soul. But those who live in Korea or have spent considerable time there know that the most popular sport, especially among the young, is computer gaming.

Flip on a television at night in Korea and you'll find at least three video game channels broadcasting famous gamers live as they perform their daring tasks of shooting down spaceships, doing battle with Orcs, and racing go-carts. Most of the time, the screen shows the same image the gamers see as they play. Once in a while, the camera shows the gamers staring rapturously at their display, fingers clicking and mouse swirling, on a stage in front of a studio audience of cheering fans. In addition to the sounds of explosions, crashes, death gurgles, and vrooms, a play-by-play announcer is breathlessly retelling the action as if it were soccer or cricket.

But computer gaming is clearly not just a spectator sport in Korea. Koreans have loved games for centuries. Most people, from young children to silver-haired *halmonis* (grandmothers), play traditional card games. These days, because nearly every home in Korea is wired for broadband Internet access, nearly everyone has the ability to play their favorite games online against virtual competitors, most of whom are in Korea. And when not at home, the average Korean has a 3G-capable phone that allows anyone to play on the subway or even sneak a few rounds at work. Those who want an even more immersive experience can walk to the nearest PC baang, most of which have optical fiber connections that allow up to 50 megabits-per-second connectivity—nearly ten times the speed of a typical broadband connection.

Gaming, of course, is popular all over the world. But in North America, Japan, and Europe it is most often done using specialized game consoles—Microsoft's Xbox, the Sony PlayStation 3, or the Nintendo Wii. In Korea, gaming is done mostly on the personal computer and smart phone. That's because in the early 1990s, right when the video game phenomenon began turning into a multibillion-dollar business, Koreans already had advanced Internet connectivity at home and on their phones, so they simply skipped over the gaming console fad. Most experts agree that the PC and smart phone are the platforms of the future for the video game industry as every other country starts to catch up with Korea's level of broadband penetration.

There's another aspect to Korean digital culture as well: piracy. It is very rare for people in Korea to pay for software. It's even common for government offices and corporate headquarters to use illegally copied word processors and databases. The same is true for games. Koreans simply never got into the habit of paying for their video games.

That reality forced Korean software companies to come up with a business model that was entirely different from their peers in the rest of the world. The shining success of the country's game industry is NeoWiz, a Seoul-based game maker that doesn't sell a single game—instead, all games are provided for free through its "Pimento" web portal. Yet NeoWiz is a highly profitable company. In 2007, it earned $28 million profit from $140 million in revenue.

While some of that revenue (about 3 percent) comes from in-game advertising, the majority of the company's money comes from in-game sales. Let's say that you are playing *Special Force*, the company's hit first-person shooter game in which the player takes on the role of a sniper who is hunted by other snipers. Suddenly you're dropped into an arctic environment, still dressed in your desert camo. A white cloak sure would be nice to camouflage yourself in the snowy environment. So you pay a few thousand won (a few dollars) on the portal for a white cloak. Now that your avatar is better accessorized for his new environment, you can go back to the joy of shooting and getting shot.

That doesn't sound like a promising way to make money, but when some 5 million Korean teenagers are addicted to your game, the small purchases add up. NeoWiz has proved better than any other company that online gaming can be free and profitable at the same time.

Already, Korea's free gaming model is starting to take off in other countries. In March 2009, when the government massively devalued the won, software makers there saw an equally dramatic rise in revenue. Foreign gamers, it turns out, were flocking to Korean online games, and even purchasing virtual items, thanks to the buying opportunity that the weaker won presented. The laws of supply and demand, it seems, work the same way in the virtual world. Meanwhile, several Silicon Valley start-ups are betting that they, too, can make money by providing online games for free. One that is supported by more than $100 million in venture capital is OnLive. In late March 2009, it introduced its first games. But OnLive suffers from a problem that Korean game makers don't have to worry about: More than half of American households have no broadband Internet access, significantly limiting the potential market.

Meanwhile, back in Korea, NeoWiz closed a multimillion-dollar contract to turn Electronic Arts' FIFA soccer game into a free online offering. While the project has grown more slowly than anticipated, it still promises to be one of the largest (by players) free online games in the history of the industry.

All told, the Korean video game sector produced more than $2 billion in revenue in 2008, nearly one-quarter of which came from exports. That's more than double the size of the country's motion picture industry. And the ride for Korean gamers is set to become even more thrilling. The government announced a $1 billion plan in early 2009 to switch all residential Internet lines to a new technology that allows service at one gigabit per second—more than ten times the speed of the current Internet.

CHAPTER 10

The Korean Wave: Ebbing or Flowing?

HER CELL PHONE plays a song by Korean pop-music sensation Rain. She often answers the phone by saying "yuh-bo-say-yo" (hello in Korean). And she knows just about every actress and actor in Korea.

Adrienne Leslie is a former schoolteacher in Queens, New York. She is Caucasian and in her sixties with a Caucasian husband and son. Leslie also is a self-professed Korean drama addict.

Leslie got hooked on Korean television shows in the mid-1990s, when she stumbled upon a late-night rerun on public television. Since then, her interest grew and she became increasingly involved with Korean immigrants in her school and community.

She became a public voice for Korean protests against Japanese moves to gain control of Dokdo Island. She spoke out against her local library's use of a children's book, written by a Japanese author, depicting negative images of Koreans. And she's traveled to Korea with sponsorship from the Korean government.

Leslie became such an ardent fan that she is writing a trilogy of novels based on Korean dramas. The first book, *Bird and Fish*, was published in late 2008 and weaves the tale of an American woman who falls in love with a Korean man. The story is full of references to Korean dramas. The second book, *Sea and Sky*, will be published in fall 2009. The third, *Wetlands*, is scheduled to be published the next year.

Leslie said she designed the books to follow the evolution she saw in Korean dramas. The first one is highly innocent, with no romantic intimacy, which is what the earlier Korean dramas were like. The second book is much more sexual, representing a later phase in the dramas. And the third one includes a murder mystery.

She said basic tales of families are missing in American entertainment. Korean dramas are "perfect, great little stories. People fall in love and fall out of love, and it's all good."

Leslie's experience represents the impact of what has become known as "Hallyu," or the Korean wave. The term refers to Korean pop culture—television, movies, and music—that has spread across Asia and to other parts of the world. Some say the wave is losing steam—and there is ample evidence to support that theory.

Exports of Korean cultural products hit $2.2 billion in 2005, but have since dropped. In 2007, the exports reached only $1.4 billion. The entertainment industry is ranked ninth in the world. The Korea Culture Content Industry, part of the Ministry of Culture, Sports, and Tourism, wants to raise that to fifth in the world.

The lull could also lead to a transition for the culture as Korea's entertainment industry evolves and finds other ways to gain popularity overseas. And there is one major bright spot. The comic and animation industry is expanding by leaps and bounds. That field is showing annual growth of 20 percent domestically and 43 percent overseas.

DYNASTY WITH DARK EYES AND DARK HAIR

When *Winter Sonata* aired on prime-time television in Korea in 2002, the show's format—twenty back-to-back episodes about modern Korean families and romance—was nothing new. Television dramas had been a mainstay in the country for decades and generally fell into two categories: historical dramas about ancient Korea and tales of present-day urban families. The format had a long track record of success among Korean viewers, especially older audiences and housewives who saw these shows as a fun way to unwind after a hectic day of errands, cooking, and taking care of the husband and children.

But *Winter Sonata* pushed Korean dramas to another level: the international stage. In 2003, it aired in Japan and became an instant sensation. The show was more popular than anything else from overseas. At one point, its viewership rating in Japan exceeded the combined ratings of U.S. blockbusters *E.R.*, *Ally McBeal*, and *Friends*. The first release of the DVD sold out in four hours.

From Japan, *Winter Sonata* became a huge success in China and Southeast Asia. It soon developed a following across the rest of the globe, including Latin America and parts of Africa.

The drama has become an emblem of Hallyu, a term coined by the Chinese press in 1999. The international success of Korean films and television programs, in particular, has propelled numerous stars to become cheerleaders for the Korean tourism industry. One of them is Bae Yong-joon. Bae was hired in 2008 to promote tourism for the Korean government. He is one of the most famous Korean stars inside and outside of the country. Born in August 1972, he is generally known as BYJ—and women around the world swoon over him. Bae played the lead male role in *Winter Sonata* and remains a megastar today, one of the highest paid actors in Korea.

Japanese fans adore him so much that they call him Yonsama. "Yon" is part of his name, of course, and "sama" is an honorific usually given only to royalty. When he flew to Japan to promote a book in 2004, around 4,000 screaming women mobbed Narita Airport. The scene was so chaotic that the airport had to be shut down temporarily.

Bae and *Winter Sonata* still command such a following that hundreds of thousands of people, mostly older women from Japan and other Asian countries, have traveled to Korea to see sites where the film was shot. Korean Airlines promoted special flights just for these tourists, and the official website of the Korean government features details of more than twenty locations appearing in the popular program.

Winter Sonata fans can sit at a table at the Dragon Valley Hotel restaurant in the YongPyong Resort, a popular skiing destination, and have the same meal that was served on the show. For an outrageous amount of money, they can stay in the same ski resort condo that was featured in the series.

Exports of Korean television dramas skyrocketed in the early 2000s. In 1998, the country exported $10 million in TV dramas. By 2002, that number had almost tripled. And in 2005, exports reached $100 million, according to the Korean Ministry of Culture, Sports, and Tourism. But exports of TV shows have since fallen off—just like they have for other Hallyu cultural products, including music and film. Exacerbating the decline is increasing piracy in other countries, especially in Southeast Asia.

Still, the fan base is expanding further west. While pop music and film have seen limited success among Americans and other Westerners, Korean television dramas continue to draw more non-Korean viewers. Mostly older Caucasian or African-American women, these American fans are so dedicated to the shows that they have formed dozens of websites to chat about them and share knowledge.

Theresa Landis, a forty-four-year-old intake worker at a county welfare office in suburban Philadelphia, started one of the most active websites devoted to Korean dramas as a Yahoo Group in 2003. Her group became Koreandramas.net with its own server in 2006 and has more than 650 active members as of early 2009. Most members are older women from the New York/Philadelphia area. But many others come from Asia, Canada, England, and Wales. In January 2009, the site had 1.6 million hits and 700,000 first-time viewers. The site now features advertising from Korean companies, and Korean broadcasters have donated films to the group's lending library. Landis coordinates this library of more than 300 titles. Fans in the more remote areas of Middle America, including Oklahoma and Montana, use the library to get shows they couldn't otherwise see on TV.

A single mother of three, Landis spends much of her free time administering the site and watching Korean dramas. Her interest started sometime around 2000, when she stumbled upon a late-night airing of the Korean historical drama *Emperor Wangong*, a 200-episode program produced by the Korean Broadcasting Systems (KBS) about King Taejo, the first emperor of the Goryeo Dynasty during the first century. Landis got hooked that night and continued watching until the series was finished. She said she wasn't a habitual television viewer until that point. The last soap operas she had watched were *Dallas* and *Dynasty* in the 1980s.

According to Landis, "The thing that kept me watching was, particularly in the daily dramas . . . a definite lack of explicit sex. Therefore the writers are forced to tell a story because they can't have people jumping from bed to bed. American TV has just gotten [to be] too much, with sex and the violence and the language. People just want almost—without sounding clichéd—almost a return to solid values and morals. Korean dramas do kind of remind me of TV, I guess, in the 1950s."

Landis said she first joined an online discussion group about Korean dramas that was focused on the intellectual analysis of historical dramas. She said she didn't like the seriousness of the group and wanted to find others who were more interested in gossiping and exchanging small talk about the shows. She found others like her with Koreandramas.net.

For Asian viewers, the dramas are polished and sophisticated, with decent to very good acting and appealing cinematography. They also convey an air of confidence and nationalism. Not only are the actors and actresses gorgeous and successful, they are proud to be Korean, and that attracts admiration.

Of course, production quality differs from one show to another, and one criticism is that the industry suffers from too much repetition (how many times can you retell the story of a person who runs into someone who looks exactly like an old flame who died in an accident?)—which brings us back to *Winter Sonata* and why it became such a blockbuster hit.

The show was about a man named Joon-sang (played by Bae Yong-joon), who has a high school romance with a woman named Yu-jin, played by Choi Ji-woo. Joon-sang dies in a car accident, but years later Yu-jin falls in love with a man who looks just like her high school sweetheart. The star-crossed lovers then embark on a complex plot that involves other suitors, lost memories, another car accident, and so on.

But the foundation of the story is its exploration of different forms of love—puppy love, jealous love, true love, and family love. Combine quality acting and cinematography with universal human traits, and you've got a hit.

It remains to be seen how Hallyu will be received in the United States. According to Landis, she has tried several times to tell advertisers for Korean broadcasting stations to air commercials in English. She said they don't understand that many viewers aren't Korean.

In addition, Hallyu isn't about promoting the lofty history of Korea, she explained. "What it is," she said, "is people getting together, having fun, [joking over] who's the worst evil mother-in-law, and poking fun at the fact that Seoul is only five blocks big. That's what Hallyu is. It was the drama that drew me into the Korean culture. It wasn't the Korean culture that drew me into the drama."

WHEN IT RAINS, IT POURS

Rain is called the Justin Timberlake of the East. BoA is called the Britney Spears of the East, minus the personal problems. Both are in their twenties and both have reached spectacular stardom not just in Korea but across Asia. In fact, BoA is now more successful in Japan and sells more albums there than in her native country.

Both performers are beautiful and masters at R&B dancing. They are highly disciplined and hardworking. And both are trying to find success in the ultimate testing ground—the U.S. music market. But they have a big drawback—they are part of a music genre that is largely copied from the United States. In a sense, they *are* Justin Timberlake and Britney Spears—just with Asian faces and accents.

Rain and BoA belong to what is known as K-pop—Korean popular music. Before the early 1990s, the country's music industry was dominated by traditional folk music (crooned by older, often gray-haired singers), ballads, and simple electronic pop music. But just as American culture has infiltrated other areas of society, American popular music seeped into the CD players and televisions of young Koreans. A group called Seo Taiji and Boys hit the scene in 1992, and their sound of rap and hip-hop, combined with slick dancing, launched a trend that is still going strong today. Most boy and girl bands are short-lived. It is rare for a band to remain popular for more than a decade.

Just as they take their music style from the Americans, the bands also adopt their look (dying their hair light brown and even blond) and names. But the names don't always make sense, and some even seem over the line. For example, one boy band is called g.o.d.

While K-pop thrives in Korea and nearby countries, few music stars have found success further west. But some are trying.

Rain, whose real name is Jeong Ji-hun, has encountered some obstacles in his attempt to enter the U.S. market. In 2006, the same year that he was named to *Time* magazine's list of 100 most influential people, the singer performed at Madison Square Garden in Manhattan. But the reviews were flat. He was not seen as much of an original.

Rain then made his Hollywood debut in the movie *Speed Racer*. But reviews were not favorable, either. He planned a U.S. tour, but had to cancel it because of a lawsuit filed by an American band with the same name. He also has faced significant legal and financial troubles as a result of canceling concerts in 2007 in several major cities, including Honolulu and Los Angeles.

In March 2009, a federal jury in Honolulu issued an $8 million fine against Rain, his former management agency JYP Entertainment, and two other promotion companies for breaching a contract and failing to pay fees after canceling the 2007 concert.

Meanwhile, singer BoA, whose real name is Kwon Boa, released an album in the United States in March 2009, and she has reportedly signed a contract with Hollywood-based Creative Artists Agency to further her work in film, music, and merchandising.

BoA was just eleven years old when she was discovered by a Korean music agency. Her first album was released in 2000 when she was thirteen, and she entered the Japanese market a year later. She was the first foreign singer to hit number one on the pop charts in Japan in 2002. Her subsequent albums have had huge success as well.

Her performing style is strikingly similar to that of Britney Spears, having the same pop/hip-hop flair. In fact, Spears came to Seoul for a Christmas concert in 2003 and spent some time onstage with BoA. BoA's voice is not powerful, and her face is fair and childlike. At five-feet-four and 99 pounds, she is smaller and less buxom than Spears. And her videos are not as racy. Her songs are most often a mix of Korean and English.

Whether or not they make it in the United States, K-pop stars face their own struggles at home. As more Koreans spent more time on the Internet, music sales have dropped—they fell 7.7 percent in 2001, another 31.4 percent in 2002, and 31.2 percent in 2003. And overseas markets haven't helped much to stem the tide, either. Exports in the music industry hit a record $22.2 million in 2005, but dropped to $16.6 million the next year.

K-pop hit its peak in 2000, when hit albums from Jo Sung-mo, g.o.d., and Seo Taiji sold more than a million records each. Jo's album, which topped the sales charts in 2000, sold 1.98 million copies. In the following years, album sales have faltered, mainly due to the popularity of illegally downloaded digital music. The last time any album sold more than one million copies was in 2001.

According to the Recording Industry Association of Korea, R&B group SG Wannabe's fourth album, *Arirang*, was the best-selling album of 2007. But it sold only 190,998 copies, less than half of the copies sold of the group's 2005 album.

Like overseas fans of Korean television dramas, overseas followers of K-pop say the industry should take better advantage of the non-Korean audience.

Liz is a thirty-two-year-old English teacher in Malaysia. She fell in love with K-pop after seeing Rain at a concert in Malaysia in January 2007. She said the quality of the music and dancing is good and the singers are sexy. They also are humble and hardworking. She loves the fact that many K-pop stars will try to interact with their fans, even celebrating birthdays with fans. "They are humble, even with all that adoration and fame. It also shows that they are human," she said.

Liz spends an average of four hours a day updating her website, k-popped.com, which she runs with two friends and fellow fans. She and her friends also splurged for a trip to Seoul in 2008. She said it's possible that K-pop will decline further, but she hopes the sponsors will make more of an effort to market outside of the country and in places like Malaysia. Going forward, she thinks Rain has the best chances of becoming a world star.

"Then there's Lee Byung-hun, who will be appearing in [the movie] *G.I. Joe*," she said. "But a global star, like Jackie Chan or Jet Li? Most Asians are still relegated to martial arts expert roles. I don't know if any of the Korean stars can break out of that mold."

MAKING THE NEXT *SHIRI*

The MegaBox Theater at the COEX Mall in Gangnam, an affluent area of Seoul, is one of the largest, most modern movie venues in the country. With eighteen screens, the theater spans two floors. There are bright signs everywhere and rows of ticket-buying machines.

On any given day, the MegaBox will show at least a handful of American films. But more than half of the offerings are Korean. Some may have English names, but they are produced in Korea. Koreans are loyal to domestic films. And the country is one of only two countries in the world where domestic films control more of the market than U.S. films. (The other country is India.)

But that doesn't mean the film industry is basking in success. Profits are dropping and production costs are skyrocketing. The average production budget rose more than six times between 1996 and 2006. These days, Korean film companies release more than a hundred films a year. Some movie ticket sales will reach into the millions—and even more than 10 million tickets sold. Still, not many films are profitable.

In 2007, one of the largest Korean film companies, CJ Entertainment, invested in thirty-six films. But only five of them made a profit. That year, the industry saw a negative growth rate (compared to an 18.5 percent increase in 2004) and lost an estimated 180 billion won—in part because of the collapse of the video rental business.

A decade ago, it seemed like the Korean film industry was headed toward a new plateau. In 1999, the film *Shiri*, directed by Jang Jae-kyu, became the country's first blockbuster. The action film centers on a North Korean spy and a South Korean security agent. It sold more than 6 million tickets and broke records at the time, achieving even more tickets sales than *Titanic* when it was released in Korea two years earlier. *Shiri* also gained acclaim overseas.

"*Shiri* in 1999 was the first breakout hit," said Robert Cagle, a cinema studies professor at the University of Illinois at Urbana-Champaign. "This was the point where there was a flood of good films onto the market."

He describes Korean films as being of higher quality overall than American films. They fare well at international film festivals and the number of respected Korean directors continues to grow. The success of films like *Shiri* spurred an investment boom in Korean films. Overseas sales rose sharply. U.S. filmmakers have been buying rights to Korean films and remaking them into American films.

The boom has been relatively new, and it's been aided by a change in screen-quota laws established by the government about the number of foreign films permitted to be shown. (Before 1996, Korean films could be shown for only about half the days of the year.) In recent years, many Korean-produced films have sold more tickets than *Shiri*. But another true blockbuster title has, for the most part, eluded the industry.

The Korean film industry also is seeing an exodus of field production staff because of poor labor conditions. And screen time is dominated by a handful of large-scale Korean productions, which hurts the ability of smaller films to get screen time.

In the last decade, too, small theaters have shut down and Mega-Boxes have opened. In 1998, there were 507 movie theaters—each with one screen and the combined ability to seat 181,512 people. In 2006, there were 321 theaters with 1,880 screens and a seating capacity of 356,691 people. This trend has made it tough for smaller films.

Director Kang Jae-kyu has directed only three films in Korea—all of them successes. He is working on a film in the United States and says the key to reviving the Korean film industry is going "back to the basics"—working on better scripts and plots and more creativity.

PART FOUR

SOCIETY

CHAPTER 11

The Culture of Business: What It's Like to Work and Play in Korea

SUNG-HEE WORKS in a cramped office on the tenth floor of an office building located along a busy, commercial thoroughfare in Gangnam, an affluent neighborhood of Seoul. At her company, an English-language school with 100 employees, the twenty-nine-year-old woman teaches a variety of English classes and helps prepare adults for college entrance tests.

For Sung-hee and her colleagues, the workday always starts by 8:40 a.m. That's when she must be seated at her desk, even though her actual start time is 9 a.m. If she comes in even five minutes late, two of her bosses lose 5,000 won from their monthly paycheck.

The office environment is strict. She is expected to wear professional attire—conservative skirts, blouses, and stockings. The boss's word is law. And the hours are long. Her day doesn't end before 6:30 p.m. According to her contract, Sung-hee must also put in at least thirty-five extra hours each month in addition to her typical fifty-hour weeks.

There's the required socializing as well—nights at karaoke bars with coworkers and managers who drink heavily. Sometimes those evenings can become uncomfortable for Sung-hee, who is single. One time, her boss got drunk and wanted to do a sexy dance with her in front of the others. She politely declined.

The work environment in Sung-hee's office and across Korea directly reflects the overall culture of the ancient society. While the booming economy offers tremendous opportunities, workers must adhere to a long list of expectations and rules. Compared to the United States and Europe, jobs in Korea come with many more strings attached.

In the workplace, just like at home, the emphasis is on the good of the group. The boundary between work and personal life often does not exist. Individualism is discouraged. Employees often even look the same. Offices are filled with men and women in black or gray suits, shiny shoes, and neatly kept hair. Workers in factories wear uniforms. Everybody comes to work at the same time. They go to lunch at the same time and brush their teeth at the same time afterward. And nobody wants to be the first to leave at night—particularly not before the boss does. Lower-level workers bow to upper-level workers. Everybody uses titles rather than first names, and communication is subtle and often based on body language rather than words.

Workplace rules and expectations are long and complex and can be perplexing to a Westerner. But the Korean work culture has also contributed greatly to the incredible success that many Korean companies have had in recent decades. Intense team spirit and worker loyalty can take an economy a long way.

A PENCHANT FOR WORKING LONG HOURS

Eddie Hollon's journey to Korea began more than three years ago at a professional conference in Las Vegas. A technical writer, the Texas native was interested in working overseas and interviewed with a Korean-owned company at the conference.

Hollon negotiated a plum deal: an apartment paid for by the company, a free car, and competitive salary. In addition, he negotiated another clause to the contract that would turn out to be crucial—an eight-hour workday.

The thirty-six-year-old Hollon said he's very glad the length of the workday was written into his contract. Since moving with his wife in January 2006 to Suwon, a city just south of Seoul, Hollon sees a clear difference between the work culture in the United States and Korea. It is not necessarily about what you do, he said, but "in general, compared to the West, there's more of an emphasis on spending a lot of time at work. They expect you to be there fifteen hours a day. You're looked on in a better light if you spend more time in the office."

His company produces user manuals for cell phones and personal electronics for companies like Samsung. Most of the company's forty employees are young, single women. And all of the Korean workers organize their professional and social lives around their job, Hollon said.

"The major difference in the philosophy is that people spend their entire lives at the office. They will sleep there. Everything is related to their work," he said. "In the West, it happens to some extent, but there's a separation between work and personal life. Here, there's no separation."

Koreans work extremely long hours—more than any other developed country. And that's even after a significant reduction over the years. In 2007, Koreans worked an average of 2,261 hours a year, by far the most of the twenty-two developed countries that make up the Organization for Economic Cooperation and Development (OECD), according to the group's 2008 report. That's still 200 fewer hours than Koreans worked in 1994.

Koreans are the only workers in the OECD who put in more than 2,000 hours a year. Poland's workers come in second, with more than 1,900 hours a year. Japanese workers put in roughly 1,800 hours, and workers in the United States come in just under that.

The reputation of Koreans as dedicated workers is no coincidence. It is rooted in the hallmark of Korean culture: Confucianism.

Confucianism is based on the belief that people need to work for the good of the group and the good of the nation. Personal needs, ambitions, and concerns are much less important. It is a philosophy that has worked well in business in Korea.

In the 1960s and 1970s, when President Park Chung-hee instituted aggressive industrial reform, his government promoted long working hours in the textile and steel factories. The government used slogans that encouraged the concept of working hard and sacrificing for the good of the country. And even in the worst working conditions, thousands of Koreans answered the call.

Confucianism also preaches loyalty and dedication to elders. In the workforce, this philosophy creates an environment that favors employers. Time and time again, Korean workers have sacrificed and worked long hours to show loyalty to their company and their bosses. Bosses are typically older than their subordinates. Workers bow to their bosses without fail. They obey without question. In fact, the culture creates little room for workers to do anything other than follow orders.

So what is Confucianism?

It is a philosophy established by Confucius, a Chinese sage and teacher who lived in northeastern China between 551 BC and 479 BC. His real name was K'ung Ch'iu, but he was also known as K'ung-Fu-tzu (Great Master K'ung) and K'ung Chung-ni. Confucius is the Romanization of his name. Koreans called him Gong Ja.

Confucius believed that people should work toward a collective good and that society should follow a strict structure and hierarchy to create harmony. Everybody had a place in society, and the hierarchy was determined by age—the oldest men had the most power, but also they had the responsibility of nurturing and caring for their subordinates. The lines of authority were clear and unwavering. But the relationship involved responsibilities on both sides. The subordinate obeyed and respected the elder, and the elder took care of the subordinate.

The philosophy, which some consider a religion, is based on five relationships, explained in the following phrases:

1. *Kun Shin Yu Eui.* Between the king and his subjects, there should be loyalty and trust.

2. *Bu Ja Yu Shin.* Between parents and children, there should be a close loving relationship.

3. *Bu Bu Yu Byul.* Between man and his wife, they each should have their own responsibilities and obligations, differing from each other.

4. *Chang Yu Yu Seo.* Between the elder and the younger, there should be clear-cut hierarchical order, where the younger should give precedence to the elder.

5. *Bong Woo Yu Shin.* Between friends, there should be trust.

The tentacles of Confucianism touch nearly every aspect of professional life. In general, Korean companies are structured according to Confucian principles. They are based on central authority by the top-level bosses and strict obedience and loyalty by the lower-level employees. The main job of the employee is to serve at the bidding of the boss, to make the boss's job easier, and to promote harmony in the company. The primary goal for a worker is to show loyalty and respect to the manager, rather than to come up with an innovative idea.

The structure of companies also depends largely on the age of the employee. Take Samsung Electronics. The huge chaebol is divided into various levels of workers. The youngest ones are hired straight out of college and do entry-level jobs. After four years, they get promoted to the next level, and they stay at that position for another four years before moving up again. So the mid-level and upper-level workers each tend to be the same age. It has been rare to see exceptions to that structure.

But that system appears to be changing. In early 2009, Samsung and LG—faced with their first profit losses in decades due to the global recession—completed a massive restructuring of the executive offices that included bringing in younger bosses. Some of Samsung's new executives are now in their fifties instead of in their late sixties.

Rahul Prabhakar, a twenty-nine-year-old native of New Delhi, India, has been working for Samsung Electronics since 2005. A senior technical communicator and trainer, he previously worked for Oracle Corporation in Bangalore before moving to Korea. Most of the other professionals in his office are Korean. About 5 percent of them are from other countries, including from Russia, Ukraine, Belarus, and the Philippines.

Prabhakar said new hires spend the first three months "on the bench"—sitting at their desk with little work to do, expected to learn the corporate culture and do menial tasks.

One lesson all Korean employees learn right off the bat is the system of titles. You never call anyone older than you by their first name. You must address them by whatever their title is—*bujang* (manager), *gwajang* (section chief), *sajang* (president)—according to their rank and relationship to you. This, again, is another rule from Confucianism.

New workers also learn that time is critical. Koreans pay close attention to the clock. "You're expected to reach the office at eight o'clock," explained Prabhakar. "If you're a minute late, your boss or someone in HR will tell you it's not good." He likens Korean corporate life to an "army-style culture."

Lunch is the same time for everybody in his division—from 11:30 a.m. to 12:30 p.m. Everybody goes to a huge cafeteria and can choose from Korean food or "International" food (usually vegetarian Indian food). Workers either eat at the cafeteria or at their desks.

According to Prabhakar, there's also a daily inspection to make sure everybody is working. A vice president in his division marches around the office to check up on the workers. If it looks like any of them are fooling around, the vice president will yell or make sure an HR person sends the message that he disapproves.

Perhaps the most significant impact of Confucianism on corporate culture is the strict line of communication and authority. Subordinates cannot criticize or disobey a decision made by a boss. It is extremely dangerous, if not impossible, to make a suggestion to a boss. "When the boss makes a decision, you don't have a choice," Prabhakar said. "You have to follow it."

And there is no room for debates in meetings. Lower-level employees remain silent, even if the boss makes a poor decision. "If you are thinking about a debate, Korea is not a good place to work," he said.

There's a well-known Korean proverb that sums up this aspect of work culture: "Sharp stones get hammered flat." That means one should not stand out or disagree with the group.

In the last decade or so, large corporations have actively recruited workers from the United States and other countries—especially English-speaking countries. Korean-American professionals will get called out of the blue by Samsung and LG recruiters looking to lure them to Korea.

That's why it is common today to see a mix of native Koreans and *kyopos* (Koreans born and/or raised in other countries) in many offices. But the kyopos learn quickly that they must adapt to the native culture. And that doesn't always happen. Many workers get the itch to leave—often to jobs in the United States. "Nobody wants to stay here for long," Prabhakar explained.

Still, there's a flip side to the Confucian coin. The bosses take their responsibilities seriously to nurture their subordinates. Bosses take extra care to make sure an employee's family is well. And even without employees' membership in a labor union, Korean companies usually provide long-term job security. Prabhakar said he's never seen a worker get laid off in his division in his four years at Samsung. This is even when some workers do little work all day.

Eddie Hollon said he is grateful for the perks of his job—an apartment, a car, and good pay, and for the eight-hour workday written into his contract. His wife is about to have a baby. "I have a really great deal here," he said.

THE GROWTH AND DECLINE OF THE LABOR MOVEMENT

Dongdaemun Market in Seoul is a dizzying sea of shops, factories, merchants, and shoppers. It is the largest retail and wholesale shopping district in the city—with twenty-six shopping malls, 30,000 specialty shops, and 50,000 manufacturers in a ten-block radius. This is where merchants buy fabric, beads, hangers, dummies for shop windows, and anything else needed for factories or stores. Men zip around the sidewalks and streets on small motorcycles saddled with all sorts of goods.

The historic Dongdaemun—or East Gate—stands a few blocks away in the middle of a busy thoroughfare. The ornate gate was originally built in 1396 as part of a fortress to protect Seoul from invaders. The other remaining gate, Namdaemun—or South Gate—was severely damaged by a fire in 2008.

The heart of Dongdaemun is a place called Pyeonghwa Si-Jang, or "Peace Market." Back in the 1960s, it was ground zero for an important part of the economic rebirth of the country. Driven by aggressive industrialization goals set by the Park Chung-hee administration, factories making clothing, shoes, and other textile items flourished in this district. Thousands of young, uneducated, and poor teens came from the villages in the south to work in the factories and become soldiers of the economic revolution.

Most of the factories were sweatshops, where young workers, mostly women, toiled for long hours in harsh conditions. Today, the narrow street directly across from the entrance to the Peace Market is called Chun Tae Il Street. In the middle of the street—now an overpass to the new and popular Cheonggyecheon river park—stands a tall statue of a young man jutting from the sidewalk from his waist up. He has extra large hands and the face of a boy, and he is wearing a long-sleeve shirt over a T-shirt. On the edge of the sidewalk is a simple black marker that reads: CHON TAE IL—1948–1970.

The statue, according to a nearby plaque, is meant to "capture and perpetuate the spirit of Chun Tae Il. Memories of him linger still in every corner of the Peace Market, forever reminding us of the tensions and conflicts of history." The surrounding sidewalk is covered with 4,000 blocks of copper and stone, and etched into this sidewalk are words in English and Korean and drawings dedicated to Chun's spirit. The statue and blocks were placed there in 2005, in part by netizens, or activists who use the Internet as their platform.

The memory of this young man remains a powerful symbol of the labor movement in Korea. Chun Tae-il was born in Daegu, an inland city in the southeast corner of the peninsula. He was the oldest of five children, and his father, a needleworker, lost his business operating a small tailor shop. When the boy was six, he and his family moved to Seoul, sometimes having to sleep under Yeomcheon Bridge near Seoul Station. At sixteen, he got a job working in the garment factory sweatshops at the Peace Market in Seoul. He was uneducated but had a strong sense of determination.

His coworkers—about 90 percent of them female—worked in horrendous conditions. Sometimes they had to kneel for fifteen hours a day, sewing clothing in the dank, dark sweatshops. They worked for a pittance; some received as little as 1,500 won a month—about enough for thirty cups of coffee. And they worked almost nonstop. When faced with tight deadlines and big orders, workers got amphetamine shots to stay awake all night at the sewing machines. In a month, they could only take two Sundays off.

Chun was pained by the suffering around him. When a young teenage girl spit up blood onto her sewing machine, he took her to the hospital, and later got fired for his action.

Dismayed by the work conditions, Chun got involved with a group that pushed for labor rights. He formed a group called the Fool Society, focusing on the fact that most workers had no idea that there was a labor law that the employers were clearly ignoring.

By 1970, when Chun was twenty-two years old, roughly 30,000 people worked in about 800 factories in the East Gate area. He made some progress organizing workers and decided to hold a demonstration on November 13, 1970, to burn a copy of the Labor Standards Act.

At first, the demonstration was typical of many seen during that time—a mass of people shouting. But after the police came to crack down, Chun disappeared for a bit. When he came back, he had a can of gasoline. The young tailor doused himself with gasoline and set himself on fire. As the flames scorched his skin, he ran in front of the Kookmin Bank and shouted: "Observe the labor standard law. We are not machines."

He died later that night in a hospital.

Chun's suicide drew intense response and reinvigorated the country's labor movement. Students at the prestigious Yonsei University took up his cause—forging a collaboration among college students and workers that would last for decades to come. Many college students joined forces with factory workers. Chun's mother created the Cheonggye Clothing Union, which would remain powerful for years.

President Park continued to quash union efforts. A year after Chun's death, strikes were deemed illegal. Still, the labor movement hobbled along for the next seventeen years. Then the summer of 1987 saw an explosion of labor unrest in the country. Just before the 1988 Summer Olympics, a series of developments in government and labor issues sparked a huge uprising across numerous sectors of the workforce.

At that time, Korean factory workers got paid 11 percent of what Americans made, and 14 percent of the hourly wage of their Japanese counterparts. They also made less than workers in Taiwan and Singapore. Third-party negotiating in union disputes was prohibited. The Park government recognized one union per company, and government intelligence officers sat in on union meetings. In 1987, 12 percent of the 17 million workers belonged to unions. In the second half of that year, workers across many sectors, including white-collar workers in finance and service jobs, staged more than 3,000 strikes.

That period was the pinnacle of labor unrest. Union membership peaked at 19.8 percent in 1989 and has been falling ever since. It dropped to 12.0 percent in 2000 and to 10.6 percent at the end of 2004, according to the Korea International Labor Foundation, or KOILAF.

Today, the labor movement suffers from disagreements in leadership and tactics, as well as from declining membership. In addition, unions have suffered as a result of corporate workforce changes instituted after the 1997 International Monetary Fund crisis, when companies changed their employee structures to include many more "irregular" workers. Those are temporary workers and subcontractors. In 2004, more than half of the workforce was composed of these irregular workers; now the government estimates that 38 percent are irregular workers, according to the KOILAF.

In general, irregular workers get about half of regular workers' wages and are typically not covered by statutory welfare policies. Most irregular workers can't join unions, even when they work at companies that have unions.

The labor movement's reputation has not been positive among economic experts and the proponents of free trade agreements with the United States and the European Union. Korea's labor issues have largely been seen as a detractor for firms looking to move to Korea. And the unions have been labeled by both foreigners and natives as militants because of extreme measures such as kidnappings and violence.

Nevertheless, working conditions are light years ahead of where they were when Chun Tae-il worked as a cutter at the factory in the Peace Market. One of the biggest changes to working life happened in the middle of 2004, when the government approved a five-day workweek. Before then, most Koreans worked Mondays through Saturdays. Average yearly wages exceed the equivalent of $20,000, but Koreans still make less than two-thirds of the salaries of other developed countries.

Most unions in Korea belong to one of two umbrella organizations: the Federation of Korean Trade Unions (FKTU) and the Korean Confederation of Trade Unions (KCTU). The FKTU has more than 100 employees who wear blue vests and work in a professionally appointed office in Seoul. The group is considered more conciliatory to employers.

The KCTU has fewer employees and operates out of a small office in another part of Seoul. The group is considered more militant. In April 2009, several transit unions withdrew from KCTU and joined FKTU, citing displeasure with the extreme stance of the KCTU and its inability to negotiate improvements for the workers.

In early 2009, the FKTU negotiated a "pain-sharing agreement" with government and employers to address the recession. The unions agreed to salary freezes or reductions in exchange for fewer layoffs. The other union group, the KCTU, did not participate.

WINE VS. SOJU

No matter how deep the economy sinks, the alcohol industry will never go out of business. In Korea, drinking is a critical part of work life. Even if they can't or don't want to drink (many Koreans have an inherited intolerance to alcohol), workers must follow the ritual of drinking at bars, karaoke bars, and room salons. That's because going out to drink with a colleague or business partner is *the* way to establish trust.

As one American living in Seoul puts it, "It's like they don't trust you unless they've gotten drunk with you." There are numerous rituals around drinking. Like so many other aspects of Korean culture, drinking is not relaxed or done in moderation. The goal is to get smashed—until you are unable to walk straight or find your way home.

To understand why drinking is so important, you must understand how the system of communication in Korea is fraught with complexities. People say one thing but mean another. Body language is subtle but important. Often people communicate without words, and it is a person's job to try to figure out the other person's feelings. Given these formalities, getting drunk is one way for people to let down their guard and see each other's true personalities. Then they can establish trust—and the workplace and business deals are built upon relationships and trust.

Without solid relationships, a businessman can't get anywhere. Sometimes the relationship is directly with someone from another company. Sometimes the relationship is with a middleman who has close ties to another party.

In the 1980s, Jim Reis worked for a company that made different types of tiles for use in buildings in Korea. On his frequent trips to Seoul, he depended on distributors to seal the deals with the construction firms. In Korea, "everybody's got their buddies," he said. "There was always a middleman." His trips to Korea involved lots of socializing. "You don't just walk in and sign a deal. It's the relationship building, the dinners, the drinks, the getting to know you," said Reis, who now serves as president of the World Trade Center Denver, which promotes international trade in Colorado.

The focus on relationships can make it very difficult for people trying to enter the workforce or start a new business. Say you've just gotten hired by an insurance company and your job is to sell policies to small businesses. One of the first things you might do is start making a list of newly established businesses, then call them on the phone or walk in the door and ask for a meeting with the manager.

This strategy would never work in Korea. Cold calls don't get you anywhere. Steve Ward learned that the hard way. He moved to Korea from Missouri in 2006 and started a business with his friend. The two had a simple business plan: to sell coin-operated game machines to bars and split the profit with them.

The machines were highly profitable in the United States, but Ward didn't get to make his pitch to any of the Korean bars he approached. He couldn't get a meeting with a manager because he had no one to introduce him. Most of the time, relationships are begun by introductions. And Ward was out of luck because he was new to the country and had only a small network of friends and colleagues.

At the bars, Ward encountered polite people. He left his card, but never got a call back. This happened at every Korean-owned establishment he approached. After months of hitting the pavement, Ward made sales only to bars owned by expats—usually Americans or Canadians. His sole sale to a Korean-owned business happened because the owner had lived in the United States for many years and was familiar with the culture there.

Ward also discovered another problem. Koreans don't stop at a bar for a leisurely drink or to drink while at play. "They go to bars to get drunk, really drunk," he said, so the concept of sipping a beer and playing a video game just didn't work. Now, he's decided to change direction and pitch to *jim-jil-bangs*—bathhouses that include arcades, lounges, and restaurants.

Once an introduction is made, businessmen follow fairly strict communication codes. Relationships, on the surface, are very formal. For instance, it is frowned upon for spouses to kiss each other or hold hands in public. But the lack of physical affection in public has no bearing on a couple's devotion to each other.

Likewise, in business dealings, the two parties follow the codes of Confucianism. The most senior executives will do the talking at meetings and the lower-level employees will remain silent unless called upon. Lower-level employees will walk behind seniors, and they will not eat before the seniors take their first bite. Employees must display their respect for and deference to bosses on many levels. And these obligations extend all the way up the corporate hierarchy.

For decades, the drink of choice for Koreans was beer. Beer consumption has grown leaps and bounds faster than any other type of alcohol in the country. And Koreans are loyal to local brands, such as OB. Only 2 percent of the market goes to imported beer.

Next in line is *soju*, a clear distilled liquor made from rice. Korea's version of sake, it is relatively inexpensive. And it gets the job done quickly. At 20 percent to 40 percent alcohol (40–80 proof), soju is much stronger than beer. While soju consumption has grown substantially in the last forty years, fewer Koreans are drinking the traditional homemade rice drink called *makgeolli*.

In the last few decades, Western food and drink have become much more prominent in the cities of Korea. Most large chain restaurants like TGI Fridays and Bennigans can be found in Seoul. Wine also is gaining prominence among Koreans. French and other European wines, especially, have gained popularity among better-heeled businessmen.

Whether you are drinking wine or soju, here are some general tips on how to behave while out with a Korean client:

- The tradition is that you don't pour your own drink.

- Fill up the other person's glass when it is empty, especially if the person is older than you or higher in status.

- Don't pour a refill if the glass still has alcohol in it. This is a good rule to remember if you don't want to drink too much. Keep your glass half empty.

- If someone is giving you a drink or pouring it into your glass, hold your glass with two hands.

- To show trust and respect, a Korean of higher rank will drink and then fill his glass again and pass it to you. You should drink it.

The tradition of going out drinking with a client or colleague often goes beyond sitting in a bar or restaurant. And that's where it could get a bit uncomfortable. Remember that Korea is a male-dominated society and the sex business is widespread. So you may be taken to a room salon—a nondescript storefront that on the inside has all the markings of a private strip joint. Groups of men will be ushered into private rooms. They will choose from lines of women, and the hostesses of their choosing will then serve drinks and sing karaoke. Then the women will strip and do a number of other things, depending on the agreement established beforehand. The cost of the evening is high—often exceeding $1,000.

The practice of going to room salons is considered an integral part of doing business, although some people are beginning to decline the opportunities. Yet the practice is so commonplace that the talk at the watercooler (among men, of course) can stray to one's exploits the night before at a room salon. And nobody will show surprise.

CHAPTER 12

Teeing Off:
Korea's Obsession with Golf

THERE IS VERY LITTLE that is natural about building golf courses in Korea. The country is small—slightly larger than the size of Indiana. The terrain is mountainous—less than a third of the land is flat. And, unlike archery and martial arts, there is no ancient historical tie to the sport on the peninsula.

Nevertheless, Koreans are obsessed with the game and golf courses are being built across the peninsula at breakneck rates. They love its high-society image, and they love the fact that their countrymen—or, shall we say, countrywomen—are excelling at the highest levels of the game. Young Korean women practically dominate the Ladies Professional Golf Association (LPGA), the top women's tour in the world. And there is every reason to believe that that level of success will continue for years, as young girls take up the sport in droves and have the money to get the best training. The sport is also popular among wealthy middle-aged housewives. Women make up roughly a third of the players in the country. For these women, golf solidifies their status and networks in high society. It also gets them out of their homes and immersed in a peaceful environment that offers health benefits.

But beyond the status and success in competition, golf is a businessperson's game. It has become a necessary part of forging relationships with clients and new partners and sealing business deals. As one president of a semiconductor company put it, he had to learn how to play golf for the sake of his business.

On any given day across Korea, tens of thousands of men and women, dressed in ultraexpensive golf outfits, pack the driving ranges and the hundreds of golf courses across the country. The demand far exceeds the supply of golf courses, so new ones are being planned wherever they are feasible. Often that means on land that can't be cultivated for crops. Accordingly, developers are blasting away mountainsides—and drawing the ire of villagers. As of early 2009, dozens of construction projects were in various stages of development. But the recession has put most of those projects on hold. Still, there's no doubt the thirst for golf will continue for years to come.

THE ULTIMATE STATUS SYMBOL

On March 1, 2006, Lee Hae-chan, the prime minister of South Korea, was seen in Busan playing golf with wealthy businessmen, including one with a criminal record. It was a national holiday, marking the day in 1919 when Koreans declared their independence during protests against Japanese colonial rule. But while Lee was rounding the greens, 17,000 railway workers across the country had gone on strike, causing massive disruptions to the transportation system. News of Lee's golf outing created a public uproar. Two weeks later, President Roh Moo-hyun accepted Lee's resignation.

This golf scandal drives home important points about the sport's impact in Korea. First, the sport has become synonymous with high society and power. Politicians play golf as a way to get to know others in power and to discuss business deals and government issues in a more informal and private setting. In a culture that emphasizes status and image, people who come from wealthy and prominent backgrounds play golf while wearing pricey, name-brand clothing and jewelry to emphasize their position in society. In the business world, golf has become such a necessity that some corporations pay for their employees to take golf lessons during lunch so that they can play a decent game while working deals on the greens.

But the sport has also been a lightning rod for criticism. Golf has been associated with corrupt government deals, with the result that the sport was banned by government officials for a certain time. The sport is also blamed for exacerbating class divisions in the country. Farmers and environmentalists have protested the construction of new golf courses on land-use grounds. Farmers and residents of small towns oppose the change such construction brings to their communities, which includes being forcibly displaced and losing their way of living. And environmentalists decry the blasting of mountains, use of chemicals to maintain the greens, and other impacts to nature caused by the building of courses.

All of these factors played into the uproar over Prime Minister Lee's golf outing, which displayed a seeming lack of concern for the welfare of the working class and demonstrated the divide between the haves and the have-nots. (Lee also had a history of golfing at the wrong time. He was golfing in April 2005 when a wildfire destroyed a 1,300-year-old Buddhist temple. In July 2005, Lee was golfing when heavy rains caused flooding in the southern part of the country.)

Golf courses, and golf players for that matter, were quite rare in Korea as recently as thirty years ago. In 1979, there were only about twenty courses across the country. But as Korea became wealthier and the upper class grew, the sport gained popularity, especially after the 1988 Olympics in Seoul.

The government helped develop the sport, too. Before 1988, the president's permission was needed to build a golf course after a decision-making process that might have involved huge sums in bribes. In 1988, President Roh Tae-woo launched an effort to make golf more accessible. The rights for building golf courses were transferred to the provincial governors, which caused a spike in construction permits. Today, there are 300 to 350 courses operating in the country.

But golf courses are difficult to build in a country where two-thirds of the land is mountainous or covered in forests. Robert Trent Jones II, an international golf architecture firm based in the United States, designed its first South Korean course in 1984. It is an eighteen-hole course that is part of the YongPyong Resort. Since then, the company has designed five more courses in Korea, among the more than 240 greens it has developed across the world. Bruce Charlton, chief design officer for the firm, said that designing courses in Korea is "definitely more challenging" than in most other countries because of the terrain.

Golfplan, another U.S.–based golf architecture firm, has so many projects in Korea that it has a full-time representative based in Seoul. According to principal David Dale, Korea is the company's largest market. Golf courses take years to build, and an eighteen-hole course can cost as much as $100 million, explained Brian Kim, the Korea-based representative for Golfplan. That includes about $25 million for the land, $30 million for construction, and up to $20 million for the clubhouse.

The regulatory process is strict and more time-consuming than in the United States, Kim said. At one point, developers needed 1,000 government permits to build a course. It takes two years to get the government approvals at a cost of about $2 million. You usually have to pay bribes, and even then, you can still lose the project. Sometimes the failure of a golf course project leads to bankruptcies, Kim said.

Still, the projects are generally profitable. Most developers are chaebol or construction companies. The CJ Group (a huge conglomerate that is affiliated with Samsung and sponsors three LPGA players) owns two courses. Samsung itself owns five. Hyundai owns a couple. The Ostar Country Club in Gangwon Province, a thirty-six-hole course, was built by Hyundai, and the twenty-seven-hole course at Rainbow Hills in North Chungcheong Province was financed by the Dongbu Corporation, a major construction and engineering firm.

Developers cover much of their costs by selling memberships. The fewer memberships, the more prestigious the course. The developers also make money from concessions (in this case, the sale of expensive food services) and greens fees.

The construction boom for golf courses is still active, but the recession has put many projects on hold. And membership fees have dropped by up to 40 percent, Kim said.

Most courses are private, requiring $500,000 to $1.5 million in membership fees and $300 for each tee time. The private clubs allow only members to reserve tee times. Country club memberships are considered major assets and are traded at an officially recognized membership market. Tee times during peak hours are sold on the black market for thousands of dollars to businessmen desperate to impress and entertain guests.

On a daily basis, 90,000 to 100,000 people can play golf on a course in Korea. That's a fraction of the 4 million players in the country. And nearly all of those players are on the greens because of a business interest.

Entertaining clients is especially crucial in doing business in Korea. And golf is seen as a perfect way to get a four-to-five-hour block of time to schmooze and talk deals. In almost every group on the course, two of the players are the hosts and the other two are the clients or people being entertained. A woman who worked for more than a year at two exclusive golf courses near Seoul said players often talk business while rounding the greens. The people hosting clients sometimes purposefully played worse to make their guests feel better. They also would sometimes wager over shots and then purposefully lose the bet so their client could make more money.

More than two-thirds of all golf courses are within a ninety-minute drive of Seoul. But some of the best courses are on Jeju Island, the tiny island south of the peninsula that is famous for honeymooners. The Pinx Golf Course and Nine Bridges have both made the list of the top 100 courses in the world. Nine Bridges was completed in 2001, at a cost of $100 million and after five years of construction. It was designed by Golfplan and developed by the CJ Group.

Since demand far exceeds supply, the number of Koreans traveling overseas to play golf has increased each year in the last decade. In 2007, more than one million Koreans traveled overseas—to China, Japan, Vietnam, Australia, and the United States—to play golf. The government is trying again to reduce costs, including taxes for tee times and barriers to construction of new courses, to keep these players and their money in the country.

Golf has also entered the leisure world. Instead of going to *noraebangs* (the Korean version of karaoke bars) or dance clubs or bars, more Koreans are spending their evenings at virtual golf cafés. An estimated 200,000 Koreans hit balls into video screens every day. That's about twice as many as the number of golfers playing on outdoor courses, according to the Korea Golf Association (KGA). In 2003, about 300 golf cafés were operating in Korea. By 2007, that number reached 2,500. In 2009, about 5,000 cafés are connected online nationwide, powered by one of the world's fastest telecommunications networks.

Each golf café has three to ten simulation rooms, and a night of practice costs around $20. Players click onto computer screens in private rooms and pick a golf course—anything from Pebble

Beach, California, to the St. Andrews course in Scotland. The wall-size screen in front of them then shows that course and records the player's performance.

In general, virtual golf is seen as a form of entertainment and training for novice players, whereas nearly all of the professional players from Korea come from wealthy or upper-middle-class families. There is, however, at least one exception to that rule.

Choi Kyung-ju (more commonly known as K. J. Choi) was born in 1970 on the island of Wando in the Korea Strait. His father was a fisherman and rice farmer. There were no golf courses on Wando. As a young teen, Choi was a gifted weight lifter. But his teacher said he was too small to remain in the sport and encouraged him to take up golf.

At age sixteen, he started learning how to swing. He'd take a bridge to the mainland and drive to Gwangju to practice. He later moved to Seoul to attend a private high school on scholarship and play on the school's golf team. He then served three years in mandatory military duty, which included teaching generals how to play golf. Choi turned pro in 1994 at age twenty-three. Two years later he won the Korean Open. By 2000, he was playing on the Professional Golfers' Association tour—the first Korean to get a card and to win a PGA tournament.

Five-foot-eight and 185 pounds, Choi goes by the nicknames "Tank" (for his stout stature) and "Hawkeye" (for his appearance on the green). He has won seven PGA tournaments. After a win at the Sony Open in Hawaii in January 2008, Choi donated $320,000 to the families of the victims of a warehouse fire in Seoul that killed forty people.

Despite his longevity on the PGA tour, Choi commands little media attention in Korea compared to the women players. Korea may be the only country in the world where women's golf is more popular as a spectator sport than men's play.

One reason is that women are flocking to the game in large numbers. Roughly 30 percent of Korea's 4 million golfers are women, compared to 22 percent of 26 million adult U.S. golfers. And the women love golf clothes. Women accounted for the majority of the $600 million in golf apparel and footwear sales in 2006. That's more than twice the $275 million spent on golfing hard goods that year.

The popularity of golf clothing and accessories can be seen at any major department store and golf course in the country. Shinsegae, one of the high-end department stores, devotes almost an entire floor to golf clothes and accessories. Shirts cost at least $200. People will spend $1,000 or more for an outfit that includes the shoes and cap.

Jay Han teaches about fifteen private lessons a day at a high-end driving range called Cheongdam Spopia, in the affluent Cheongdam section of Seoul. He wears a gray polo sweater and a Tag Heuer watch. A shiny black Mercedes sedan is parked outside, and a handful of people are hitting balls on the first and second floor.

They are all dressed in the expensive golf clothes sold at the department stores. According to Han, people dress up because appearance is important in Korea. And because Koreans are serious about golf, that means brisk business at the driving range. From sunrise to 11:30 p.m., the place is busy. Even at eleven at night, fifteen to twenty people are still hitting balls. "Koreans are very competitive, so they work hard," says Han.

KOREA'S GOLF GODDESS

Pak Se-ri had been playing for just seven years and was more than 6,700 miles away from her hometown when she changed women's golf forever, both in the United States and her native South Korea.

It was June 1998, and Pak was playing her fourth round at the unforgiving Blackwolf Run course in Kohler, Wisconsin, about a two-hour drive north of Chicago. She had played the previous three rounds in rain and driving winds. The fourth round was just between Pak and another young player, Jenny Chausiriporn. The two had tied for the top spot in the third round.

Pak began the game with some poor shots that put her four strokes behind her opponent after five holes. But by the twelfth hole, she had pulled even with two straight birdies. At the eighteenth hole, disaster struck.

Pak misplayed a shot and watched her ball roll down an embankment and into a pond. But rather than take a one-shot penalty that would allow her to take the ball out of the water, Pak took off her shoes and socks (an informality that shocked and delighted the millions of Koreans watching at home) and waded into the pond. She shot the ball out of the water, over a tall embankment, and back into play. By the end of that hole, the two women were tied again.

The tie put the game into sudden death. Whoever won the next hole would take home the title.

Both women made par on the first hole, a par five. The second hole was a par four. Both women got onto the green in two shots. Chausiriporn missed a birdie try from eighteen feet. Pak, also from eighteen feet, found the cup. Cheering fans in living rooms across South Korea watched their national hero battle to the end on television. Pak burst into tears and jumped into her father's arms.

That was Pak's rookie year on the LPGA tour. She won two majors that year—a rare accomplishment for any player. But beyond her triumphs on the golf course, Pak helped to energize women's golf across the world, and especially in her home country. Her story is both unusual and full of Korean quirks.

Pak was born on September 28, 1977, in Daejeon, South Korea. She was the second of three daughters. Her father, Pak Joon-chul, worked in the construction industry, may have been involved in organized crime, and described himself as a "thug." Her mother, Jeong-sook, was a stay-at-home mom.

The Paks were not the typical golf family in Korea. In the first place, there weren't many golfers in the country at that time. And those who did golf tended to come from wealthy, elite families. Pak's father could play a decent game, but he couldn't afford to join a private golf club.

As a young girl, Se-ri excelled in track and had developed thick, muscular thighs from that training. She took up golf at age eleven, not with the intention of becoming a worldwide star, but just wanting to please her father. Her father quickly saw the girl's talent and decided to pour his life into making her a star.

There was only one public course in the country, so Se-ri didn't have the luxury of unlimited practice time on the course. But she had a natural talent and a beautiful swing. Her father worked her hard to develop discipline and a tough mind. She woke up every day at 5:30 a.m., ran up and down fifteen flights of stairs in her apartment building, and practiced for hours wherever she could.

To develop in Se-ri an unflinching mental toughness, her father made her hit balls in the cemetery where her grandfather was buried. He also forced her to sleep in a tent overnight at the same cemetery to force her to overcome her fears. He took her to dog fights and often pushed Se-ri to tears. She had no friends or social life. Just golf and a hard-driving father.

But the hard work quickly paid off. She won thirty amateur tournaments in Korea, and then went on to rack up a number of titles on the Korean LPGA tour in 1996 and 1997. Money was extremely tight at this time. Se-ri sometimes traveled to tournaments by bus and was not always embraced by the wealthier women on the tour.

The young woman's financial problems were solved when Samsung gave her a $10 million endorsement contract and sent her to the United States to be coached by legendary tutor David Leadbetter in Florida. She would take the golfing world by storm in 1998 when, during her rookie year on the LPGA, she won four tournaments, including two majors. She was named Rookie of the Year.

While her success was noticed by golfing enthusiasts in the United States, millions of people in her home country who had never heard of golf instantly saw Pak as a savior. During her rookie year, Korea was suffering through a tremendous economic crisis—what has now become known as the International Monetary Fund (IMF) crisis that began in 1997. Scores of people lost their jobs and saw their savings reduced to almost nothing. Companies closed left and right, and panic was widespread. (See chapter 3 for an in-depth discussion of the crisis.)

Pak's success on the world stage gave the Koreans a sense of hope that they desperately needed. And they looked to her to continue the magic.

When she returned to Korea in late 1998, the twenty-one-year-old was overwhelmed and exhausted. The press followed her every move. President Kim Dae-jung threw a parade for her and presented her with the Blue Dragon, the highest sports medal in the country. She ended up collapsing from exhaustion and was admitted into a hospital for several days.

Since that storybook rookie year, Pak has had her ups and downs. But she has retained the title of queen of golf in Korea. She's won twenty-four LPGA tournaments, including six majors. No other

Korean player has come close. In 2007, Pak was inducted into the LPGA Hall of Fame. At age twenty-nine, she was the youngest woman ever to make it to that level.

THE NEXT GENERATION OF GOLFERS

At 3 a.m. on a humid summer morning in 1998, little Park Inbee's life changed forever.

The nine-year-old girl was jarred awake by the sound of her parents screaming. Inbee got out of bed to investigate and found her parents celebrating in the living room of their apartment outside Seoul. On the television, they had just seen Pak Se-ri win the U.S. Women's Open in Wisconsin. Inbee didn't know anything about golf that night, but was impressed to see a young Korean woman become a national hero.

Two days later, Inbee wrapped her hands around a golf club and took her first swing. Ten years later, the nineteen-year-old made history herself, becoming the youngest woman to win the U.S. Women's Open—one of four majors on the LPGA tour. That day, she thanked her inspiration as she held the silver trophy.

"I really would like to thank Se-ri for what she's done for golf, for Korean golf," Inbee said to the world that day. "Ten years ago, I was watching her winning this event on TV. I didn't know anything about golf back then. But I was watching her. It was very impressive for a little girl. I just thought that I could do it, too."

Park Inbee is part of an army of South Korean girls who think they can do it—or at least have fathers who want them to. Since 1998, interest in women's golf has exploded. Young Korean girls are taking up the game and facing intense pressure to succeed. Korean parents are using all their finances and turning their lives upside down to help the girls train. Some families move to Australia, where golf is cheaper to play and available year-round. Others send their daughters to the United States, Thailand, or the Philippines to practice.

There are at least a half dozen young women—all born in 1988—who took up golf after Pak Se-ri's legendary rookie year in the LPGA. Ji Eun-hee won the Wegmans tournament in New York a week before Inbee's big win. Oh Ji-young took top place at the State Farm Classic in July. Choi Na-yeon was one of the top rookies of 2008 and almost won the Evian Masters in late July of that year.

All of these young women are known as the Se Ri Kids. In just ten years, they have joined a growing legion of Korean players who have become a dominant force in the LPGA. The pro golf tour has more than forty Korean women—by far the most players from a single country. And dozens more South Korean girls are practicing feverishly back in South Korea, or in Australia, or in the United States. They are all hoping to become the next Pak Se-ri.

Ron Sirak covers the LPGA for a number of golf magazines in the United States. He said the Korean women have permanently changed the face of the tour. He credits their work ethic. "The Koreans are the first ones on the range in the morning and the last ones to leave at night," he said.

And South Koreans have become much bigger fans of women's golf than men's golf. Two television channels in South Korea air the women's tournaments around the clock. And the broadcasting fees paid by Korean television companies account for the single largest revenue stream to the LPGA. According to a deal made in February 2009 with Korean broadcasting company J Golf, the LPGA website will soon be translated into Korean, and women's tour events will continue to be televised in Korea for years to come.

In the last decade, the LPGA has undergone a dramatic shift away from American dominance. The tour has struggled with declining prominence and fewer tournaments, although one is played in Korea. Between 1950 and 1994, the LPGA Player of the Year was an American every year but one. Since 1994, no American has been Player of the Year. "There haven't been Koreans there, either," Sirak said. The Players of the Year have been Swede Annika Sorenstam, Mexican Lorena Ochoa, and Karrie Webb of Australia. Of the top twenty players in the world, four are Americans and five are South Koreans.

According to Sirak, the growing number of South Koreans on the women's tour has effectively shut out second-tier American players—which has caused some grumbling. Cultural tensions have also been apparent. In 2005, the LPGA commissioner called all the Korean players and parents to a meeting to discuss rules. In the previous months, several instances of attempted cheating had been reported to the officials. They included Korean parents giving instruction to their daughters in Korean from the sidelines. Only caddies can give instruction. In another case, the mothers were opening their umbrellas and pointing them in a certain direction to signal blind shots. But the most egregious case was one in which the father of a Korean player allegedly kicked a ball out from the bushes during the Canadian Women's Open in December 2005.

Over the years, Korean fathers have often been seen as trouble by LPGA officials. Hovering over their daughters, yelling at them, and directing their careers, the fathers have become notorious for firing caddies when their daughters play poorly. The LPGA employs a Korean American to serve as liaison to the Korean players.

In 2008, LPGA Commissioner Carolyn Bivens issued a new rule ordering all players to attain a certain level of English proficiency within two years of joining the tour or face suspension. The announcement immediately drew a firestorm of criticism and was seen largely as a move against the Korean players. Within two weeks, Bivens retracted the rule.

Sirak and several coaches in Korea and other countries describe the Korean zeal for women's golf as driven largely by fathers. Gaining success in the game has also become a fairly foolproof way for young Korean women to become national heroes.

"Korea, to the best of my knowledge, is a place where women are not going to rise to upper levels of corporate leadership," Sirak said. "If you have a daughter, sports is the only field really open. Dads channel their daughters a lot toward sports and toward golf because there's economic opportunity there."

So far, Pak Se-ri has not lost her throne among Koreans. But some golf watchers expect that to change someday soon. More Korean players are winning majors on the LPGA tour. As of early 2009, the highest-ranked Korean player was Shin Ji-yai at number five.

A plump, five-feet-two (perhaps five-one) student at the prestigious Yonsei University, Shin is the oldest of three children. She is one of the Se Ri Kids, also born in 1988.

In 2004, she was practicing at a course when she received a call that her mother had just been killed in a car accident. Her younger siblings were seriously hurt and spent almost a year in the hospital. Shin spent most of her nongolf time at the hospital with them. And she dedicates every victory to her mother's memory.

There are many more young Korean women training feverishly with hopes of turning pro. Kwon Min-kyung spends about six hours a day hitting balls from the second floor of the posh Cheongdam Spopia driving range, with its marble floors and team of fifteen instructors. Kwon is nineteen years old and lives in Ilsan, a suburb of Seoul. She started playing at age fourteen because her father plays golf and he wanted her to learn the game. Today, she is semiprofessional.

On a recent evening at the driving range, Kwon takes a break and flips through a thick fashion magazine. Standing in a foyer to get a break from the chill, she is wearing black pants, a hot pink shirt, and black vest. She grins and giggles, joking with her coach.

With heavy makeup and gold Minnie Mouse earrings, Kwon says her idol is Tiger Woods and her favorite female player is Julie Inkster. Although Kwon also attends college ("sometimes," she says), she likes golf as a career because she can travel and play.

Her dream?

"To make it to the LPGA."

CHAPTER 13

From Homogeneity
to Multiculturalism:
The World Comes to Korea

TWO THOUSAND YEARS AGO, Buyeo was the center of the world for
the people of Baekje, one of the three kingdoms that made up Korea
at the time. Nestled in the most fertile region of the peninsula, along
the Paengmagang River in southwestern Korea, Buyeo was the last
capital of the powerful, aristocratic Baekje Dynasty. For more than
a hundred years, the kingdom flourished in Buyeo.

It was here that one of the most famous legends from the three
kingdom period occurred. In AD 660, Baekje was besieged by fighters from the neighboring Silla Kingdom with help from the Chinese.
According to legend, 3,000 ladies of the Baekje court leaped to their
death from a cliff top of Mt. Busosan, committing suicide rather than
becoming slaves to the conquerors. That site is now known as Nakhwaam Rock, or the "rock of falling flowers"—evoking the image of
the women falling in their colorful dresses that look like flowers.

Many relics of that time can still be seen today. But the town is largely forgotten, lost in the fast-paced development of the country. Dwarfed by much larger cities that are situated along major highways, Buyeo has roughly 80,000 people and can be reached only by small roads.

But even in a town as remote as this one, a recent but growing demographic trend can be seen. Across the street from the main tourist attraction, the park leading to the most famous historical sites, including Nakhwaam Rock, is a restaurant called Baekje House.

The three-story restaurant serves traditional food from the region and is filled with relics and black-and-white photos from decades ago. Hidden away in the back of the kitchen, a middle-aged woman washes dishes. Unlike the maids of Buyeo that dashed themselves against the rocks 2,000 years ago, she's not from around here. She's from Russia. Her name is Nina, and she is about fifty years old and has been working there for two years. She came to Korea seeking a decent living and stays in a dorm nearby with the other workers at the restaurant.

During a slow hour in the afternoon, Nina and the Korean restaurant workers sit down for a meal of rice and soup. She smiles and chats with them in Korean.

It was not too long ago that foreigners—other than American military—came to Korea only as tourists or conquerors. Today, demographic and economic shifts have made Korea a popular destination for workers from across the world—and especially from across Asia.

Today, you can find foreigners in any village and city in the country. They work on construction sites and in restaurants, and they are marrying Koreans at a fast pace. The population of Korea now boasts more than one million foreign-born residents, accounting for more than 2 percent of the population.

Where did all these people come from? The majority of them are of Chinese-Korean origin. They traveled to Korea for marriage or for jobs. They speak the language and understand the nuances of the culture. Thousands of them are Koreans from Japan who have resettled in South Korea after a tough sojourn in North Korea. Then there are the Western expatriates, many of whom came to Korea to teach English and never left. Finally, there are laborers from all over the world who, for one reason or another, made their way to Korea to find work. It is this last group, ranging from Filipino factory workers to Uzbek bar girls to Nigerian dockworkers, that is most at risk of falling victim to crime, abuse, and neglect. But the Korean government, aided by civil society organizations, has been working to protect them and provide basic medical and food aid when needed.

Altogether, Korea looks a lot different today than it did just a few years ago. And the flow of foreigners into the country is expected to increase as the country ages and the native workforce shrinks.

HINES WARD: AN UNLIKELY HERO

When Hines Ward caught the first pass in Super Bowl XLIII, it was a very minor play. A twelve-yard-out pattern, a catch of a lazily thrown ball, and then a push out of bounds. True, it resulted in a first down, but it wasn't the kind of play that would show up on highlight reels. Nevertheless, the bars throughout western Pennsylvania erupted in cheers for one of Pittsburgh's most popular players. There were also raucous cheers in the bars and noodle rooms of Seoul, where the February 2009 game was being watched in the late morning.

Around the same time, a meeting was getting underway in the boardroom of LG, one of South Korea's largest corporations. A group

of the seven most senior executives of the company were discussing
the worsening economic situation and how to respond to it. It could
have been any meeting room at any Korean corporation, but there
was one odd thing about it: Only two of the executives were Korean.
The other five were from other parts of the world, having been hired
by LG to lead the now multinational corporation.

What do a black football player and five non-Koreans in a conference room in Seoul have to do with each other? They are each, in
their own way, stretching the bounds of what it means to be Korean.
Hines Ward is the son of a black U.S. Army officer and a Korean immigrant. The five foreign executives at LG are part of new wave of
high-level migrants who are turning Seoul into a truly international
city. In the last few years, multiculturalism has come to Korea in
a big way.

If there were a poster boy for the wave of multiculturalism that
has washed over the country, it is Hines Ward. Although he would
catch only a couple of passes in Super Bowl XLIII, he was a revelation in the Super Bowl in 2006. In that game, after which he was
voted Most Valuable Player, he caught one touchdown and threw for
another, a rare feat for the average wide receiver. But Hines Ward
was never average.

Born in 1976 to a black soldier and a Korean seamstress in Seoul,
Ward moved with his family to the United States as a toddler. His
parents' marriage soon fell apart and by the age of five, Ward was
living with his mother. But being the only half-Korean, half-black kid
in the Atlanta suburbs was not easy. He would often hide in the car
when his mother drove him to school so that his friends wouldn't
see that he had an Asian mother. He found an outlet in sports, and
soon became a star in several games. When it came time for college, the University of Georgia recruited him as their quarterback.
Ward went on to lead Georgia to several bowl games, but, after
graduation, the National Football League didn't show much interest in him. He was too small to play quarterback in the professional
league, and too slow to make the switch to wide receiver. Nonethe-

less, the Pittsburgh Steelers selected him with a second-round draft pick and started teaching him the nuances of the wide receiver role. Within a couple of years, he was a verified NFL star, overcoming his lack of speed with the disciplined manner in which he ran his routes and the sheer gumption that he showed every time he put his cleats on the field.

After his MVP performance, Ward gave the cameras the obligatory line: "I'm going to Disney World." He should have said "I'm going to Korea." Because in April 2006, that's just what he did. It was his first visit since leaving the country at the age of two. His whole life, he told reporters, he felt that there was a hole in his heart where Korea should have been. It was time, he said, to discover Korea. What he didn't expect was that Korea had found him.

Koreans watched the Super Bowl, too. And when they discovered that there was a superstar football player who was half-Korean and half-black, they did a very uncharacteristic thing: They embraced him.

For decades, there has been a tiny underclass of Amerasians in Korea, the products of American soldiers and their Korean girlfriends. Outcasts, they inhabited the nether zones of Korean identity—fluent in the language, vaguely resembling the physical characteristics of Koreans, but never to be accepted. That underclass accepted Ward and his story as its own.

What was more surprising was how accepting the rest of Korea was to Ward, too. Hundreds of journalists showed up when his plane touched down at Incheon. The Seoul metropolitan district handed him the keys to the city. President Roh Moo-hyun passed the football around with him in front of cameras. Ward wasn't just the hero of the Amerasians in Korea. He was the hero of all of Korea.

Still, Korea is not a multicultural paradise. In a visit to Korea before Ward became a star, Ward's mother was reportedly savagely beaten by her sisters for returning to Korea after bringing shame to the family. And Korea is still a lonely, alienating place for most interethnic children. A recent poll of schoolchildren showed that 10 percent of respondents wouldn't allow themselves to become friends with an ethnically mixed classmate. The seeds of racism and chauvinism remain strong in the culture.

Nevertheless, it is clear that Hines Ward came to a different Korea in 2006 than had ever existed before. Among other things, old Korea was built on the concept of undiluted blood ties to ancestors. The concept of interracial marriage—or even interethnic marriage with non-Korean partners—was considered a horrible sin. Korean nationalism, unlike nationalism as it exists in multiethnic countries, is partially based on the concept of pure bloodlines. For Koreans to accept a non-full-blooded Korean like Hines Ward as "one of our own" shows just how far the country has come.

"Before Korea became aware of Hines Ward, Koreans just didn't think very much about multiracial offspring of intermarriages, and when they did, it was in a negative sense," said Timothy Lim, a professor at California State University, Los Angeles, who was a visiting professor at Korea University in Seoul when Hines Ward visited the country. "If nothing else, Hines Ward got Koreans talking about multiculturalism, and he got the government to open debate on policies about interethnic marriages." In that sense, Hines Ward is a real hero, and not for anything he did on the football field.

THE NEW MULTICULTURAL WORKFORCE

In January 2007, Yong Nam took the reins as CEO of LG Group, one of Korea's leading chaebol (see chapter 8). His job was to continue the spectacular growth of the previous decades, when LG rose from

a chemicals manufacturer to become one of the world's five largest purveyors of premium electronics. Nam's role was to increase
growth even more.

After a few months in the corner office, Nam realized that LG
was held back by the yes-man culture of senior executives. He
wanted people who would argue with him and with each other, who
would be passionate about their beliefs and their jobs, so much
so that they would be willing to blaze a trail independent from
their supervisors.

To find executives like that, he looked outside the country. He
hired multiple headhunting firms and gave them one directive: Find
the best people for the highest jobs in LG. Fast-forward two years,
and five out of seven of the top LG executives are non-Koreans.
Among them are Irish-born chief marketing officer Dermot Boden,
who left global soap giant Unilever to take the LG job; Tom Linton,
a career IBMer who left Big Blue to take the chief procurement officer position; and Didier Chenneveau, a Swiss supply chain guru
for Hewlett-Packard who took over that part of LG's business. After
overcoming some initial resistance from employees ("It gave me a
headache to speak English to my boss all the time," one LG worker
told *BusinessWeek*), the five foreigners have since overhauled many
of LG's internal and external operations, helping the company, for
instance, move from the number-four spot in global mobile phone
sales to the number-three position. Even more telling is the fact that
Samsung, LG's archrival in many businesses, went on a foreign hiring
spree for its executive suite in late 2008, replacing many longtime
employees with new foreign transplants.

While the move toward a more global executive suite might seem
a logical step for a multinational company like LG or Samsung, the
fact is that most levels of the Korean economy are taking in foreign
workers. They take the most senior positions at global conglomerates as well as the most unwanted jobs—known as 3D (dirty, dangerous, and demeaning) jobs.

Nazrul Chaudhury came to Korea from Bangladesh in 1991 because he wanted work that would pay decent wages. He worked for three years in a plastic factory in Hwasung, a city in Gyeonggi Province, outside Seoul. In March 1994, Chaudhury was involved in a horrific accident at the factory. A mortar belt almost amputated his left leg. He spent the next four years in various hospitals and underwent twelve operations.

Today, the forty-six-year-old father can't work. He's been living for years in a shelter operated by the Seongnam Migrant Workers House, a nonprofit group that is operated out of a church in the city of Seongnam, Gyeonggi Province. He stays in a room with other men from Bangladesh and Iran, and he helps translate for the staff when they are helping other workers.

"My life now—it's just going on," he said quietly. He hasn't seen his seventeen-year-old son and wife for many years and does not have plans to go back to his country.

The director of the service agency is Lee Sang-rin, a former CEO of an electronics company in China. Lee has worked with the agency since 1997. The agency was established by two pastors and is supported by twenty or thirty churches and about ten companies, including Korea Gas Corporation, in addition to receiving financial donations from members. There are twelve full-time staff members.

The agency helps about 180 foreign workers a month. Most of them come from Bangladesh, Pakistan, Sri Lanka, Mongolia, and China. They work in the 3D jobs—mostly in factories and in construction.

"Foreigners think Korea is a rich country, but when they come here to work they find a different situation," Lee said. "More than three-quarters don't have a good job."

Lee and his staff help the workers get salary that they are owed, and help them resolve immigration problems, among other things.

They also provide shelter, housing sixty people in a handful of rooms in the church basement. The workers are supposed to stay in the shelter for a maximum of three months, but some stay for ten years, he said.

Lee, a gray-haired man who speaks good English, walks down the hall of the basement and points to a door on the left.

"This is for Bangladesh and Iran."

Inside, three men, including Chaudhury, are sitting on the raised yellow *ondol* floor, watching television or reading news from their home country on a computer.

Lee walks to the next door and says, "This is for Koreans and Chinese."

Inside, a handful of older Asian women organize their belongings in bags.

Lee walks to the next door and says, "This is for men from Korea and Chinese."

Inside, a few older Asian men sit on the ondol floor watching television. There is a faint smell of cigarettes.

Lee walks down the hall to another room and says, "This is the multicultural library. We have 1,700 books from other countries, for kids."

The tour continues upstairs. Lee opens the door of another large room. There are five Chinese students learning Korean in one group on the floor. In another, smaller room, three Vietnamese women learn Korean. In an adjacent room, four women from Vietnam and the Philippines learn Korean. Nearby, in another space, there are twelve women from Bangladesh and the Philippines learning the language.

This is the other major part of the agency's work. The agency works with many foreign women who come here to marry Korean men (more on that later in the chapter).

There are many agencies like Lee's working to help foreign workers and wives adjust to the culture and language of Korea. It is not an easy transition. Traditional Korean culture is less experienced in globalization on its home shores than most cultures. Korea, after all, has been an ethnically homogenous country, with a single culture, language, and ethnicity (Koreans refer to it as a race, setting themselves genetically apart from their Chinese and Japanese neighbors). They have guarded that exclusivity for generations, fighting against Japanese attempts to merge them into that country's national tradition. And then, suddenly, in the mid-1990s, they opened their doors to a trickle of foreign migrants.

Within the last five years, that trickle has become a torrent. Korean government officials now place orders for workers from other countries to meet labor needs on the peninsula. Of the workers who come, a little more than half are ethnic Koreans from China. Many thousands more are ethnic Koreans from Japan, the United States, and other countries. But a large portion of the workers are non-Koreans—household maids from the Philippines, nightclub singers from Thailand, and factory workers from Bangladesh.

The struggle and exploitation of low-level workers have led to intervention by social service agencies and even the powerful unions. Trade unions interceded on their behalf in the early 1990s, pushing for equal pay for foreign and Korean workers. The unions are not gaining much ground organizing these workers, but some unions still provide services to them.

Francis Kim, assistant director of education and publicity at the Federation of Korean Trade Unions, one of the two largest umbrella unions, said his organization does not see foreign workers as a threat because most migrant workers "are concentrated on 3D jobs, which Korean workers don't want."

Union involvement in organizing and advocating foreign workers soon led to a trend that had other civil society organizations working on behalf of the foreigners. Still more groups lobbied the government for better treatment of the workers and for benefits, including healthcare.

The two most recent presidents, Roh Moo-hyun and Lee Myung-bak, have instituted policies and programs to encourage openness to and equal treatment of foreign workers. Still, the economic downturn could hurt the livelihoods of these workers, as the government has made moves to reduce the number of visas issued to foreign workers in an effort to provide more jobs to native workers.

The difficulties for foreign workers are both cultural and practical. Koreans follow a collective culture that focuses on groups that are established in school—from elementary school to college—through families, or by geographic regions. Once those groups are formed, it is difficult to gain entry. This goes for foreigners as well as Koreans who grew up in other countries.

"Because of the group thing, you're in or you're out," said Anne Ladouceur, a Canadian woman who has lived in Korea for more than a dozen years and operates her own business and website for expatriates.

On the practical side, foreign workers are restricted by matters as simple as the number on their ID cards (identification cards are issued to every person living in Korea). About a decade ago, the Korean government changed the foreigner registration card system. The ID number for everyone in Korea is thirteen digits. It includes your birth date and a number telling whether you are male or female. If you are a foreign woman or man, you have a different number (a five-digit ID for a foreign male and a six-digit number for a foreign female). This different type of ID number makes it impossible for foreigners to do certain things in Korea. For instance, many Koreans shop online using their ID number, but foreign ID numbers are not accepted to purchase items such as plane tickets or movie tickets.

Foreigners also have trouble opening bank accounts. Many of them have to wait three months after arriving in the country to open a bank account and then still can't use the bank's ATM for another three months.

Cell phones are difficult to get, and foreigners can't have more than one cell phone. One major company does not allow foreigners to get cell phone service. Another charges a 300,000 won security deposit. So, while the government advocates a welcoming attitude toward foreigners, more work needs to be done to make that attitude reach down to the level of everyday matters.

MAIL-ORDER BRIDES

The tiny farming village of Chulpo, on the western coast of Korea, has about twenty families. They grow rice, fruit, and vegetables. Centuries ago, the village was known for master artisans of the light green pottery known as celadon.

Today, as in so many villages across rural Korea, the farmers are having trouble finding Korean wives. Most of the young women who grow up on the farms move to the cities in search of a better life—one that does not require long days of back-breaking work in the fields.

So the men in Chulpo are doing what many rural men have been doing over the last decade: finding wives from other countries. The village already has at least two wives transplanted from overseas. One forty-seven-year-old farmer married a twenty-two-year-old woman from Vietnam. They have a daughter and son, and the wife is pregnant again. The husband has a small farm where they grow watermelons and green onions. Another villager, a sixty-five-year-old man, recently married a twenty-five-year-old woman from Vietnam.

The man has no job. They are supported by the husband's grown children and the government. One man paid 10 million won to get married. Now the government will give the family 5 million won to pay for marriages to foreign women.

The trend of Korean men marrying women from other countries began in the early 1990s and saw a huge rate of increase in the first half of this decade. The number of international marriages peaked at more than 31,000 in 2005 and has dropped slightly since. In 2007, more than 29,000 men in Korea married foreign women. Overall, more than 11 percent of all marriages that year were to foreign wives or husbands, according to government statistics.

The number of international marriages is so high that banners can be seen in villages across rural Korea that advertise wedding halls and banquet services for Vietnamese women coming over here. In Hangul, the signs say "Vietnam Shin Bu" (Vietnam Bride).

The trend was spurred by demographic and economic changes in the country. Rural women have been moving in large numbers to the cities. Fewer women are marrying. The birth rate has dropped sharply. And farmers need wives to have children and keep up the family business.

The gender imbalance grew without a solution until 1992, when South Korea and China established diplomatic relations for the first time. China is home to more than 2 million ethnic Koreans, most of whom live in poverty and half of whom are women. Starting that year, the first Chinese-Korean brides began moving to Korea to marry eligible Korean farmer bachelors. Although foreigners, they shared a language and cultural traditions with their husbands-to-be. They also wanted to live in a more prosperous country and to marry men who were, by Chinese standards, wealthy.

The trickle of brides quickly became a flood and rural Korea soon became host to tens of thousands of transplanted Chinese women. Some of the marriages fell apart—as often happens in such arranged social contracts. In parts of China, it is common for husbands to cook, and Chinese women received a rude awakening in Korea. Still, many marriages held together and there was a renaissance of child-rearing in rural Korea.

But the pool of potential brides in China wasn't bottomless. Soon, new husbands found themselves in competition for the few remaining bachelorettes and the phenomenon of unmarried farmers started to appear again. As a result, some bachelors resorted to ordering brides from Taiwan, Vietnam, and the Philippines. These brides, unlike those who arrived from China, didn't speak Korean and found themselves in relatively prosperous circumstances, but in the midst of a rare and foreign culture.

Today, there are more than 150,000 foreign brides in Korea, a significant portion of them nonethnic Korean. In response to this trend, the government of Korea launched an ambitious program in 2008 to culturally acclimate foreign wives. More than a hundred rural community centers were established in just two years. Korean classes are offered at these community centers free of charge and Korean tutors are even sometimes sent to the women's homes to help them learn the language. Additionally, health classes, parenting classes, and even breastfeeding tutorials are offered. "The idea is to make the acculturation to Korea easier and to lessen the culture shock between international spouses," says Joon Kim, a professor of ethnic studies at Colorado State University, who has studied the new network of community centers. "But it's important to note that it doesn't make Korea any more multicultural. They are teaching the foreigners to be more Korean. You notice that they don't offer any Vietnamese-language classes for the husbands."

Thanh Hoa Le Ngoc is from a small farming village in Vietnam and has been married to a Korean man in Seongnam since 2005. She is twenty-seven and her husband is forty-three. They met through a friend, another Vietnamese woman who married a Korean man.

Thanh Hoa dated the Korean man in Vietnam a few times and then got married in Vietnam. Her husband works in construction. They have two daughters and she is pregnant.

Thanh Hoa is the oldest of four daughters. Since she got married, she has introduced two of her younger sisters to Korean men. The connections were made through her husband, who is from Gangwon Province in the south. Her sisters married men from his hometown, Hongchon. They live on farms, growing chili peppers, rice, and cattle. She predicts that the number of Vietnamese women coming to Korea as wives will continue growing.

CHAPTER 14

A Changing Society:
Shifting Roles in Modern Korea

IT'S ELEVEN O'CLOCK on a chilly spring weeknight and the subways across Seoul are brimming with men and women in dark suits, heading home from work or an after-work outing. High school and college students stand in the subway cars, chatting with friends or playing games on their cell phones.

Outside, residential neighborhoods are generally quiet. But not all the children are in bed asleep.

In a sprawling apartment complex in the suburb of Seongnam, Choi So-young walks her eight-year-old daughter home from a *hakwon*—a private tutoring school. Such schools are well attended across the country. The mother carries her two-year-old daughter Min-se on her back. The toddler is barefoot, in her pajamas, and fast asleep. The second grader, Min-je, carries a book bag on her back and talks quietly about her day, including about the swimming and belly-dancing classes she took that evening. They walk into building 108, ride the elevator to the fifteenth floor, and shuffle to their apartment.

The eight-year-old comes home at 11 p.m. two nights a week. On the other weeknights, she comes home from hakwon at about 9 p.m.

This scene plays out nearly every night across every city and village in the country. Soon after children learn how to read and write, they begin an intense, arduous journey to college. The process requires long days and nights at tutoring schools, music lessons, tae kwon do for the boys, and sports, followed by hours of studying and cramming for tests. The days get longer and the sleep gets shorter as the children near the college entrance exam.

In many cases, mothers endure as much stress as the children. Responsible for the success or failure of their children, mothers shuttle their children to and from the schools and activities, closely monitor their studies, and push them to study harder.

In Korea, education has long been the key to a person's future. What college you attend most often determines your social network and what job you get after school. It also plays a major role in who you will marry and your overall status in society. Education can also be the best way to display filial piety—the virtue of showing respect to your parents. That's because a person's education and job reflects on the entire family. Many centuries ago, people who obtained the highest level of education and scored the best on tests became government officials—and that title was inscribed on the family gravestone. This was considered a tremendous mark of honor for the family.

Until the twentieth century, only a small portion of Korean society—the aristocrats, or *yangban*—obtained advanced education. But when Korea modernized after the Korean War, the government applied the yangban attitude toward education to everybody. Korea established essentially universal education for children, whether they lived in tiny villages or in major cities. Today, Korea boasts the highest educational attainment in the world.

As in the rest of society, the educational system has favored men. But that is changing. More women are going to college and passing exams for government jobs. They represent a growing portion of the workforce. And as that trend grows, marriage and childbearing rates have been dropping.

Today, Korea faces a major problem: It has one of the lowest birth rates in the world. This, in turn, has caused another significant demographic trend: a rapidly aging population.

The country is aging at a faster rate than any other country. By 2026, one-fifth of all Koreans will be elderly. And by 2050, more than one-third will be elderly, with life expectancy expected to hit eighty-six.

A KOREAN CHILDHOOD

Koreans go to extensive lengths to avoid coldness, especially when it comes to babies and children. Women with babies are discouraged from drinking cold liquids and ordered to cover their bodies (no short sleeves or bare feet) for at least a month after giving birth.

Babies aren't supposed to leave the house for the first month. They are bathed nightly in hot water. And they are always double layered—in cotton long johns and an outfit. Throughout early childhood, many little ones wear long johns under their clothes during cold months, plus thick coats, gloves, and hats. The avoidance of chill is rooted in traditional medicine, which believes coldness in the inner organs is the origin of disease.

It is common to see strollers that are outfitted to protect babies from the cold. Koreans put thick clear plastic covers across the front of strollers so that they resemble an airplane cockpit. You often can't see the child underneath because of several layers of coats and blankets.

The children in these strollers are protected as if they're going out in a winter blizzard—even though it may actually be a cool, dry spring afternoon. This attitude about bundling babies and young children echoes the overall view toward parenting in Korea. There is no such thing as a casual parent. The responsibility is taken very seriously. If the child gets sick or fails in school or even as an adult, it is considered the parents' fault. In other words, the well-being of the child—no matter how old—is a direct reflection of the actions of the parents.

So babies are treated as if they are made out of porcelain. They spend much of their time tied to their mother's back with a fabric wrap that encircles the baby's back and buttocks. Women carry their babies on their back while they cook, clean, and travel.

In the past, children were free to play until it was time to enter school. But in recent years, it has become more common for children as young as three to start going to school and getting tutored in English and other subjects. These days, most children already know how to read when they start school.

Yoo-bin began attending an English preschool when she was four. That school cost her parents $1,000 a month, with the school day lasting six hours. At age five, she started one-on-one tutoring in English, science, piano, and violin. She's now seven years old and attending elementary school during the day and hakwon in the evenings. On top of that, she has a lot of homework.

Competition is fierce and kids are pushed to be the best in their class. Some students even live at tutoring school dormitories. If parents identify a special talent in their children, some will devote their lives to turning the child into a star. Behind nearly every famous young Korean star—in sports, music, or acting—you will find parents who have sacrificed deeply to nurture the child's talents.

A NATION OF SCHOOLS

It's about 10 a.m. on a Friday morning and the classrooms at Seongnam Elementary School are bustling with activity. In one second-grade class, a girl marches up to the front of the class, stands under a Korean flag, and recites a short speech as some of her classmates giggle.

Outside on the dirt playground, a row of students do sit-ups on mats as their classmates sit on their legs and count. In a first-floor classroom, fourth graders practice pounding in unison on a traditional Korean drum. And in one corner of the L-shaped building, a group of fifth graders starts an English class.

"Hello, everyone," the teacher calls out. "Attention!"

"Hello, teacher!" the students respond in unison.

"How are you?" she asks.

"How are you?" they respond.

Like the rest of Korean society, and nearly every school across the country, the students at Seongnam Elementary School learn and move as a group. All public schools follow a core curriculum chosen by the federal government. So a second grader in a village in the southern provinces follows the same textbook as a second grader in Seoul.

The education system is geared strongly toward rote memorization and standardized tests, although there are moves underway to place less emphasis on tests. What hasn't changed, though, is the universal focus on one goal: achieving the highest score possible on the college entrance exam.

It is difficult to overstate the importance of the college entrance exam. All high school seniors take the test on the same day. And it happens only once a year: the second Thursday of November. It is the only day of the year where multiple segments of society, from taxi drivers to members of the military, make special accommodations to help the students score well.

Preparations for the test begin months before. Parents—especially mothers—go to great lengths trying to bring good luck to their children for the exam. They seek out the advice of fortune-tellers. They go to temple or church and pray. The students themselves sleep little—studying into the wee hours every morning for months on end. In many high schools, older students don't leave until about 10 p.m. and then they go to hakwon until one or two in the morning before heading home.

And when the day of the exam finally arrives, all schools close so that the test takers are not disturbed by other students. Some of the younger students come to school anyway to lend a hand—standing by the doors to cheer the seniors on as they arrive.

Many businesses will open at 10 a.m. to reduce traffic and crowds while students are trying to make it to their test sites by 9 a.m. Utility companies will make special arrangements to make sure the heat and power is on at the schools. Taxi drivers will give free rides to test takers. And parking will be prohibited near schools so that parents will have ample space to drop off their kids.

The test takes all day. There are four subjects—Korean, math, society/science, and English. You can get extra points for taking tests in other languages. The test is multiple-choice, except for math.

While the test is going on, airlines will adjust schedules to avoid flying over schools during the listening portion of the test. Cars are not allowed to honk their horns near schools. The military will halt exercises with jets and helicopters to keep things quiet.

The goal for most students is to earn a high enough score to make it into one of the top three universities in the country. They are known as the SKY schools: S stands for Seoul National University. K stands for Korea University. And Y stands for Yonsei University. All of them are in Seoul. For young women, the top school is Ewha Womans University, also in Seoul.

Students who make it to those schools are essentially set for life. Once they graduate, job choices are plentiful. The friends and networks they make in school will stay with them for the rest of their lives—often helping them and their children to find work and gain social status. And their social status will remain high because many of them will marry alumni from the same schools.

Testing has been a major focus in the history of the country. In ancient times, tests were required to enter the civil service and the military.

The education system underwent major changes during the Japanese occupation, and then again after the Korean War. The country established almost universal, free education at least for elementary school. Today, the high school graduation rate is nearly 100 percent, and four out of five high school graduates go on to college. Korea ranks first among member countries of the Organization for Economic Cooperation and Development (OECD) in the percentage of adults aged twenty-five to forty-three with a college degree. Compared to other countries, Korean students rank near or at the top of developed countries in reading, math, science, and problem solving.

Those successes, however, come at a hefty price. Korean parents are spending more and more of their income on hakwon. The conventional wisdom is that the more money a family has, the better the schools (and hakwon) their children attend—and the better their chances of getting into a top college.

In 2007, Korean families spent $13.6 billion on private schooling. Parents spend the most money on teaching their children English. English education has been part of the public school curriculum for years, but the push nowadays is to begin the classes at a younger age. By 2005, the federal government had mandated that all elementary schools teach English. At Seongnam Elementary, English classes begin in the third year—one hour a week for third and fourth graders, and two hours a week for fifth and sixth graders.

Parents with financial means will send their three- to five-year-olds to English preschools, where they are taught by foreign teachers. They will pay for one-on-one English tutoring and then send their children to English tutoring schools in the evenings.

Higher-income families will go to even greater lengths. They'll move to English-speaking countries and enroll their children there for a few years. They'll try to get foreign citizenship for their children to qualify them for foreign schools in Korea. And some mothers will even give birth to their children in English-speaking countries like Australia, Canada, and the United States so that their children will have foreign citizenship and can enter foreign school in Korea.

Korean parents spend more money on English education than on any other subject. Lee Hye-ji started learning English in third grade, both at a hakwon and at school. She is now in sixth grade and considered one of the best English-speakers in her thirty-six-student class.

"I'm thirteen years old. I started to learn English in third grade," she said, looking down because of her shyness. She said she is learning English "because English is a global language."

The focus on English is one of many changes occurring in the education system. Foreign countries view Korea's education system as highly successful because of the high literacy and college-going rate. But Koreans and overseas education experts have been hotly debating the effectiveness of a system that emphasizes rote memorization and test taking.

There also is concern about the caliber of college graduates. The road to college is so arduous that many students slack off once they get to college. In addition, even the top universities in Korea are not highly ranked internationally.

ENTER THE WOMEN

In February 2009, U.S. Secretary of State Hillary Clinton visited Korea as part of her first overseas trip in her new position. During that trip she conducted a town hall at Ewha Womans University in Seoul.

There were 3,000 people at that event and a few students were chosen beforehand to ask questions. They asked Clinton about her childhood aspirations to work for NASA, her experience at Wellesley College, and how she handles countries that don't respect women in high positions. Then Clinton began taking questions from the general audience. Many of these questions focused on relationships: her marriage to Bill Clinton and her experience raising Chelsea. One student asked how she knew Bill Clinton was the right person to support her.

At one point, Clinton talked about how difficult it was to take care of her daughter Chelsea when she was a baby. She described the struggles she faced learning to be a mother on her own.

Upon hearing this, a woman in the audience snickered to her fellow alumni. "How stupid! She could've called her mom," the woman said. "That's what moms are for."

The tenor of that event underscores the mind-set of women in Korean society. At a time when the government is striving to improve the status of women, the visit by Clinton to the top women's university in the country was a clear attempt to demonstrate the progress that had been made. But the fact that the students didn't ask questions about foreign policy, instead quizzing her about relationships and her experience as a woman, shows the priorities of many young women in the country today. And these questions came from the most intelligent and best educated young women in the country. At one point during the event, Clinton said, "I feel more like an advice columnist than secretary of state today."

That's not to say that the status of women hasn't improved. It was not that long ago when women were confined to the home. As recently as a century ago, upper-class women weren't permitted to leave the house during daylight. They scurried around at night with their heads covered. And they had few legal rights.

For instance, until about twenty years ago, Korean women could not get custody of their children in a divorce. Inheritance rights were also limited. The federal government took more aggressive measures to improve women's rights in the mid-1980s. The Equal Employment Act—the first major nondiscrimination law for women—was passed in the mid-1980s. A few years later, the government established a gender equality ministry under the prime minister's office.

Since then, legal protections have increased significantly. On paper, Korea's laws protecting women are strong compared to other countries, said Jung Soon-young, who has been working for many years at various agencies promoting women's rights in Korea. "But the problem is de facto discrimination," she said. "De facto discrimination against women still exists. We can say that it has changed a lot, the attitude of men . . . but still it is very difficult."

The percentage of women ages fifteen and older who are working increased from 39.3 percent in 1970 to 50.2 percent in 2007. At the same time, the proportion of young women who are married decreased significantly. In the twenty-to-twenty-four age group, the percent who are married dropped from 42.8 percent in 1970 to 6.3 percent in 2005. In the twenty-five-to-twenty-nine age group, the percent of married women dropped from 90.3 percent to 40.9 percent.

The vast majority of working women are employed in temporary or otherwise irregular jobs that offer little job security and low pay. They still make far less than their male counterparts. In 1995, women made less than sixty cents for every dollar earned by men. In 2003, their earnings rose to 64.2 percent of men's salaries, according to the Ministry of Gender Equality.

In 2003, almost 90 percent of male college graduates entered the workforce, compared to about two-thirds of female college graduates. Men still far exceed women in participating in the workforce at all ages and education levels. It is rare to see a woman CEO except for small companies. And while women make up about 25 percent of the public sector, very few hold managerial positions.

Federal law requires large companies to provide childcare, but very few follow through. And the government operates a small number of childcare centers. So the overall lack of quality childcare also hurts the ability of women to maintain steady employment.

Social expectations make the problem even worse. Women are pressured to leave work once they get married, and especially after they have children.

Esther Hahm is a partner at the Seoul office of Ernst & Young. She worked for many years in the United States and is active with professional women's groups in Korea. She has taken numerous steps to improve the treatment of women in her office. She arranged for a female accountant to have a private room to pump breast milk at the office. She also has encouraged the promotion of women to higher positions, including partner.

Hahm is not married and has no children. She faces difficulties when other staff members assume she is married. At black-tie events, she has been seated at a table next to an empty chair assigned for Mr. Esther Hahm. She said some employees at the firm still believe that women should not work as accountants—that they belong at home.

KOREA'S AGE PROBLEM

So far, retired life has been good for Song Bok-ku. The seventy-year-old man retired thirteen years ago from an electronics company where he worked for many years. He lives with his wife in an apartment in Seoul and spends his days hiking and taking nature photos that he sells to different agencies. He also goes to church and meets with friends at least once a month.

A few times a year, Song travels to a park near city hall called Top-Gol-Gong-Won. The square features an ornate pagoda and the remains of a twelve-meter-high stone pagoda that was originally built in 1467 during the Joseon Dynasty. The park is known as a gathering place for seniors. They sit on the pagoda steps and talk or just gaze at their surroundings.

The park is serene, and flowering trees are beginning to bloom. On this day, Song is taking photos of trees that bloom small pink flowers like cherry blossoms. He wears hiking boots and specialized hiking pants made by Kolon, a Korean sportswear company. He wears a beret that bears the Izod emblem.

Song doesn't plan to live with his children, who work as researchers in Daejeon. He said most of his friends also don't want to live with their children. When he reaches a point where he can't take care of himself, he will move to a nursing home for seniors.

Society has changed a lot in the last few decades, he said: "More people don't want to live with their children. This is the trend. The young generation, they know just themselves."

Not far from the senior park is the Chong-no-sahm-kah subway station. It is a hub where subway lines 3, 1, and 5 intersect. The underground hallways are spacious and lined with stores. Dozens of elderly men and women mill about the station. Many of them sit on the stairs. Some are homeless.

On an elevated platform near the center of the station, volunteers wear green vests that say "Korea Dream Mission Team." Two women in vests cut the hair of two elderly men. About six other men sit in chairs nearby waiting for a cut.

Subway fare is free for the elderly, so it is easy for them to travel to the station. A man wearing a Levi's cap walks up to us and says he wants to talk. He says his name is Song Moo-lim and he is eighty-two years old. "Please shake hands," he says to a young Korean woman, and then vigorously shakes her hand while counting up to twenty in English.

His breath smells of alcohol. He points to a row of elderly people sitting on steps nearby and says, "They don't have even 300 won for coffee. No money."

He spends a few minutes ranting about the condition of seniors. Then he says, "I'm a gentleman." He looks at the woman and asks, "Do you have a husband?"

Scenes like the one at the senior park and the subway station will become more common in Korea in coming decades. Korea already is considered an aging society. But the demographic shift is moving quickly.

The essential problem is the low birth rate. In 1960, women had an average of six children. Today, it is just over one. The drop came about in part because of a government campaign that lasted until the mid-1990s, where the aim was to control population growth and discourage the birth of babies. Now, Korea is aging faster than any other country, and the government is scrambling to reverse the trend.

But the damage has already been done. Population growth has dropped to 0.33 percent compared to 3 percent in 1961. The population is expected to start declining in 2019. By 2050, the population is expected to drop by 1.71 percent.

At the same time, life expectancy is increasing. In 1970, the average life expectancy was sixty-two years; now it is seventy-nine. It is expected to continue going up.

The tradition in Korea is for seniors to live with their eldest son. That was one reason for the emphasis on having boys. It also is closely tied to the notion of filial piety. But today, across the country, fewer seniors are living with their children. In 1980, 72 percent of seniors over age sixty were largely dependent on their grown-up children. In 2003, less than a third of this population was taken care of by their children.

This trend is happening for a number of reasons. First, the younger generation may not have the means to support their parents, and they are becoming less interested in doing so. Second, the parents don't always want to live together with their grown children, and they also don't want to raise the grandchildren.

As a result, more nursing homes and residential facilities are being built for seniors. They are often known as Silver Towns.

In addition, older Koreans are staying in the workforce longer. About one-third of people over age sixty-five are working now. The government has implemented regulations to encourage the hiring of seniors. It has also invested in more services for this growing population.

Still, many seniors are living alone and struggling to survive. Roughly half of seniors aged sixty-five and older are living in poverty, according to data from the Korea National Statistical Office (NSO) and the OECD. That rate is higher than many other developed countries.

The economic struggles of seniors are primary factors behind a growing suicide rate. In 2006, 4,644 people older than the age of sixty committed suicide in the country. That's an average of twelve senior suicides a day. Elderly suicides in South Korea are the highest in number, and the rate is the fourth highest among thirty OECD countries.

Many organizations are stepping forward to address this problem and provide care for the growing senior population. A Buddhist temple operates the Chun Ju Yo Yang Won residential senior center in northern Chunju, a major city and the capital of North Jeolla Province. The two-story brick building is located on the edge of a bumpy road and next to a big empty lot with trash. It is surrounded by a metal fence and is next to a school and a modern apartment complex called Jin Hung Apartments.

The center was first established in 1949 and serves seniors with serious illnesses and Alzheimer's disease. There were seventy-four people living there in early 2009, and four out of five are low-income. Most of the seniors come from the smaller villages outside the city. The government pays 80 percent of their expenses and the residents have to pay 20 percent. The center costs about 37,000 won a day per person.

A doctor comes twice a week to see the residents. They live two to a room. Their names and ages are typed on a paper that's posted to each person's bed board. One woman is 100 years old. Of the seventy-four residents, twelve are men and the rest are women. Of all the residents, about eight of them never get visitors. Some have lived there for thirty years.

In addition to the Chun Ju Yo Yang Won residence, there are fourteen other senior centers in Chunju. The city built more senior centers after 2003 because of the growing senior population, said the center's general manager, Hwang Sung-chol. Team manager Choi Young-sul emphasizes the importance of making the seniors feel comfortable and mentally at ease. The center's brochure also stresses those points. The brochure contains this statement: "The elderly people gave birth to us, and worked to help society, so we respect what they contributed for us. We have to demonstrate our values to help them live comfortably. And we have to work harder to take better care of them."

PART FIVE

THE FUTURE

CHAPTER 15

Whither the North?
Four Scenarios for the
Future of North Korea

BEING A NORTH KOREA EXPERT is not an easy task. Imagine if your job was to observe, collect data on, and analyze a country you were rarely allowed to visit, you had no access to the locals, and the main written material you had to work with was propaganda from the government-controlled press.

So it's not really a surprise that people who are paid to be North Korea experts are a testy bunch who argue with one another. Take Bruce Cumings, whose 2003 book *North Korea: Another Country* is one of the best descriptions of modern North Korea. In it, he derides another North Korea expert, Nicholas Eberstadt, proclaiming that "Eberstadt has also been wrong-wrong-wrong about his prognostications. . . ." A page later, he is criticizing U.S. intelligence experts on North Korea by saying "My long-standing impression is that 'intelligence' inside the beltway is a euphemism for the blind leading the blind. . . ."

The other side gets in its fair share of jabs, too. Johns Hopkins professor Jae Ku, head of the school's U.S.–Korea Institute, said that "anybody who calls themselves a North Korea expert doesn't know what he's talking about. The only people who have taught me about North Korea are those in other lines of work who have some insight that might also apply to North Korea."

Why are these "experts" so upset with each other? It most likely has to do with the fact that they have all been wrong at different times. Most have prophesied the end of the North Korean regime at least once in their career. Some have predicted that the North will outcompete the South. And all have at some point said something that is demonstrably wrong.

That's what happens when your job is to analyze a group of people whose entire mind-set is based on the unpredictable and the unexpected. That's why we are not going to try to predict what will happen with North Korea. Instead, we look at the four most likely scenarios and predict what each one would look like. We start with the ugliest scenario: another war.

ANOTHER WAR

A future war between the Koreas would not look like the first Korean War. Casualties would be in the tens of thousands in the first few days. Chemical and possibly nuclear weapons would be used. And the war wouldn't end in a stalemate. It would probably end in total defeat of the North Koreans.

But the toll would be enormous. It is assumed that no war would be initiated by the United States or South Korea, as both have far too much to lose in such a conflagration. The only logical start to such a war would be a surprise attack by the North Koreans along the

Southern end of the demilitarized zone (DMZ) and a rapid attempted thrust into Seoul, just forty miles from the border.

The war would begin with an artillery barrage. In fact, it would be one of the largest artillery barrages ever known to mankind. North Korea has more than 4,000 artillery tubes (cannons and rocket launchers) situated within a few miles of Southern forces. The Northern generals would be motivated to "use it before you lose it" because—over time—the artillery of North Korea would make a relatively easy target for U.S. air bombers. Thus, it is estimated that more than 200,000 artillery projectiles would fall on Seoul within the first few hours of the conflict. Within the first few days, that number would be in the tens of millions.

Right behind this thunderous barrage, North Korean armored units consisting of more than half a million soldiers, all of whom have been in position for a rapid strike right along the border for decades, would roll across the 38th parallel through the Chorwon and Munsan mountain passes, both of which lead directly to Seoul.

At the same time, hundreds of North Korean commando units would embark from submarines, speedboats, and helicopters and parachute throughout the soft rear defenses of the South's army and would begin to commit ambushes and acts of sabotage. It is estimated that there are more than 100,000 highly trained special forces in the North Korean Army, all of whom are prepared to fight behind enemy lines.

The North Korean Air Force, which consists of about 500 planes, would strike at land targets and engage the U.S. and South Korean air combat units. Because of U.S. technical superiority (the average North Korean pilot gets only about twenty hours of training time in 1960s vintage planes; U.S. flyboys are not allowed to fly combat missions without more than 600 hours of in-flight training), this fight wouldn't last very long. But in the first hours of the conflict, it would be fierce.

How far the North Korean ground offensive would get is the greatest unknown if such a war were to break out. According to Operation Plan 5027, the U.S. military's publicly available plan for attack and counterattack, it is estimated that the assault would move forward across the eastern plains of Seoul but would be halted by South Korean ground forces with some help from the U.S. Air Force. Destroying an advancing armored column, after all, is the U.S. Air Force's primary task. Thanks to smart bombs, laser range finders, and advanced targeting techniques, such an attack force would be decimated, especially considering that U.S. pilots would have little opposition in the skies after the first few hours of battle.

But OpPlan 5027 recognizes that things don't always go as planned, and that the North Korean Army could conceivably break through and reach Seoul. If that were the case, the allied forces would concede the capital city in order to avoid an urban fight that would leave too many civilian casualties. Instead, they would fall back below the Han River, where the first U.S. units would encounter the North Korean attackers. At this point, the war would degrade into a grinding tank and infantry battle, as U.S. and South Korean forces would fight a running retreat southward while as many as 690,000 U.S. reinforcements started to pour into the port of Busan.

So far, this sounds very much like a repeat of the first Korean War. But it is hard to believe that, with all the technological superiority of the allied forces, such a running retreat would go very far south. The ability of the United States to airlift tens of thousands of soldiers and all their equipment in twenty-four hours means that the North Koreans would be facing a tactically superior enemy within a few days of battle. Within a few days more, along with the help of U.S. air power, the allied forces would have a significant upper hand.

According to OpPlan 5027, the counterattack would begin once a critical mass of about 100,000 reinforcements had arrived. These soldiers would strike back right at the spear edge of the North Korean attack line and wouldn't stop until they reached the Yalu River and the border with China. The U.S. strategic command is very explicit in the goals of the counterattack: to extinguish the North Korean regime. Within a few weeks, the U.S. buildup would have reached its full planned contingent of 690,000 troops and the final thrust into the North would begin. And probably end not too long afterward.

That's when things start to get very scary. As of late 2008, North Korea was believed to have about six nuclear weapons. Just as destructive is its chemical arsenal, believed to number in the thousands of mortar and artillery shells of nerve gas. Once the North's existence is threatened, there would be little reason for the Northern generals to avoid using these weapons. The advancing U.S. forces would be targeted with nuclear and chemical weapons, as would the city of Seoul.

The implications for this city of 10 million are devastating. Hundreds of thousands of civilians would be killed and hundreds of thousands more would be left with nightmarish injuries. The city itself would be leveled and contaminated with toxic residue.

Another unknown would be the reaction of China. Assuming that the North did strike first against Republic of Korea (ROK) and U.S. forces, it will be a very difficult move for China to come to the rescue of the North once again. The world is a very different place than it was in 1950, when China saved the North from extinction because it was competing with Russia to become the vanguard of the communist revolution.

Today, China's primary interest in its bordering countries is stability. Its secondary interest is in the reduction of U.S. influence in the region. If the United States sensitively telegraphs to China that it will make a significant withdrawal from the peninsula once the North has been vanquished, there's little reason for China to enter the fighting. Likewise, tensions can be further reduced if South Korea sends out diplomatic couriers to China to ensure that its leaders understand that the Yalu will not be crossed.

If China does enter the fighting, it will be ugly for the Chinese. U.S. forces will have guaranteed air superiority and the conventional Chinese tactics of human wave formations will be decidedly ineffective in the face of modern air weapons at the disposal of U.S. F-16s. Nuclear brinksmanship will surely come into play as well, but what China has to lose compared to what it has to gain from defending North Korea points to a probable end game of a negotiated solution.

The aftermath of such a war will probably look much like the aftermath of regime collapse, which is discussed in our second scenario.

REGIME COLLAPSE

All-out war isn't the only scenario for which the U.S. military is planning. In 2002, the U.S. military commanders in Korea ordered the creation of a new type of operational plan, one that would detail how U.S. and South Korean forces would deal with a full or partial regime collapse north of the border.

While such an eventuality is not necessarily a military affair, the implications of it most certainly are. A splinter faction of a fractured North Korean military might initiate hostilities against the South. Or the North Korean military might launch a preemptive strike against the South, as a way of preempting regime collapse by involving the two countries in a broad war. Even if there is no outright fighting, North Korea would surely descend into lawlessness and chaos—a situation that would require Southern military forces taking up positions in the North.

In OpPlan 5029, the name of the plan for regime collapse, U.S. military planners call for an occupation of North Korea by South Korean forces and the gradual digestion of the North into the Republic of Korea. Unlike OpPlan 5027, its details are still a closely guarded secret. U.S. and ROK military officials fear that North Koreans would consider disclosure of the plan a hostile act, so they have kept the lid shut on this document. All that is publicly known for sure is that it tackles a number of different scenarios, from complete regime collapse to partial fracturing or even a civil war between military factions in the North.

If regime collapse were to happen, it would probably be sudden and severe. It is known that there are three prominent centers of power within North Korea: the army, the intelligence agencies, and the Korean Workers Party. For regime collapse to occur, each would have to individually disintegrate to the point where it couldn't step into the power vacuum. The chances are, foreigners would hear very little about this disintegrative process. By the time it would be revealed to the external world, collapse would have already happened.

As the military, the intelligence agencies, and the party lose their grip on power there would be little evidence of it from the outside. Then, some sudden event—such as the death of Kim Jong-il—would cause the center to become undone. And in a system that is as centralized as North Korea, when the center falls apart, there would be nothing else left.

According to most North Korea watchers, regime collapse would be immediately followed by a flood of refugees desperately attempting to reach the South. The military's first goal would be to stem that flood. "It is important in the early stages to keep the two populations separate," said a ROK military officer who has helped to prepare plans for a post–North Korea world. "We can't fix the chaos in the North if there is chaos in the South, too."

ROK forces would quickly stream into North Korea and occupy strategic positions like airfields, ports, the country's borders, and military encampments. They would then ensure that transportation routes were secure so that convoys of relief material could begin moving into the North. The border with China would also have to be secured militarily to avoid a refugee flood into that country.

From that point on, reconstruction would become the main theme of the occupation. "There would be a stepping-stone policy of revitalizing one region at a time," said an ROK military official who did not want to be named. "First Gaeseong [the bordering city located just across the DMZ with Seoul] would be rebuilt from the ground up and then its border with the South would be dismantled. Then Pyongyang, then Sinuju . . .," he said, naming other Northern provinces.

All of this would be done, he said, in the midst of low-level warfare. "In addition to civilian chaos, there would be military conflict as well," he said of the Southern military's expectations. "But it won't look like the last Korean war. It will instead resemble . . . the Vietnam War: guerrilla ambush warfare where the enemy is difficult to differentiate from the general population. . . . But as reconstruction continued, the level of fighting would decrease, too." Altogether, this military officer expects, the reintegration process would take two decades and cost several trillion dollars. Pouring massive resources into the North would be a difficult sell to the population in the South. The greatest fear among North Korea experts is that civil society in the South would weaken because of the tensions caused by the burden of the reconstruction of the North.

A much more positive scenario—some would say hopelessly optimistic—is gradual peaceful reunification. How it might work is addressed in the next section.

PEACEFUL UNIFICATION

There are many different visions of what reunification between the North and South might look like. There's the "doom and ashes" scenario, which foresees a cataclysmic war on the peninsula, resulting in a win by the South and a long period of rebuilding. Then there's the seamless "give peace a chance" scenario, in which the Northern generals and the Southern business tycoons agree to peacefully unify their countries over the course of several decades.

Such a vision transformed into partial reality when the two countries agreed to establish the Gaeseong Industrial Complex in 2002. Prior to the Korean War, Gaeseong was the summer capital of Korea, a place where the wealthy elite of the country kept their mansions. It is in Gaeseong that a broad experiment of economic cooperation is taking place. The results are impressive, albeit much messier than planned. Its existence is always overshadowed by the diplomatic brinksmanship of the North Korean government.

In Gaeseong, there is an industrial zone that is the first of its kind. If you believe the claims of the diplomats' declarations when the zone was established, it is a spectacular success. But if you are aware of the mostly empty trains shuttling nonexistent goods from the industrial zone back to the South, then it becomes apparent that it hasn't realized all of the grand dreams of success.

Yet, to call the Gaeseong Industrial Complex something other than a success would be a difficult exercise in semantics. More than 30,000 North Koreans work in the zone for South Korean corporations, earning more than $50 per month, although much of that goes to the communist regime. Even with the cut taken by the government, the workers make much more than the average North Korean, so it is not as exploitative as it might seem. The laborers work peacefully with their South Korean managers to produce a multitude of products, from textiles to plastic toys.

On the one hand, the Gaeseong Industrial Complex looks a lot like the worst fears of some Korean observers. If the experiment were to stop here, then it would mean that North Korea represents nothing more than a large, untapped pool of slave labor for South Korea's megacorporations. Hopefully, it will not stop there. Hopefully, more industrial parks will open in the North, luring firms from all over the world. And hopefully, the Northern factories will quickly morph into places where value-added goods and services are produced.

The future of peaceful integration comes into sharper focus if the observer could view a different kind of factory, located in a gray industrial building in Pyongyang. Unfortunately, it is closed to foreigners and very few have actually seen inside. It is the animation center for SEK Studio, the company that was founded in 1997 to make children's animated films. It employs more than 1,500 illustrators, colorists, and computer graphics technicians. It has become one of the prime outsourcing factories for global animators, offering some of the cheapest production prices in the world.

The company benefited greatly from its relationship with Nelson Shin, a South Korean native who went to Hollywood in the 1970s to find his fortune. Shin is more than a famous animator. In the industry, he is more like a living god. He first found fame as the creator of the animation sequences featured at the beginning of the *Pink Panther* movies. Later, it was Shin who designed the light saber wielded by Jedi Knights and Darth Vader in the *Star Wars* series. Shin would go on to lead the Akom Production Co. in South Korea, which became famous as the first foreign animation house that was outsourced work on such U.S. television hits as *The Simpsons* and *Transformers*. He formulated the concept of animation outsourcing to Asia and then helped to build the South Korean animation industry from a backwater into one of the world's largest.

As its economy grew, however, South Korea lost the main attribute that brought in the Hollywood contracts to begin with—cheap artists. Soon, animation workshops blossomed in the Philippines, Vietnam, and Cambodia. Now these countries are evolving the same way South Korea did, and Hollywood is in search of the next animation outsourcing paradise.

Shin thinks that he's found it: North Korea. Akom began an unprecedented alliance with SEK and went on to produce one of the most symbolic inter-Korean projects ever made: *Empress Chung*. It was a movie based on a Korean fable about a princess who sacrifices her life to cure her father's blindness. The movie, unfortunately, was a loser at the box office. But the project led to a flourishing of SEK and established it as a legitimate competitor for animation contracts. Today, scores of workers toil away at drawing children's animation projects in that building in Pyongyang.

It used to be considered controversial to suggest that the South and North would reunify in peace. Now it's becoming conventional wisdom. But the conventional wisdom isn't necessarily correct, either. Nelson Shin's Akom Production Co. is now bankrupt, even if its North Korean partner is doing well. The Gaeseong Industrial Complex became a victim of inter-Korean power politics when the North demanded that half the South Korean managers leave the complex in November 2008. Its future continues to be tentative and fragile. In other words, the process will surely not be steady and linear. If it is to grow, it will do so in fits and starts. The more successful the enterprise of South-North cooperative economic development becomes, the more it will likely be held as ransom by North Korean government negotiators.

It is also important to note that the dream of integration through peaceful economic cooperation must progress beyond the model of the Gaeseong Industrial Complex, where experienced South Korean managers oversee poorly paid North Korean unskilled laborers. Success will be far more likely if, at some point, North Korean managers are overseeing skilled North Korean workers making high value-added products. That, for now, is still a dream.

If the future is to be based on the past, however, then our fourth scenario, that of things continuing as they have in the past into the foreseeable future, is probably the likeliest of all the scenarios described in this chapter.

SAME AS IT EVER WAS

In March 1999, two North Korea experts, Oh Kong-dan and Ralph Hassig, published a paper titled "North Korea: Between Collapse and Reform" in the journal *Asian Survey*. In it, they prophesied that things were either headed toward peaceful reunification through a fundamental change to the nature of the North Korean regime, or toward total collapse of the government of North Korea, to be followed a forced and difficult integration with South Korea.

It's more than ten years later and neither event has seen the light of day. Instead, we've seen a slow and steady degradation of the regime as it loses more and more of its economic viability. Yet no collapse. Likewise, there have been spurts of minor economic reform, but nothing that resembles the economic liberalizations that Deng Xiaoping led in China in 1979. Instead, things in North Korea have, much to the astonishment of everyone on the outside, stayed almost exactly the same.

Recent events have added substance to this view. Take the theory of regime collapse. It is assumed that any collapse will be precipitated by the death of Kim Jong-il, the "Dear Leader" who has ruled the country since his father's death in 1994. The assumption is based on the fact that there is no codified succession plan for when Kim Jong-il dies. Therefore, some predict an inescapable power struggle between the different factions in the country.

That's not the only possible outcome of a Kim Jong-il funeral. For all we know, there is a solid plan of succession and it is understood by all those in the halls of power in Pyongyang. In other words, the power struggle has already been fought and won by an as-yet-unnamed successor.

There are signs that hint that this is the realistic scenario for a post–Kim Jong-il world. In the fall of 2008, rumors of Kim's imminent death were rife. A reporter in Paris snapped pictures of a famed brain surgeon getting out of a car and onto a plane with Kim's eldest son, Kim Yong-nam. In September, Kim missed a parade that was held to celebrate the sixtieth birthday of the state, a sure sign of trouble. Later, the official North Korean press issued photographs of Kim "proving" that he was still alive. The photographs clearly showed flowers in bloom and lush greenery in the background, belying the fact that they had been taken sometime in the spring, not the fall.

At the same time, North Korean border guard units went on alert along the frontier with China. "If it's true that they are repositioning their military, it means that something momentous is about to be announced," said Scott Snyder, a North Korea expert. "It's probably not an attempt to instill order. They just want to control the flow of information into and out of Korea."

All signs pointed to an imminent announcement of Kim's death. Instead, the world learned in early December 2008 that the Dear Leader was alive and doing relatively well. The French surgeon reported that he had indeed visited with Kim, who had suffered a stroke. But the doctor reassured the world press that Kim was well and healthy after the surgery and was prepared to reassume full duties soon thereafter.

What's important here is that it is clear that for a few weeks in the fall of 2008, the world, and the North Korean regime, didn't know if Kim Jong-il was going to make it. That should have been enough to set the wheels of regime collapse in motion. Yet nothing happened.

If Kim had been on the verge of death, North Korea didn't behave the way it was supposed to. Gun battles in the streets of Pyongyang didn't erupt. The work camps in the mountains didn't suddenly swell with the losing faction's leadership. Newspapers didn't denounce as traitors those who were losing the battle for dominance. In fact, North Korea kept functioning in its own unique way, launching propagandistic rebukes against the United States and the South and engaging in its usual brinkmanship during nuclear negotiations with the outside world. That probably means that the regime has planned for its post-Kim future and that those plans are in place and ready to be executed during his illness. If he does die soon, don't expect it to lead to immediate regime collapse.

At the same time that Kim was suffering through his medical maladies, another strange tale was unfolding. The North Korean military announced an end to the Gaeseong trips that some South Korean tourists were allowed to take. Coincidentally, the number of South Korean managers at the Gaeseong Industrial Complex was ordered to be cut in half. At the same time that their Dear Leader was on the verge of death, the North appeared to be sharpening its resistance to inter-Korean ties, even though such moves seemed to bite the hand that fed them. The Gaeseong tours and the industrial zone in that same city are among the only means to bring foreign exchange into North Korea, and are thus very valuable to the regime. So why were they shutting the operations down?

The answer to that question most likely lies in the actual statistics of the Gaeseong Industrial Complex. While the number of South Koreans allowed into the zone were cut in half, the number of North Korean laborers increased between the months of October and November 2008—from 36,618 to 37,168. Since the North Korean regime gets paid directly for each worker who gets paid in the industrial zone, the move can be seen as a method of increasing, not decreasing, the country's engagement with capitalism.

If North Korea was trying to send a message to the world by cracking down on the Gaeseong Industrial Complex, it was this: We are going to manage this thing better. Why, after all, did the operation require more than 8,000 supervisors for a staff of less than 40,000 workers? That's an unusually high manager-to-employee ratio, especially in the labor-intensive industries that dominate the zone, like textiles and kitchenware manufacturing. Whereas much of the world interpreted the crackdown in Gaeseong as a slap in the face of capitalism, it was probably more a proclamation by the North that it will adopt capitalism, but only on its terms.

What does that mean for the future of North Korea? Probably that it will be a very long time before free market capitalism appears in the country. Instead, the regime will continue to take baby steps toward economic reform, but will forever fail to make the "Great Leap" that everyone hopes for.

So, without economic reform to return North Korea to self-sufficiency, won't the political system inevitably fail? Not if the outside world has as much invested in its staying power as the regime itself has, which appears to be the case. Each of the major geopolitical players in the region (with the possible exception of the United States) wants North Korea to remain in place. China fears that a unified Korea would have designs on its Korean-speaking provinces, and maybe even all of Manchuria. Japan fears that a unified Korea will challenge it for regional hegemony. Russia, too, would prefer a divided Korean peninsula: Unification would only dampen Russia's power reach in the area. Even the United States has some conflicts with a unified Korea because it would probably mean the end to the presence of its troops on the peninsula.

If we had to place a bet on the future of North Korea, our money would be safest if it were placed on the scenario of things staying the same. A powerless but stable North Korea makes the most sense for everyone concerned—except the Koreans.

CHAPTER 16

Toward Korea 3.0: Challenges and Opportunities for the Next Forty Years

IF WE ARE CORRECT in our hypothesis that the Korean economy has fundamentally changed from the economy of its "Asian tiger" years of the 1960s through the 1990s, the logical question to ask is: What's next? Korea could follow two very different paths in the next few decades. The first is to follow in Japan's footsteps. After that country reached developed status, many people collectively sat back and engaged in a "safety first" mentality (at all costs, let's not lose what we have built). As a result, Japan's economy entered the wilderness of the lost decade of the 1990s, in which there was no net economic growth. It should, in fact, now be called the lost decades, because the country remains in essentially zero-growth mode.

The other path that Korea can take is the one overgrown with brambles because it is rarely followed. It involves continuing to take great risks. It involves staying lean and hungry, rather than growing fat off the success of Korea 1.0. It involves staying true to the essentials of Korean nature and demonstrating extreme mental discipline, collective sacrifice, and hard work. At the same time, it is clear that Korea needs to change the way some things have been done in the country. It is our opinion that Korea's future progress is hampered by its dependence on fossil fuels, inadequate progress on environmental issues, too much centralized planning, closed social networking systems, and social and political unrest. The real test for Korea's future success is whether the country can adjust to the changing times and shed the last vestiges of the Hermit Kingdom mind-set.

KOREA'S ENERGY CHALLENGE

The Korean economy of today, with its $1.25 trillion gross domestic product (GDP), low interest rates, and low inflation, wouldn't have been possible without cheap fossil fuels. Korea's economy is export-driven, and exports can't get to their destination countries unless they are cheap to transport across the globe. And the goods themselves wouldn't be possible to make unless the energy inputs, primarily in the form of petroleum, natural gas, and coal, were not cheap and plentiful. Korean steel mills, for instance, are fueled by Australian coal and Iranian oil. Korean homes are heated by liquefied natural gas (LNG) from Qatar. Korean cars are fueled by Saudi gasoline. Without those energy sources, there would be no Korean steel industry and no Korean car industry, and winters would be very cold for most Koreans.

But 2009, when this book is being written, is a very different time from the 1960s and 1970s. While oil prices have settled from their 2008 high of $140 per barrel, they are still expensive at $50 per barrel when compared to the equivalent prices in early 1970, when they peaked at around $15 per barrel (in 2009 dollars). Coal and natural gas, likewise, are moderately expensive when compared to their prices during the heydays of Korean growth. And, as we continue to consume our dwindling fossil fuel resources, there is no doubt that prices will go up, rather than down. It is now almost universally accepted that cheap fossil fuels are a relic of the past.

That's very bad news for Korea, which imports 97 percent of its fossil fuels. The reliance upon these fuels leaves the country at great risk of price fluctuations in these commodities. What happens, for instance, if there is a major war in the Persian Gulf and the supply of oil is strangled to a drip? The major losers will be countries like Korea and Japan, which rely on that oil to fuel their economies.

Korea's answer to that potentiality thus far has been a national drive toward nuclear energy. As of 2009, 20 percent of the country's electricity came from nuclear reactors. A government plan is in place to increase that percentage to 40 percent by 2020, a goal that entails the construction of some eleven large nuclear reactors in the next ten years. While it is logistically plausible, newly emboldened municipalities and regional governments might rise up against the construction of such plants in their backyards. Until now, there has been no such political opposition to nuclear power plants, but then, no plants have been constructed in the last few years, a time of great political coming-of-age over various other issues.

If Korea can succeed at building so many reactors in such a short time frame, it will certainly be good for the country. However, it still leaves the other 60 percent of electricity production, not to mention all transportation fuel consumption, to fossil fuels. Right now, there are no significant plans to address that dilemma. And that, in our opinion, is a tremendous mistake.

Other countries, including the United States and the European Union countries, have boldly declared plans to reduce carbon-based fuels by as much as 80 percent in the next forty years. Korea's grand ambition: to increase renewable production to 11 percent of total electricity production by 2030. Not only does that leave the Korean economy at the whim of the oil markets, but it also does little to reduce greenhouse gas emissions—a drive that has dramatic popular support throughout the world, including in Korea.

A three-pronged renewable energy policy emphasizing wind power, solar power, and electric vehicles would do a great service for the country in many ways. First of all, it would reduce the country's reliance on foreign suppliers like Iran, Saudi Arabia, and Venezuela. Second, if the country could generate electricity domestically from renewable sources, the economy would enjoy the benefits of paying itself, rather than foreign suppliers, the enormous amounts of capital it requires to fuel the country. Nearly 15 percent of South Korea's imports are in the form of fossil fuels. Every kilowatt of Korean-produced electricity would go toward reducing that portion of imports, improving the country's balance of trade and turning its current account deficit into a consistent account surplus.

Wind power represents an enormous opportunity for Korea, thanks to its mountainous land mass and extensive coastline, which funnels trade winds from the ocean onto breezy shores. According to the Korean Wind Energy Research Center, the country could easily produce 3,000 megawatts of wind power onshore and 8,800 megawatts of wind power if turbines were also put on Korean territory offshore. All told, that represents almost 25 percent of South Korea's electricity demand.

One of the reasons the Korean government and corporations have been so slow in building new wind production facilities is that the technology is already dominated by U.S. and European companies such as General Electric, Vestas, and Siemens. The idea of subsidizing a new industry in which the main pieces of equipment are foreign made is one that is alien to the Korean heritage. That's understandable. But there is a window of opportunity in one facet of the Korean wind market that could lead to massive overseas sales, too: the offshore wind market. Currently, there are only a few thousand megawatts of wind turbines sited offshore globally (mostly off of Denmark and Germany). And those turbines are planted underground in very shallow water. If Korea were to set as a national goal the creation of a new industry of floating wind turbines for place-ment in deep water, it would be able to supply itself with enormous amounts of domestically produced power while also creating an in-dustry for export in the coming decades. The U.S. offshore regions, for instance, have the potential to produce hundreds of thousands of megawatts, and hundreds of billions of dollars in capital to the producers of all those turbines.

The potential for solar power in Korea is tremendous as well, de-spite the high latitude and relatively cloudy weather of the country. Japan, which has a similar climate, has heavily subsidized solar pho-tovoltaic installations, which in turn created a new industry (today Sharp and Kyocera are two of the world's largest manufacturers of silicon photovoltaic panels).

If Korea were to engage in the same kind of subsidization that Japan has, it would be well served if it were to target a new type of solar cell, called thin-film photovoltaics. These devices are manu-factured on rolls upon which minute amounts of active compo-nents are sprayed. The same basic manufacturing process is used in hundreds of Korean factories to produce the screens for LCD television sets and computer displays. With an enormous amount of experience and installed manufacturing base in the thin-film arena, Korea is uniquely positioned to take a dominant position in this field, which is expected to grow from a collective $2 billion in revenue in 2009 to hundreds of billions of annual revenue by 2020. It is conceivable that if the country were to build a large thin-film industry, it could easily produce 50 percent of its electricity from photovoltaic panels placed on top of preexisting houses, factories, and warehouses.

If both the solar and the wind goals are achieved, along with the nuclear ambitions already mentioned, that would mean that South Korea could produce 115 percent of its current electricity demand. That figure allows for a little room for growth in demand. It also allows for the realization of the third leg of a renewable energy pro-gram: the electrification of the vehicle market in Korea.

Korea is, in fact, an ideal candidate for electric vehicles. Unlike the United States or Australia, where vast expanses mean long driving distances, there is no point in the country that is more than four hours away from any other point. The vast majority of driving in the country is done within stop-and-go city traffic. That suits the strengths of electric vehicles even more so than gasoline vehicles.

Korea already has a fundamental lead on the core technology behind electric vehicles: Lithium-ion battery manufacturer LG Chem is the world's leader in making batteries for electric vehicles, as discussed in chapter 8. The country that won the Chevy Volt battery contract should be following through with an extensive electric vehicle program of its own. True, the government has declared that it hopes to have 40,000 electric vehicles on the road by 2012, but that includes simple hybrids like the Toyota Prius, which doesn't plug in to the grid and gets all of its power from regenerative braking. For the country to make a fundamental change in how its transportation system works, it needs to commit to a far greater proportion of all-electric vehicles. Assuming that it follows through on a major push toward solar power, wind power, and nuclear power, the electricity that will be consumed in order to power electric cars will mostly come from zero-carbon, domestically produced sources.

THE GREENING OF KOREA

According to legend, the Korean nation was born when a tiger and a bear prayed to the gods to become human. They were granted their wish. They were each given mugwort and garlic to eat for twenty-one days straight; only then would each of them be transformed into a human being. The tiger soon gave up and requited himself to being a tiger for all ages. The bear, however, survived the diet and became a beautiful woman. She would later marry Hwanung, the embodiment of the gods, and then give birth to Tangun, the founder of the Korean race.

As a result of this founding myth, tigers and bears have always had a special place in Korean culture, tigers for their unique tiger spirit that can't be changed and bears for their humanlike qualities. Yet being a wild tiger in Korea is a lonely existence, now that almost all available land in South Korea has been developed. No tiger has been spotted in the wild since 1922. Only a small population of some 400 Amur tigers, the breed that once roamed the hills and mountains of Korea, still exists in western Siberia.

Bears have it a little bit better: They still exist in the wilds of Jiri-san, the mountain that crosses the border between North Jeolla and South Jeolla provinces in the far south of the country. Eleven Asiatic black bears are known to still live in the woodlands surrounding that mountain. Yet they continue to be hunted by poachers, despite being named living national monuments. More than a thousand bears live in captivity in bear farms, where they are milked of their bile for traditional medicinal potions.

In other words, Koreans don't have a good track record protecting the living relatives of the founders of their nation. Environmentalism is weak in the country, despite the repeated mentions of the word *green* in consumer packaging and political speeches.

The government has implemented a series of lengthy policies and laws regarding environmental issues. There are taxes on gasoline for vehicles. There are standards imposed on environmental pollutants. "We have all kinds of environmental policies," said Park Ho-jeong, assistant professor and environmental economist at Korea University. "But we need more focus."

The government passed the first major environment-focused regulation—the Pollution Prevention Law—in 1963. But industrialization efforts took priority and that law was largely ignored. The government replaced that law with the Environment Preservation Act in 1977, which introduced standards, total pollution load management, and impact assessments. Environmental rights were added to the constitution in 1980. And in 1990, the law was divided into five more specific laws related to air quality, water quality, noise and vibration control, hazardous chemicals, and environmental dispute resolution. More laws followed. As of 2002, there were thirty-three environmental laws under the directive of the Ministry of Environment. Despite the laws, economic and business concerns have taken precedence.

That's not to say that the country has failed to make progress on this front. Until the 1990s, most homes in Korea were heated with systems that burn charcoal briquettes. With government aid, the vast majority of those systems were switched to natural gas, which significantly reduces particulates and nitrous oxide pollution.

The Korean government imposes one of the steepest gas taxes in the world on vehicles. Roughly 65 percent of the price of gas is tax. But even with such high gas prices, Koreans still like their cars, and they continue to buy more each year.

The effects of global warming have already impacted the country. Take certain fruits and plants, for example. The city of Daegu in the southern part of the peninsula has historically been famous for growing the country's best apples. But in recent years, the apples grown in that region are reported to have lost some of their taste, and apples are being grown further north, according to Park Ho-Jeong, the Korea University professor.

Another example is the camellia flower. The delicate, small flower that comes in a vibrant coral color historically grew only in the Busan area and Jeju Island. Now it can be found as far north as Seoul, Park said.

These changes are due to the warming of the climate in recent decades, said Park. While the country faces the consequences of industrialization and global warming, politicians are trying to develop platforms based on the growing popularity of "green growth."

In January 2009, President Lee Myung-bak announced the "Green New Deal," a $10 billion stimulus package meant to cultivate new economic growth by investing in environmentally friendly technologies and public works projects. The problem with the Green New Deal is that it is neither green nor new. The program's main element is a $6 billion project to dredge several rivers, thereby reinforcing their banks and reducing soil erosion. The project has long been on the backburner of national planning and was resurrected as part of the stimulus package. The only thing "green" about dredging rivers is that rivers seem to be somehow connected to the Earth. And the Earth, as we all know, is green.

The bulk of the other $4 billion to be spent on the Green New Deal is to be invested in previously planned rail networks and roads and bike paths. While there is an argument to be made that travel by rail is arguably greener than travel by bus or car, there is little rationale for labeling new roads as being "green." The bike paths, which account for only about $10 million of the public monies to be spent on the overall project (that's less than one-tenth of one percentage point), are indeed green, although it has yet to be seen how many bike paths can be constructed with only $10 million. On top of these programs, there are several directives for the development of renewable energy, although these proclamations are unfunded.

FROM CENTRALIZED PLANNING TO DISPERSED LEADERSHIP

It seemed like an offhand comment. Upon being handed a Nintendo DS, the Japanese-made portable gaming console, President Lee Myung-bak was purported to have said, "Why can't we make a console like this in Korea?" He then mocked his country's scientific establishment, which has been able to shoot rockets into space and clone dogs, but can't keep up with the Japanese in the console market.

His words were soon flashed across blog postings and newspaper headlines. The president has commanded us to make a game console, the masses seemed to have interpreted him as saying. It was just like back in 1970, when President Park Chung-hee ordered a domestic car industry to be founded, or in 1988, when President Roh Tae-woo demanded the country be cleaned up for the Olympics. Soon, a state-sponsored research institute announced a new program to crash-build a gaming console in a few months' time.

The problem with all this is the fact that Korea's gaming industry is actually far more advanced than Japan's. As mentioned in chapter 9, the Japanese, North American, and European gaming markets are dominated by consoles, special machines that the consumer has to buy in order to play games. In Korea, most games are downloaded from the Internet and then played online. Everyone in the industry agrees that online, free gaming is the future of the industry. Instead of a game maker asking consumers to buy the games, money is made inside the games themselves whenever players customize their in-game experience, which they do by making many small online transactions. Korea is at the vanguard of this new movement and is in a dominant position as other countries move toward this model.

In other words, it was as if the president of Finland, while traveling in the Third World, observed an old-fashioned rotary landline phone and then went home and demanded of his country that it too produce such fancy technology, imploring the engineers at Nokia to reengineer one of those big black phones that you plug into a wall instead of wasting their time with all those handheld wireless devices.

In the last decade, Korea's attempts at centralized economic planning have also been problematic. In the IT 839 initiative of 2004, the government issued a clarion call for a focus on twenty different technologies and sectors within the information technology industry. Six years later, almost all of those targets have been failures, despite the great cost in developing them. Digital mobile television, as discussed in chapter 9, has few subscribers willing to pay $20 per month to watch TV on two-inch screens on the subway. Another focus of the 839 program was WiBro, a wireless data standard that is unique to Korea. Unlike its cousin WiMax, which is now being used in more than fifty countries, WiBro has found little traction outside the Korean peninsula. Even in Korea, its adoption rate has been disappointing, as Koreans would rather avoid the high monthly costs of the service and instead rely on the very high speed Internet access they can get from their landline-based PCs and good enough access from traditional WiFi outlets for their mobile gear. In other words, the Korean government proved to be absolutely awful at picking winners in emerging technologies.

The fact is that Korea and the industries in which it participates, from electronics to automobiles to software to television dramas, are beyond the five-year planning stages. They are beyond economic directives from the president and the advice and wisdom of central planning authorities, no matter how prescient those technocrats may be. Korea should accept this fact and allow for the organic development of its major industries. A thousand hands at the wheels of a thousand boats are far more effective in today's global marketplace than a single set of hands on the wheel of a supertanker.

OPENING THE NETWORKING SYSTEM

When Kim Chang-won moved to the San Jose area after graduate school, he was amazed by the openness of the culture of Silicon Valley. "So what happens is, while I'm meeting someone, if I mention this person's name that I saw on tech news in the morning (whom I would have never expected to be able to meet if I was in Korea), the guy I'm meeting with goes, 'Oh, I did my previous start-up with him and hung out with him in the bar the other night. Would you like to meet him?' And I'm, like, damn—was it that easy?" he writes in his blog, www.web20asia.com.

Kim has achieved much with the access he was given. He went on to cofound a blog software company whose platform would become the most popular blogging software in Korea (sixty-five of the 100 top-ranked bloggers in the country use it). Then he cashed in by selling the firm to Google and becoming a Google executive. He is a Korean technology entrepreneur success story.

For someone who has lived in Silicon Valley and in Korea, Kim is often asked how the latter can create a new version of the former. It can't, is Kim's terse answer. Silicon Valley is based on open access to capital for anyone with a good idea and a strong track record. Korean business culture works very differently. He writes:

> You want to meet the "movers and shakers" of the industry? You will probably have to meet their secretaries first. You have this crazy idea that you think will change the world? You will likely find there's not enough capital or other necessary ingredients that will let you build a business around that idea. So the next thing you do is to bring that idea to this established company, most likely a portal or a big company's IT arm. If they don't understand what the heck you are talking about (which is the most likely scenario), they will basically tell you to get a real job. If they do see the potential, they will either try to rip you off by offering a cheap labor opportunity on an exclusive business deal, or copy the idea altogether.

Making business deals in Korea is extremely difficult—if not impossible—without knowing the right people or getting an introduction to the right person. It isn't that Koreans don't want the business. It's just that they rely heavily on social networks that are established from as long ago as elementary school and stay intact all their lives.

These networks are formed through family ties, friends from your school or hometown, and work colleagues. The networks create the foundation for a person's social and professional life. That's one major reason why Koreans push their children to go to a top university. The networks established in college often will determine the opportunities a person gets in the workforce.

This process has worked for decades because of the importance placed on trust. In the business world, Koreans will not work with just anybody. They will find people from their networks. If they go outside the group, it is only through an introduction from someone they trust. Once an introduction is made, Koreans will make deals—but only after developing a relationship with someone, which means after a period of socializing, drinking, and getting to know each other. Then, the relationship will be sealed for life.

The problem with this process is that many people, even if they are talented and have good ideas, are shut out simply because they don't know the right people. This dilemma is especially worrisome for foreigners who come to Korea to do business. They won't get traction even with the most innovative business plans. That's why many foreigners describe Korea as having an unfriendly business climate.

But the problem goes much further than that. The reliance on networks creates a thick wall between Korean society—including government, business, and social groups—and the outside world. Many Koreans simply ignore attempts at contact from foreigners—even when the intent is good.

That attitude also applies to the media. Many in the foreign press face high hurdles getting access to Korean leaders. Their requests for interviews often get ignored or rejected. And the rejections happen even when the exposure would be helpful. Take this book, for example. The authors encountered tremendous obstacles—and closed doors—when trying to talk to officials.

The lack of engagement with the media, and especially the foreign press, can only be harmful. Like every other country in the world, Korea's image is significantly affected by coverage on television and radio and in print media. Any politician or business leader will tell you that it is important to make friends in the media and to actively seek out positive press. Just as effective public relations can make or break a company or a government agency, a productive relationship with journalists can make or break a country's image. Avoiding the media—and especially the foreign media—can lead to incomplete news reports and features and a distorted perspective on Korean affairs. But more important, Korea loses a terrific opportunity to tell its story and shape its image.

In light of these cultural barriers, it is no surprise that Korea's name recognition and reputation across the globe is weak. The country's brand recognition ranks thirty-third among developed countries, even though its economy is ranked fifteenth, according to the Anholt-GfK Roper Nation Brands Index. This underscores the fact that Korea's rich culture and powerful economy are not well known across the world.

Many Korean leaders recognize the public relations problem, including the president. The Lee Myung-bak administration has launched a major and expensive effort to improve Korea's brand across the globe. In April 2009, a new National Branding Council, led by Euh Yoon-deh, the former president of Korea University, announced an ambitious set of plans to improve the country's image in the world. Those efforts include increasing the number of Korean volunteers for overseas humanitarian projects from 2,000 to 3,000 a year, sending IT experts to developing countries to teach them computer skills, increasing the number of students who come to Korea to study, and promoting the country's advanced technology with a "Premium Korea" logo.

Dr. Euh said the nation brand index is "just a gimmick," but even so, the branding council appears to want Korea to make the fifteenth spot on the Anholt nation branding index by 2013. The council's work is not about advertising but about turning the country into a place where the people's attitudes and behavior match where Korea should be on the global stage, he said.

Korea's rightful place on the global stage is alongside the most advanced countries in the world. This tiny country has proved time and again that it is capable of competing with the best and the brightest. The nation has succeeded through sheer willpower, hard work, and an emphasis on education and setting ambitious goals. The country's list of achievements is stunning, and there is ample reason to believe that Korea will continue to be successful, while holding on to its rich history and culture.

But not nearly enough people outside of the country know about Korea's achievements. To spread their story more effectively, Koreans should take a hard look at how they treat outsiders. The tools that made Korea 2.0 successful will not necessarily work for Korea 3.0. A centrally planned economy is not the answer to future growth, and neither is a rigid networking and communication system. It is time to shed the Hermit Kingdom label once and for all, and to show the world all that Korea has to offer.

INDEX

A123Systems, 146
Afghanistan, Korean Air Force for resupply missions, 93
aging population, 157, 226, 235–239
agricultural collective, 35
Ah Jong, 74–75
AIBO robot, 158
Akom Production Co., 251–252
alcohol industry, 188–192
alternative fuel vehicles, from Hyundai, 101
Amerasians, as outcasts, 213
American Chamber of Commerce in Korea, 83–84
Amsden, Alice, *Asia's Next Giant*, 114
Anholt-GfK Roper Nation Brands Index, 270
animation outsourcing to Asia, 251
antenna for cell phone, 141
anti-Americanism in Korea, 16–17, 80
appliance industry, in South Korea, 137–139
archery (*kuk kung*), 2
archery in Olympic games, 5
Asian financial crisis (IMF crisis), 46–62, 203
Asia's Next Giant (Amsden), 114
astronomical observatories, 18
automobile industry, 58, 100–117
    Pony, 109–113
    Samsung entry, 124–125
    steel for, 102–106
    U.S. in Korea, 83

babies, 226
Bae Yong-joon, 165–166, 168
Baekje House, 210
Baekje kingdom, 14, 15, 18, 209

baht (Thai currency), 48
Bank of Korea, 59
bathhouses, 95
beef from U.S., 85, 86, 87–89
beer, 191
Bell, B. B., 92
Bird and Fish, 164
birth rates, 226, 237
Bivens, Carolyn, 206
bloodlines, purity of, 214
BoA, 169, 170–171
Boden, Dermot, 215
border guards, 39
branding, 113, 133–137
Brazil, 112
bribery, 29, 32–33, 39
Buddhism, 14
Buddhist temple, senior center operation, 238
bulgogi (barbequed ribs), 8
Busan, 26, 107
Busan-Seoul highway, 107
Bush, George W., 17, 83–85
business culture, 176–192, 268
Buyeo, 209–210

Cagle, Robert, 173
camellia, 264
can-do attitude, 10–11
capitalism, 256
cathode ray tube (CRT) technology, change from, 125
CDMA (code-division multiple access) standard, for cell phones, 153–154

revitalization of North Korea, 249
Rhee Syng-man, 13, 90, 135
roads in Korea, 106–109
Robert Trent Jones II (golf architecture firm), 196
robots, 156–159
Rodgers, John, 30
Roh Moo-hyun, 13, 32, 82, 87, 89, 194, 213, 219
Roh Tae-woo, 13, 72, 196
room salon, 192
Rumsfeld, Donald, 92

Saemauel Undong (New Community Movement), 11
Samkkuk Sagi ("History of the Three Kingdoms"), 9
Samsung, 56, 68, 118–131, 133, 134, 181, 197, 203
  divisions, 130–131
  early history, 119–123
  entry in auto industry, 124–125
  future, 129–131
Samsung Heavy Industries, 11
Saudi Arabia, 112
Scud missiles, North Korean launch of, 23
Sea and Sky, 164
SEK Studio, 251
semiconductors, 122
senior executives, interaction with, 190–191
Seo Taiji and Boys, 169
Seongnam Migrant Workers House, 216–218
Seoul, 16, 18, 26, 123, 183–184
Seoul National University, 230
Se Ri Kids, 205, 207
sex business, 192
SG Wannabe, 171
shamanism, 15
Shin, Nelson, 251–252
Shin Ji-yai, 207
shipbuilding, 60–61
Shiri (film), 173
Silicon Valley, 268
Silla kingdom, 14, 17–18
Silver Towns, 237
Singapore, 70
Sino-Japanese War, 22
Sinse-gae, 200

Sirak, Ron, 205
SKY schools, 230
slaves, 18
Snyder, Scott, 29, 254
social networks, changing, 267–271
social prejudice, 16
socializing, worker requirements for, 177
soju (liquor), 191
solar power, 261
Sony, Playstation, 142
Sony Ericsson, 133
South Gyeongsang Province, 13, 14
South Jeolla Province, 13, 14
South Korea
  appliance industry in, 137–139
  culture and society change, 3–4
  current account deficit, 49
  economic conditions in 1997, 49–50
  economic conditions in 2008/09, 59
  economic growth, 51
  impact of North Korea, 24
  interest in new technology, 148–149
  IT 839 policy, 152–153
  military spending, 93
  national debt, 59–60
  negotiation stances, 32
  normalized relations with Japan, 76
  North Korea invasion of, 91
  North Koreans in, 37–43
  recession in 1998, 56
  U.S. relationship, 79–87
spas, 95
Star Wars series, 251
state-sponsored research institute, 266
steel, for automobile industry, 102–106
Steers, Richard, *Made in Korea: Chung Ju Yung and the Rise of Hyundai*, 111
Stiglitz, Joseph, 57
subway, 236
Sui Dynasty (China), army invasion of Goguryeo, 19
suicide rate of seniors, 238
Sung-hee, 176
"Sunshine Policy," 32

Taean, crude oil spill near, 11
Taejo (king), 15, 18
Taiwan, 70
Tangun, 263
Tangun Wangom, 17